ISLAMIC THEMES IN US HIP-HOP CULTURE

Music and Performance in Muslim Contexts

Published in Association with the Aga Khan University Institute for the Study of Muslim Civilisations and the Aga Khan Music Programme

Series Editors: Theodore Levin and Jonas Otterbeck

This series presents innovative scholarship in music, dance, theatre and other performative practices and varieties of expressive culture inspired or shaped by Muslim artistic, cultural, intellectual, religious and social heritage, including in new creative forms. Bringing together outstanding new work by leading scholars from a variety of disciplines across the humanities and social sciences, the series embraces contemporary and historical cultural spheres both within Muslim-majority societies and in diasporic subcultures and micro-cultures around the world.

The Awakening of Islamic Pop Music
Jonas Otterbeck

From Rumi to the Whirling Dervishes: Music, Poetry and Mysticism in the Ottoman Empire
Walter Feldman

Music Making in Iran from the 15th to the Early 20th Century
Amir Hosein Pourjavady

Islamic Themes in US Hip-Hop Culture
Anders Ackfeldt

edinburghuniversitypress.com/series/mpmc

ISLAMIC THEMES IN US HIP-HOP CULTURE

Anders Ackfeldt

EDINBURGH
University Press

IN ASSOCIATION WITH

THE AGA KHAN UNIVERSITY
(International) in the United Kingdom
Institute for the Study of Muslim Civilisations

AGA KHAN MUSIC
PROGRAMME

Edinburgh University Press is one of the leading university presses in the UK. Publishing new research in the arts and humanities, EUP connects people and ideas to inspire creative thinking, open new perspectives and shape the world we live in. For more information, visit www.edinburghuniversitypress.com.

Edinburgh University Press Ltd
13 Infirmary Street, Edinburgh EH1 1LT

First published in hardback by Edinburgh University Press 2025

Typeset in 11/15 EB Garamond by
IDSUK (DataConnection) Ltd
Printed and bound by CPI Group (UK) Ltd,
Croydon, CR0 4YY

A CIP record for this book is available from the British Library

ISBN 978 1 3995 3753 7 (hardback)
ISBN 978 1 3995 3754 4 (paperback)
ISBN 978 1 3995 3755 1 (webready PDF)
ISBN 978 1 3995 3756 8 (epub)

MIX
Paper | Supporting responsible forestry
FSC
www.fsc.org
FSC® C013604

This book is printed using paper from well-managed forests, recycling and other controlled sources

CONTENTS

FIGURES

ACKNOWLEDGEMENTS

This book first saw the light as a doctoral dissertation entitled 'Islamic Semiotic Resources in US Hip-Hop Culture' at Lund University's Centre for Theology and Religious Studies, under the supervision of Professor Jonas Otterbeck. I owe a profound debt of gratitude to Professor Otterbeck for his boundless patience; neither this book nor the thesis would have been completed without it. His intellectual generosity and ability to transform complex discussions into enlightening conversation filled with humour were pivotal during this process.

I consider myself lucky to have such supportive colleagues that they often double as my friends. Among others, Dr Dan-Erik Andersson, Dr Olof Heilo, Dr Andreas Johansson, Professor Mark Levine, Douglas Mattsson, Dr Jesper Petersen, Darcy Thompson, Professor Leif Stenberg and Dr Simon Stjernholm have helped blur the lines between camaraderie and work.

My deepest thanks go to my wonderful family – Zinaida, Elma and Eira – whose unwavering love and motivation formed the foundation upon which this book was built. Without their support, this venture would have remained incomplete.

Malmö, 5 January 2024

1

INTRODUCTION
SIGNS, SYMBOLS AND ARTEFACTS

This book examines how Islamic themes feature in US hip-hop culture.[1] The empirical material analysed in the following pages is a heterogeneous collection of lyrics, sounds and pictures produced primarily by US-based hip-hop artists, Muslim and non-Muslim alike. While I will be looking at the articulations of Islamic themes within the US context, I also seek to contribute to the broader field of Islamic studies by analysing how the production of Islam can be seen as the outcome of interactions between actors who define themselves as Muslims as well as those who do not. To give empirical weight to this novel argument, theoretical tools from the field of social semiotics are utilised through three case-studies or gateways.

First of all, I will discuss this research field in more detail, situating this study within the growing body of scholarly literature on Islam and US hip-hop. I will then state the specific aims and research questions that have guided my work, concluding with a brief overview of the study.

A Glimpse of the Divine?

The use of Islamic themes within African American cultural settings pre-dates hip-hop culture. Although there is still much research to be done when it

[1] Hip-hop can also be spelled 'hip hop' or 'hip-hop' (with or without capital H). Here, I use the spelling hip-hop. Hip-hop is also commonly referred to as rap music. I use only hip-hop for the sake of consistency.

comes to early Islamic presence in the US, some scholars have suggested that the relationship between Islam and music was already forged during the transatlantic slave trade.[2] The scholar Alan Lomax has suggested that it would have taken only one skilled musician to transmit the musical tradition from Central and West Africa to the New World.[3] Moving forward in the history of music, despite sparse evidence scholars have inferred that there is a link between Islam's call to prayer, the *adhan*, and the minor scale and phrasing in blues music.[4] To give another example, jazz historians have noted that there was a tendency among some African American jazz musicians to embrace the message of the Ahmadiyya Muslim Community in the late 1940s and early 1950s.[5]

In the 1960s, the artists of the Black Arts Movement (BAM) defined the African American political struggle as a cultural struggle. The playwrights, musicians and poets of this movement fused their art with Islamic themes to create a revolutionary new African American aesthetic. In an interview titled 'Islam and Black Art', published in *Negro Digest* in January 1969, the controversial poet and activist Amiri Baraka (1934–2014), then still using his birth name LeRoi Jones, has discussed the possibilities of an Islamic state and economy in the US, as well as Islam's role in 'Black Art':[6]

> The closeness of man with natural evidence of Divinity is what art was all about in the beginning – to reveal, to manifest Divinity that man can understand: to make marks, to make symbols, to make signs, to make sounds, to make images that reveal Divinity, that reveal the presences of the One Force that animates everything. And that's what art is supposed to be about: to collect Divinity, to show its existence, to praise it, and to damn things that are seemingly trying

[2] Diouf 1998: 194.

[3] Lomax 2002: 334.

[4] Shibli 2007.

[5] Chase 2010.

[6] Amiri Baraka has on several occasions expressed controversial opinions and lashed out against LGBTQ+ people, women, white people in general and Jews. For example, in his poem 'Somebody Blew Up America?' (2002), published only months after the 9/11 attacks, he has suggested that the Israelis had prior knowledge of the attacks and therefore evacuated Israeli workers from the Twin Towers ahead of the attacks. For a general overview of the Black Arts Movement, see Smethurst 2005.

> to throw themselves against it. The artist's words, the signs, the symbols, the artifacts, are magic things, they're supposed to be able to suggest the presences of Allah (God). Just by hearing them (words), showing them, they're supposed to place you in close contact with the Divinity; they're supposed to make you come face to face with the Divinity.[7]

By invoking 'magic', 'symbols', 'signs' and 'sounds', Baraka envisioned 'Black Art' as a unique and original art form that serves as a conduit for bringing African Americans closer to Allah. The 'artefacts', symbols and signs possessed a magical potential to show a glimpse of the divine. Baraka's influence on the BAM during the 1960s was immense. His poem 'Black Art' served as a manifesto for the movement, and even though the majority of the poets, writers and artists of the BAM did not use Islamic themes in their artistic productions, those who did participated in making Islamic themes a part of African American political consciousness, even outside of the relatively small avant-garde circles of the BAM.[8]

The author and scholar Edward E. Curtis IV has noted that 'Many African American Muslims literally drew and rhymed themselves closer to the imagined worldwide community of Muslim believers'.[9] The artistic production of musicians, writers and other artists helped African Americans to discover Islam as a vehicle for protest and self-expression. The hip-hop artists studied in this book did something similar for their generations. The history of the use of Islamic themes in African American arts and culture therefore stands as an informative and important background for later uses of Islam in hip-hop music. The BAM writers' words inspired and continue to inspire. This historical background will be further explored in Chapters 2 and 3.

[7] 'Islam and Black Art – An Interview with LeRoi Jones', *Negro Digest*, January 1969, https://books.google.se/books?id=2rIDAAAAMBAJ&hl=sv&source=gbs_slider_cls_metadata_9_mylibrary (accessed 7 May 2024).

[8] McAlister 2001, 108–10. The anthology *Black Fire* (edited by Amiri Baraka and Larry Neal) includes several poems and writings that use Islamic themes, for example, Gaston Neal's 'Personal Jihad', Larry Neal's 'Malcolm X: An Autobiography' and Marvin E. Jackmon's 'That Old Time Religion'. See Baraka and Neal 2007.

[9] Curtis 2007: 684.

The Hip-Hop Zone Emerges from the Ruins

Just as the Black Arts Movement provided disillusioned African Americans with an artistic platform for expressing dissent and venting critique against the majority society, the emergence of hip-hop culture in New York in the 1970s provided a comparable artistic space.[10] As the media scholar Todd Boyd has put it, '[i]n the same way that civil rights leaders spoke to the conditions back in the day, hip-hop artists now speak to a populace often disillusioned by those considered overtly political in a traditional sense'.[11] With the emergence of hip-hop, the use of Islamic themes was extended into the post-civil rights era, just as Baraka had envisioned. Islamic 'artefacts', 'symbols' and 'signs' would become a part of the culture from the very beginning, just not primarily to celebrate God or to glimpse the divine.

Figure 1.1 Aerial view showing the Cross-Bronx Expressway, looking east at Webster Avenue, under construction in New York City in 1960. Source: AP Photo/Alamy.

[10] For discussions concerning the emergence of hip-hop, see, for example, Chang 2005a; Rose 1994; Rivera 2003.

[11] Boyd 2002: 10.

Most hip-hop historians and commentators see the construction of the Cross-Bronx Expressway as one of the starting points for hip-hop. The philosopher Marshall Berman's life was entangled with New York City, particularly the Bronx, to which he continuously returned in his lectures and writings. In 1982, Berman published *All That Is Solid Melts into Air: The Experience of Modernity*. The book was completed around the same time as hip-hop culture began to gain exposure outside of the Bronx. It contains a chapter on the construction of the Cross-Bronx Expressway and the devastating impact that it had on his community. Berman encountered the early writers, DJs, MCs and b-boys and b-girls in the Bronx. Later in his career, he described the blossoming hip-hop culture as 'a proof that modernity still lived' as a direct furtherance of other modernist writings and cultural expressions that drew power from 'the flow and the convulsions of the modern city streets', from Baudelaire to Billy Bragg.[12] Berman died on 11 September 2013, aged seventy-two. His last public lecture was delivered at the City College of New York on 2 May 2013, and when he took the podium the speakers in the auditorium blasted Boogie Down Productions' 'South Bronx' from their hip-hop album *Criminal Minded* (1987). A more fitting introduction is hard to imagine. During his speech, Berman revisited the ruins of the Bronx in the 1970s for the last time:[13]

> Meanwhile, the demos of the Bronx was finding voices. One voice was the explosion of graffiti on our subways. I loved it! The kids who made it were thrown into a public transit system that was far more broken down than today's. They told the world, 'We are not helpless; we can make this world colorful, exuberant, exciting'. I was thrilled. I took my mother to the 149th Street subway stop, near where we had lived, with a good view of the trains. She was a very reserved woman, but she said, 'It's a rainbow, in a place where who would expect one?'[14]

In the lecture, Berman suggested that the 'wholetrain' graffiti[15] passing through the 149th Street subway stop and the rhymes of the MCs in the Bronx revealed

[12] Berman 1996: 163.

[13] An adapted version of the lecture is available online: 'Emerging from the Ruins', https://www.dissentmagazine.org/article/emerging-from-the-ruins (accessed 22 December 2023).

[14] Ibid.

[15] 'Wholetrain' is a term used by graffiti writers to describe a train where all wagons are painted from top to bottom.

that residents wanted to demonstrate that they were not helpless but had the power to change their world. Furthermore, the haunted ruins came to life, and shouts in the streets echoed through the urban wasteland: 'We come from ruins, but we are not ruined'.

In Berman's dialectics, hip-hop became 'shouts in the streets' against the 'expressway world', a way to make sense of and react to a world in constant change. While making sense of the world around them, American hip-hop artists have continued the practice of using Islamic signs and symbols, not only in ways similar to what was envisioned by Baraka in the radical cultural climate of the 1960s, but also in ways that differ from Baraka's ideas of art celebrating and revealing the divine.[16]

Hip-hop culture is usually conceptualised, by practitioners as well as by outside observers, as a cultural phenomenon that encompasses four artistic expressions, commonly referred to as elements. These are: graffiti or writing; the dance form known as breaking or breakdancing (which gave rise to b-boys and b-girls); MCing (also referred to as rhyming or rapping); and DJing. The latter two constitute the foundation for rap music (here referred to as hip-hop music or hip-hop), which is the aural expression of hip-hop culture.

I have neither the intention to define what hip-hop culture is or should be, nor the desire to pass essentialist judgments on what constitutes 'authentic' or 'real' hip-hop. Definitions of hip-hop are best kept vague. To paraphrase the American anthropologist Clifford Geertz when discussing the concept *baraka* (in Islamic traditions often viewed as a continuity of spiritual presence that begins with Allah and flows through those closest to Allah), hip-hop is 'one of those resonant words it is better to talk about than to define'.[17] However, for an academic conceptualisation of the term, Raquel Rivera's definition of hip-hop as a zone has marked a good start:

> Hip hop is a fluid cultural space, a zone whose boundaries are an internal and external matter of debate. A profoundly diverse, translocal, multiethnic and multiracial cultural phenomenon, hip hop expressions also can present

[16] For a closer comparison between the jazz avant-garde of the 1960s and African American Muslim artists (from the website muslimhiphop.com), see Poutiainen and Rantakallio 2016.

[17] Geertz 1999: 32–33.

> themselves as exclusionary, for aesthetic, regional, gender, sexual-orientation, national, ethnic, racial, class or myriad other reasons. The dynamic tensions within hip hop and its constant drawing and crossing of borders are better addressed by the somewhat ambiguous concept of a 'hip hop zone' than by frequently adopted but more limiting (and, in my opinion, questionable) terms like 'hip hop community' and 'hip hop nation'.[18]

Rivera's conceptualisation of hip-hop as a 'fluid cultural space' fits well with my own understanding of hip-hop as a set of cultural expressions in constant conversation with surrounding societies. Like Berman, I view hip-hop as the product of a society in constant change. With a rich and multifaceted history reaching back some four decades, hip-hop arguably stands as one of the most significant cultural movements of the twenty-first century.

If we, like Berman, imagine modernism as a struggle to make ourselves at home in a world of constant change, we will realise that no strain of modernism can be definitive. Herein lie the many paradoxes of hip-hop and the reason for its transience. Depending on one's ideology, hip-hop can serve both as a beacon of commercialism and as a cross-cultural glue for the marginalised. On the one hand, as feminist scholar bell hooks has argued, hip-hop can be understood as a chauvinist fantasy for the mainstream, feeding multiple forms of oppressions: political, economic and social. It can reproduce misrepresentations and reinforce stereotypes.[19] Hip-hop can be about geopolitics, big business, ice grills and blood diamonds.[20] But on the other hand, as Boyd has argued, hip-hop can also be seen as a natural extension of the Civil Rights and Black Power movements, an inspiration for marginalised groups all over the world, providing grand narratives through which these groups can give meaning to perceived injustices on multiple socio-political scales.[21]

Much has happened since the young artists from the Bronx first forged cultural and artistic expressions of New York City, and hip-hop today is arguably a global story. In 2008, scholars estimated the total number of hip-hop

[18] Rivera 2003: 15.

[19] 'bell hooks pt 8 cultural criticism (rap music)', https://www.youtube.com/watch?v=EnN3EFmNyIM&t=64s (accessed 6 May 2024).

[20] See, for instance, Aidi 2014; Charnas 2010; Cepeda 2007.

[21] Boyd 2002.

fans around the globe to be around 100 million.[22] This number has probably increased since then. In 2015, the streaming service Spotify analysed the listening habits of its users. Spotify found that hip-hop was the most popular and listened to genre in its catalogue of nearly 20 billion songs.[23] The trend seems to be constant. In 2017, hip-hop streaming on Spotify was up 74 per cent since 2016, while the hip-hop playlist RapCaviar has millions of followers.[24] As of June 2018, Spotify had 83 million paying subscribers worldwide, while it was quickly approaching 200 million active users (including non-paid users) during the second quarter of 2018.[25] By 2023, Spotify had established its significant global reach, being accessible in more than 183 countries worldwide. As of the third quarter of the same year, the platform boasted approximately 574 million active users.[26] Among the various music genres available, hip-hop emerged as a particularly prominent category. It was reported that over 400 million users globally engaged with hip-hop music through Spotify in 2023. Additionally, the renowned 'RapCaviar' playlist achieved considerable popularity, securing its position as the secondmost-followed playlist on the platform. These data underscore the substantial impact and widespread appeal of hip-hop music within the digital streaming landscape.[27]

When it comes to hip-hop consumption in the US, data analysis agency Nielsen's Audience Insights report on hip-hop shows that the typical hip-hop listener is male and between eighteen and twenty-four years old. Despite the popular notion that white listeners constitute the lion's share of hip-hop

[22] Motley and Henderson 2008: 243.

[23] 'Hip-hop is the Most Listened to Genre in the World, According to Spotify Analysis of 20 Billion Tracks', https://www.independent.co.uk/arts-entertainment/music/news/hiphop-is-the-most-listened-to-genre-in-the-world-according-to-spotify-analysis-of-20-billion-tracks-10388091.html (accessed 8 August 2018).

[24] 'Hip-Hop Is the Most-Streamed Genre on Spotify Globally, up 74% Year Over Year', https://djbooth.net/features/2017-12-05-spotify-year-end-report (accessed 8 August 2018).

[25] 'Spotify Hits 83 Million Paid Subscribers', https://www.theverge.com/2018/7/26/17616404/spotify-paid-subscribers-83-million-streaming-music-quarterly-results (accessed 8 August 2018).

[26] 'Spotify Statistics for 2024: Users, Demographics', https://whatsthebigdata.com/spotify-statistics/ (accessed 6 May 2024).

[27] 'Nearly a Quarter of All Streams on Spotify are Hip-Hop: Spotify's Global Editors Reflect on the Genre's Growth', https://newsroom.spotify.com/2023-08-10/hip-hop-50-murals-new-york-atlanta-miami-los-angeles/ (accessed 6 May 2024).

consumers, Hispanics and African Americans are more likely to be hip-hop fans than the average white American. Hip-hop fans also seem to be more tech-savvy than the average American. Therefore, they are more likely to express their love for and interest in hip-hop on social media platforms such as Instagram, Snapchat and TikTok.[28]

Although these numbers should be taken with a grain of salt, most scholars would argue that, in its four-decade history, hip-hop has become one of the world's most far-reaching cultural forms.[29] It has been something of a cliché for culture commentators, general pundits and scholars alike to point to the global impact of hip-hop culture. As stated by the American journalist and music critic Jeff Chang in his article 'It's a Hip-Hop World', published in *Foreign Policy* magazine, 'that message [of hip-hop music] has proven its appeal to youth all around the world. Now, from Shanghai to Nairobi to São Paulo, hip-hop is evolving into a truly global art of communication'.[30]

Far from all hip-hop songs contain political undertones. The most-streamed rap song on Spotify in 2023, with over 730 million streams, was Doja Cat's 'Paint the Town Red', which can be viewed as a testament to her flamboyant style: living a fast life, young and carefree, encouraging the listeners to let loose and 'paint the town red',[31] a metaphor for breaking free from constraints. The song utilises a funky sample from the 1964 Grammy-nominated song 'Walk on By' by Dionne Warwick, which makes it a perfect anthem for nights out and celebrations.

[28] 'Hip-Hop Nation: How the Genre is Turning it up in 2015', https://www.nielsen.com/insights/2015/hip-hop-nation-how-the-genre-is-turning-up-in-2015/ (accessed 6 May 2024).

[29] The regional diversity of hip-hop is echoed in the vast academic literature investigating the culture outside the US. The first edited volume on hip-hop culture outside the US, Tony Mitchell's *Global Noise: Rap and Hip-Hop outside the USA* (2001), has provided insights into local hip-hop cultures in places as diverse as New Zealand, Korea and Japan. More recently, two German scholars, Sina A. Nitzsche and Walter Grünzweig, have contributed to hip-hop scholarship with the first edited volume on hip-hop culture focusing solely on Europe. The book, *Hip-Hop in Europe: Cultural Identities and Transnational Flows* (2013), has presented a much-needed European perspective on hip-hop culture in past and present Europe. Finally, a large number of monographs and articles on hip-hop have appeared, covering expressions of hip-hop in most corners of the world.

[30] Chang 2007: 58.

[31] 'Doja Cat Had Spotify's Most Popular Rap Song of 2023', https://www.hotnewhiphop.com/749528-doja-cat-spotify-most-popular-rap-song-2023 (accessed 3 January 2024).

Nevertheless, the hip-hop audience represents a possible global arena for the broadcasting of radical political and religious ideas. Next, I will show in detail how the literature on hip-hop has conceptualised and analysed the artists and songs that have made use of political and religious symbols, images and discourses.

A Review of the Scholarly Literature on Islam and Hip-Hop in the US

Contemporary music with Islamic themes is not bound to any specific geographical space, interpretation of Islam or musical genre. The plurality of musical expressions with Islamic themes has been studied from a multiplicity of perspectives across academic disciplines, including sociology, ethnomusicology, social anthropology, political science, hip-hop studies, cultural studies and Islamic studies. Nevertheless, in an effort to meaningfully demarcate the literature relevant to this book, this review will train a specific focus on the growing scholarly output (within various fields) on hip-hop music with Islamic themes, with a geographical emphasis on the US context.[32] With a few exceptions, most studies on the topic do not emanate from the field of Islamic studies.

One of the first researchers to highlight the fact that US hip-hop artists incorporated Islamic themes in their music was the French Islamic studies scholar Gilles Kepel. His book *Allah in the West* (1997), first published in French as *A l'ouest d'Allah* (1994), contains a section titled 'The Islam Rap'.[33] The section, mainly based on an interview with Conrad Muhammad, who at the time was a youth minister in Nation of Islam (NOI), has briefly described the relationship between hip-hop artists such as Public Enemy, Ice Cube and Sister Souljah, on the one hand, and NOI, on the other. Kepel has also noted that some of the songs on Public Enemy's sophomore album *It Takes a Nation of Millions to Hold Us Back* (1988) contain references to Allah and NOI.

Another early account has been provided by Swedish historian of religion Mattias Gardell in his seminal dissertation on the modern history of NOI: *Countdown to Armageddon: Minister Farrakhan and the Nation of Islam in the Latter Days* (1995).[34] Gardell has focused on what he labels 'message rap' and the role that artists ('raptivists') – such as Brand Nubian, Ice Cube

[32] Ackfeldt 2016; Daulatzai 2012; Nieuwkerk, LeVine and Stokes (eds) 2016; Otterbeck and Larsson 2017.

[33] Kepel 1997: 54–57.

[34] Gardell's dissertation was later published by Duke University Press, under the title *In the Name of Elijah Muhammad: Louis Farrakhan and the Nation of Islam* (1996).

and Paris – have played in popularising the message of NOI as well as the Five Percenters movement in the late 1980s and early 1990s. He has written: 'Teenagers dance into black consciousness and internalise the NOI creed through hip hop albums'.[35] Even though Gardell has emphasised political aspects such as police brutality, economic inequality and drugs, he has also been one of the first scholars to underline that artists directly allude to theological aspects and teachings of NOI. This is particularly important as other scholars at the time tended to underemphasise, or even neglect, these aspects.[36]

In his important and widely cited article from 1997, 'Islam in the Mix: Lessons of the Five Percent', the anthropologist Ted Swedenburg has been intrigued by the fact that Islamic references in the output of artists such as, for example, Public Enemy and Eric B. & Rakim had 'gone virtually without comment' among scholars at the time.[37] Many scholars and observers of hip-hop in general have ignored, consciously or unconsciously, the Islamic references that such artists make and instead highlighted the significance of Afrocentricity and Black nationalism.[38] Swedenburg's article has provided the first serious attempt to understand and analyse what he has labelled 'Islamic Rap' in the US. The article has stressed the fact that Islam is no marginal occurrence and that many Islamic Rap groups have reached mainstream fame.[39] Swedenburg has used the term 'Islamic Rap' for the sake of convenience. It is not completely clear which artists Swedenburg's concept is intended to capture. The text is mainly driven by the ambition to introduce and illuminate the teachings of the Five Percenters;[40] Swedenburg has introduced their history, key beliefs and

[35] Gardell 1995: 252.

[36] Ibid. pp. 250–57.

[37] Swedenburg 1997: 3.

[38] For example, Tricia Rose has failed to register Islamic themes when discussing groups such as Eric B. & Rakim and Public Enemy in her groundbreaking book on hip-hop culture, *Black Noise: Rap Music and Black Culture in Contemporary America* (1994). Jeffery Louis Decker's article, 'The State of Rap: Time and Place in Hip Hop Nationalism' (1993), to take another salient example, has described NOI and The Five Percenters in detail, but not recognised the religious dimensions of their music and instead focused on Afrocentristic and nationalistic themes.

[39] Swedenburg 1997: 2.

[40] The Five Percenters, occasionally referred to as NGE or NOGE, the Nation of Gods and Earths, or The Five Percent Nation, is an Islamic movement founded in 1964 in Harlem, New York City, by a former member of NOI: Clarence 13X. The movement is of utmost importance for understanding the usage of Islamic themes in hip-hop music. NGE will be discussed below.

concepts, pointing out that they are a crucial reference point for understanding the uses of Islamic themes in US hip-hop.[41] Swedenburg has done well in narrating the usage of Islamic themes among Five Percenter artists, but he does not take into account the influence of the movement on hip-hop aesthetics and the fact that non-Five Percenter artists use Islamic themes associated with the movement as well. Swedenburg, moreover, seems restricted to comparing and contrasting the Five Percenters' teachings 'to the type of Islamic teachings that one encounters in the Middle East'.[42]

In 2003, the religious studies scholar Anthony Pinn edited the innovative anthology *Noise and Spirit: The Religious and Spiritual Sensibilities of Rap Music* (2003). The book has scrutinised, in various ways, how different religious traditions – such as Islam, Christianity and Rastafari – are expressed within hip-hop music. One chapter has been dedicated to examining Islam and hip-hop, titled 'A Jihad of Words: The Evolution of African American Islam and Contemporary Hip-Hop', by the theologian Juan M. Floyd-Thomas. Floyd-Thomas has argued that the concept 'jihad of words' can help us to better understand Islamic expressions within hip-hop music.[43] The concept is taken from Richard Brent Turner, a scholar of African American religious history, and his description of Malcolm X's religious, social and political critique of US society. Floyd-Thomas has suggested that this is also in line with 'the greater Islamic tradition'. Floyd-Thomas has viewed the influence of Islam on hip-hop as a counterweight to more 'facile, materialistic and thuggish elements' of 'mainstream rap music'.[44]

In the exploratory article 'A New Research Agenda: Exploring the Transglobal Hip Hop Umma' (2005), H. Samy Alim, a scholar of education studies, has raised important questions concerning the diversity of Islamic expressions of Islam (what he labels as the 'Transglobal Hip Hop Umma') within global hip-hop culture:

[41] Swedenburg has examined global hip-hop culture in relation to Islam in other articles. See, for instance, 'Islamic Hip-hop vs. Islamophobia' (2001) and 'Hip Hop Music in the Transglobal Islamic Underground' (2002).

[42] Swedenburg 1997: 12.

[43] Floyd-Thomas 2003: 49–51.

[44] Ibid. p. 67.

> We can begin with general questions: How much do we know about the relationship between 'hip hop' and 'Islam'? Do we even see these two communities as compatible? We can further problematize the notion of 'Islamic hip hop' by reconsidering what it means to be an 'Islamic artist'[45] [. . .]. What is the relationship between African American Muslim movements in the hip hop cultural movement and the global Islamic world? What kinds of nation-building activities are occurring when Wu-Tang Clan's Rza visits with his Muslim brethren in Egypt, or when the Sunz of Man meet up with IAM in France?[46]

While raising interesting questions, Alim has not attempted to answer them. But he has made clear that it is crucial to develop a sensitivity to the concepts used, such as 'Islamic', to understand the broader context of Islamic themes in US-based hip-hop.

In his article 'Fear of a Muslim Planet: Hip-Hop's Hidden History' (2008), the cultural critic Naeem Mohaiemen has discussed the various ways in which Islam has influenced American hip-hop culture. He is one of the first scholars to recognise the link between the use of 'Islamic symbols' among the musical predecessor of hip-hop, not least the spoken word group of the Last Poets and today's hip-hop artists. Mohaiemen has suggested: 'When rappers rhyme over the *azaan* or Quranic *ayaats*, mainstream society's perceptions of an "alien" religion are flipped. Enhanced visibility through music can create a dynamic that moves America from hyper Islamophobia to a dialogue among equals'.[47]

In the aftermath of the tragic events of 9/11, numerous scholars have started to investigate Islam, resistance and American hip-hop music at the intersection of entangled transnational connections. This most likely had to do with the increased visibility and popularity of Muslim hip-hop artists in the US and beyond. The international affairs scholar Peter Mandaville has attributed this development to the disillusionment with 'conventional Islamist groups' among many young Muslims:

> While these new arenas of Muslim politics do not yet represent mainstream political Islam, it's significant that the actors and networks largely bypass the

[45] Alim 2005: 265.
[46] Ibid. p. 271.
[47] Mohaiemen 2008: 332.

> established 'old guard' of modern Islamism such as the Muslim Brotherhood. In other words, young Muslims, dissatisfied with the failure of conventional Islamist groups to deliver results, may be searching for alternative avenues of political expression and mobilisation – iPods firmly in hand.[48]

For Mandaville, hip-hop provides a new arena for Muslim politics and protest with a future potential to circumvent the 'old guard' of Muslim political activism. This rising form of Muslim social-justice activism is, according to Mandaville, driven by a shared urban experience characterised by racial tensions, unemployment, drugs and other social ills.

One scholar that has engaged deeply with the cultural experiences of young Muslims in the decade after 9/11 is the political scientist Hisham Aidi. Between 2002 and 2011, Aidi published several influential articles that have provided the foundation for his highly praised book *Rebel Music: Race, Empire and the New Muslim Youth Culture* (2014).[49] Aidi has explored Black internationalism and politics, as well as their encounters with Islam, from a variety of perspectives. A diverse set of social movements and counter-hegemonic practices are explored and carefully mapped on both sides of the 'Black Atlantic', often through the lens of music. Aidi has moved with ease across national borders, musical genres and language barriers as he has sketched a wide range of Muslim counter-politicking in the post-9/11 world. He has written:

> For over a century, African-American thinkers – Muslim and non-Muslim – have attempted to harness the black struggle to global Islam, while leaders in the Islamic world have tried to yoke their political causes to African-American liberation. Islamism, in the US context, has come to refer to differing ideologies adopted by Muslim groups to galvanize social movements for 'Islamic' political ends.[50]

Aidi has traced the intellectual roots of these Muslim countercultures to the Pan-African writings of Edward W. Blyden and Dusé Mohamed at the turn of

[48] Peter Mandaville, 'The Rise of Islamic Rap on the Streets of Britain, Hip Hop Jabs at Muslim Politics', *Yale Global*, 19 August 2010, http://yaleglobal.yale.edu/content/rise-islamic-rap (accessed 22 July 2016).

[49] The book received the American Book Award in 2015.

[50] Mohaiemen 2008: 332.

the twentieth century, through the speeches and writings of American Muslim leaders such as Malcolm X. In doing so, he has blurred the lines of the two fictive entities 'East' (the Muslim world) and 'West' (the rest). For Aidi, music is one of the strongest means used to disseminate African American politics – Muslim as well as non-Muslim – internationally. Hip-hop is just the latest execution, serving as the glue holding together marginalised youth around the world:

> Hip-hop has emerged as the idiom for the urban activism of minority youth in Europe. For Muslim youth experiencing the crackdown on immigrants, as well as state withdrawal and welfare cuts, hip-hop offers a chance to express critiques, vent rage, declare solidarity with other marginalised youth (particularly African Americans) and display cultural pride.[51]

Furthermore, Aidi has stressed that the politics of the 'Hip-hop Ummah' serve as a counterweight to other Muslim political projects on the 'Islamic shores of the Black Atlantic'.[52] As an example, he has highlighted the failure of boycotting American brands and substituting them with Halal alternatives marketed as 'Cool Islam', such as Mecca Cola or different Muslim streetwear brands. Such attempts have largely been unsuccessful, according to Aidi, because of the fact that young Muslims of the hip-hop generation remain loyal to US brands.[53]

But Aidi's research has done more than merely describing the bond between Islam and hip-hop in the US context as purely oppositional. In his article 'The Grand (Hip-Hop) Chessboard: Race, Rap and Raison d'État' (2011), he has investigated the other side of the coin. The article has put the spotlight on how the US State Department has used Muslim hip-hop artists to combat 'radical' political Islam in the Middle East and beyond. These 'hip-hop ambassadors' are sent to perform in hotspots around the world, in order to market 'American values' such as multiculturalism and democracy and to strengthen the image of the US overseas. Aidi has also discussed the tensions that US 'soft power' has created within hip-hop culture, perhaps best captured in the words of the English-Iraqi rapper Lowkey (as quoted in Aidi): 'When the US government loves the same rappers as you love, whose interest are those

[51] Aidi 2003: 47.

[52] For an informative discussion concerning 'cultural blackness' and Islam, see de Araújo and Gebauer 2016.

[53] Aidi 2004: 117.

rappers serving?'[54] Overall, Aidi's research has provided a bird's-eye view that combines a deep understanding of the topic with rich empirical material and historical knowledge. His writings have opened up and beged for further investigations of African American internationalism and Islam.

One work that delves deep into the research field is the musicologist Felicia Miyakawa's book *Five Percenter Rap: God Hop's Music, Message, and Black Muslim Mission* (2005). Miyakawa has provided a comprehensive evaluation of the Five Percenters' ideology, as well as the movement's influence on hip-hop music, and delivered a detailed account of the doctrines and teachings as they are reflected in hip-hop lyrics. Her study, however, is not restricted to textual references; she has extensively dealt with aural allusions as well as visual content, such as album cover art, music videos and liner notes. For Miyakawa, hip-hop music becomes a tool for the Nation of Gods and Earths to 'market' their 'way of life'. She has written: 'Rap is a perfect medium for spreading the Nation's doctrine. Rap not only captures the attention of an international audience, but also capitalises on the Nation's emphasis on verbal ability'.[55]

Although, strictly speaking, not an academic work, Michael Muhammed Knight's *The Five Percenters: Islam, Hip Hop and the Gods of New York* (2007) has provided a personal account of the movement, with a focus on its history. The chapter 'Songs of the Gods' provides unique information concerning the Five Percenters and their involvement in early hip-hop culture, as well as reflections on hip-hop lyrics influenced by the teachings of the movement.

In the context of studies dealing with the Five Percenters, it is worth mentioning two that have offered insight into specific facets of the movement in relation to hip-hop music. Travis L. Gosa, a scholar of African American studies, has presented an important contribution to the limited research on the Five Percenters in his article 'Counterknowledge, Racial Paranoia, and the Cultic Milieu' (2011). Gosa's study has discussed the Five Percenters and hip-hop music in relationship to 'counterknowledge' and conspiratorial ideas, which constitutes an insufficiently studied area.[56] The second study, 'I Can be Your Sun, You Can be My Earth: Masculinity, Hip Hop and the Nation of Gods and Earths' (2010) by Edward Onaci, has explored how gender relations, and

[54] Aidi 2011: 38.

[55] Miyakawa 2005: 37.

[56] Onaci 2010; Gosa 2011.

more specifically masculinity, are portrayed in hip-hop lyrics produced by artists influenced by the teachings of the Five Percenters. For Onaci, the Nation of Gods and Earths' views on gender and masculinity 'mirrors Black nationalism and American patriarchy'.[57]

In connection with research on gender, hip-hop and Islam, it is worth mentioning Anaya McMurray's article 'Hotep and Hip-Hop' (2007). In this article, the author has explored how two African American female artists, Erykah Badu and Eve, in their respective artistic productions negotiate their belief in Islam within the strictures of hip-hop culture. McMurray has argued that African American Muslim female artists create 'music spaces of resistance' for themselves and other African American women, where political and religious experiences can be expressed.[58]

In her often-cited article 'Rep that Islam: The Rhyme and Reason of American Islamic Hip Hop' (2007), the anthropologist Su'ad Abdul Khabeer has discussed different aspects of 'American Islamic Hip Hop'. The article is based on interviews with nine American Muslims involved with hip-hop. Although Khabeer has recognised the influence of what she has called 'Islamicate theologies', such as the Five Percenters and Nation of Islam, the focus of her article is on Sunni Muslim artists who, according to her observations, 'offer an alternative to the unfettered consumption and misogyny that dominates contemporary commercial hip hop'.[59] They also, according to Khabeer, evince 'a serious commitment to hip hop music and culture' and 'share an even more serious commitment to their religious beliefs and practices'.[60] In consequence, the author has argued for a change of terminology from American *Muslim* hip-hop to American *Islamic* hip-hop to describe the interlocutors interviewed for the article:

> I use the term Islamic rather than Muslim to distinguish a genre of hip hop music and culture created by American Muslims that seeks to comply with

[57] Onaci 2010: 145.

[58] McMurray 2008.

[59] Khabeer 2007: 138. Khabeer has drawn on Marshall Hodgson's term 'Islamicate' to 'describe things related to Islam in a more holistic sense rather than simply tied to strict doctrine'. Khabeer has not elaborated on this concept.

[60] Khabeer 2007: 127.

> Islamic religious standards and practices and whose current and primary audience is Muslims. For example, Islamic hip hop may restrict the types of musical instruments used, generally does not employ expletives and frequently refers to issues of doctrinal import. By foregrounding religious identity in these ways, Islamic hip hop artists are distinct from other American Muslim hip hop artists who are more integrated in the music industry, whether they are mainstream or underground artists.[61]

Some of the artists discussed in the article are Tyson, the members of the Maryland-based rap trio Native Deen, and Miss Undastood. Specific issues covered in the article include the permissibility of music within the realm of Islam, women, Islam and hip-hop, as well as the future of Islam and hip-hop.

In her ethnographic monograph *Muslim Cool: Race, Religion and Hip Hop in the United States* (2016), Khabeer has built on her earlier work and examined how African American youth construct and perform their 'Muslim Cool' identity. For Khabeer, the concept of 'Muslim Cool' represents a 'counterpoint to the hegemonic norms of Whiteness as well as to Arab and South Asian US American communities'. Furthermore, she has argued that the concept 'pushes back against the pervasive phenomena of anti-Blackness'.[62] In the article 'Muslimhiphop.com: Constructing Muslim Hip Hop Identities on the Internet' (2013), Inka Rantakallio has investigated how Muslim identities are constructed and negotiated on the American website Muslimhiphop.com which was launched in 2004.[63] Rantakallio's work, like Khabeer's, has focused on 'conscious Muslims who clearly bring forward their religion in their music', which is also the stated goal for the website studied.

Sohail Daulatzai's book *Black Star, Crescent Moon: The Muslim International and Black Freedom Beyond America* (2012) has offered an original examination of African American internationalism and Islam as a unifying global symbol of resistance. Not restricted to a critical analysis of popular culture, the study has offered a broad survey of positions and political engagements in what Daulatzai has branded 'the Muslim International':

[61] Ibid. p. 126.

[62] Khabeer 2016: 5.

[63] Rantakallio 2013.

> In this way, the Muslim International acts as a permeable contact zone, sharing territories of struggle with the larger Afro-diasporic imagination, in which ideas about community, resistance, and belonging can be engaged. [. . .] the Muslim International is not geographically located. Instead it is composed of not only multiple and overlapping diasporas that have resulted from slavery, colonialism, and migration, but also by communities and collectives that have been shaped by uneven and disparate relationships to nation-states, capitalism, and imperial power, a zone of struggles and solidarity in which new kinds of politics emerge.[64]

One chapter in this study has been dedicated to the exploration of the political terrain of 'the Muslim International' through the lens of American hip-hop music. In the chapter 'Return of the Mecca: Public Enemies, Reaganism, and the Birth of Hip-Hop',[65] Daulatzai has analysed how American hip-hop became a vehicle for artists to extend 'Malcolm X's internationalist vision in the post-Civil Rights era'. Artists such as Ice Cube, Public Enemy and Gang Starr have been discussed in detail; there is also a fine reading of Eric B. & Rakim's song 'Casualties of War' (1992), which in the author's interpretation is 'a vivid narrative about race and belief, slavery and imperialism, national allegiance and international belonging', which 'potently links US power and violence with the Muslim Third World of Iraq'.[66] For Daulatzai, American hip-hop artists who incorporate Islamic themes in their musical and lyrical productions play a crucial role in shaping and developing 'the Muslim International'. *Black Star, Crescent Moon* has provided a historical and contextual backdrop to the connection between Islam and hip-hop music in the US.

In *Representing Islam: Hip-Hop of the September 11 Generation* (2020), Kamaludeen Mohamed Nasir has woven together the threads of Islam and hip-hop within the fabric of a generation marked by the events of 11 September 2001. Nasir has drawn inspiration from Karl Mannheim's seminal essay 'The Problem of Generations' and identified the existence of a 9/11 generation – those born between 1980 and the eve of 9/11 – who are unified by the symbolic

[64] Daulatzai 2012: xxiii.

[65] An earlier version of this chapter was first published as 'War at 33 1/3: Hip-Hop, the Language of the Unheard, and the Afro-Asian Atlantic', in Basu and Lemelle 2006.

[66] Daulatzai 2012: 129.

significance of the terror attacks: these events serve as a cohesive force, placing them under the same analytical lens.[67] The book has portrayed the 9/11 attacks as a central motif in the creative endeavours of young Muslim hip-hop artists, whose work is saturated with references that appear in auditory, visual and textual forms – ranging from t-shirt designs to lyrical punchlines, metaphors, album covers and sound clips. This generation has made the memory of 9/11 a persistent theme, an echo that reverberates through their art and commentary.[68] Nasir's research has distinguished itself by stepping beyond the typical American or European contexts that have traditionally dominated generational studies. He has approached the subject as a global sociologist with a keen understanding of hip-hop culture across various locales, from the streets of New York to the hip-hop scenes in Kuala Lumpur and Sydney. By stressing the fluidity between these scenes, Nasir has given substantial empirical depth to his analysis, offering a richly textured perspective that underscores the global resonance of the 9/11 generation's experience. *Representing Islam: Hip-Hop of the September 11 Generation* is a noteworthy study of how a paradigmatic moment in history has left a lasting mark on a diverse group of hip-hop artists around the globe.

In the chapter 'Islam and Hip Hop in Black America: Oral Tradition as Critical Liberatory Praxis' from the book *The Complexities of Race: Identity, Power, and Justice in an Evolving America* (2021), Amer F. Ahmed has explored the intersection of Islam and hip-hop within the African American community as a form of resistance against systemic racism. Through the lens of the philosopher Paulo Friere's notions of critical pedagogy and praxis, Ahmed has highlighted how what he calls Islamic-based ideologies provide an alternative to Western hegemony and connect Black Americans to their African heritage.[69] Hip-hop, influenced by Islamic ideologies and rooted in African oral traditions, so he has argued, emerges as a powerful medium for self-expression, resistance and social critique. The personal study has emphasised hip-hop's role in educational and community settings as a tool for empowerment, transformative action and social justice.

To sum up, as hip-hop continues to evolve, the intersection of music and Islam has remained a vibrant field of cultural and political significance, offering

[67] Nasir 2020: 4.

[68] Nasir 2020: 181.

[69] Ahmed 2021: 193f.

rich opportunities for further academic exploration and understanding. The previous research, beginning in the mid-1990s, has demonstrated that Islamic themes, stemming from different Islamic traditions (especially African American ones), are present in US hip-hop. Hip-hop has also been shown to play an important role for mobilising a countercultural African American political awareness and Muslim political awareness more generally. Above all, hip-hop lyrics inspired by Five Percenter ideology have gained much attention. Research has provided several excellent case-studies of artists and songs, along with general overviews, most with a focus on the textual production of artists or themes addressed from ethnographical and anthropological perspectives. What is particularly important for the present study are studies of the Five Percenter worldview and how this worldview finds its way into hip-hop. The results of this research will be expanded upon in this book.

There are a few areas that have been left out in the literature. Firstly, there is a lack of studies that seek to understand or explain the dynamics of how Islamic themes, symbols and signs are crafted and used. This, as I will argue in Chapter 2, requires a new form of theorising in regard to the uses of Islamic themes. Secondly, hip-hop in the last decades needs to be more firmly understood in relation to an African American musical history in which Islamic themes have played a prominent, indeed formative, part. Such a contextualisation delimits a crucial research field that will be explored in Chapter 3. Finally, while many artists (and their music) have been previously discussed, others still remain to be situated in hip-hop culture and history. Here, too, my study seeks to make a contribution.

Directions and Essential Questions

In order to unearth, present and analyse the use of Islamic themes in hip-hop, I will employ theoretical perspectives and concepts from the field of social semiotics, in particular the concept of semiotic resources and the concept of semiotic regimes (see Chapter 2). This study thus seeks to examine how semiotic resources previously not associated with Islam have the potential to be perceived as Islamic. The present book departs in two ways from earlier research on the topic. Firstly, it *analyses* the artistic production of US hip-hop artists as containing semiotic resources that relate to Islam, while the existing research has remained content by merely *describing* the music as Islamic or influenced by Islam. Secondly, to my knowledge, this book represents the first major research on the uses of Islamic themes in hip-hop culture conducted within the field of Islamic studies. I want to contribute not only to the understanding of Islam and hip-hop, but also to the larger field of Islamic studies, by providing new theoretical angles for studying the innumerable faces of Islam. The work has largely been motivated by my desire to highlight and better integrate the study of African American Islam into the larger field of Islamic studies, as well as into the sub-field of Islam and music.

This is an urge that I feel I share with many scholars of African American Islam. As a testimony to this, I would like to highlight the great Twitter/X initiative started by Kayla R. Wheeler, a PhD candidate in the Department of Religious Studies at the University of Iowa. At the end of 2015, Wheeler started the hashtag #BlackIslamSyllabus, with the stated goal being 'to provide teachers, professors, researchers, journalists and people interested in learning more about Islam with resources on Black Muslims to promote a more inclusive approach to the study of Islam'. At the time of writing, this amazingly useful project contained more than forty pages with articles and Internet resources on the topic.[70]

This is a theoretically driven, sustained and systematic effort to bridge the gap between the literature on the topic and Islamic studies; in order to close this gap, this book seeks to explore and answer the following research questions: (1) Given the results, insights and shortcomings found in the literature review, the first research question asks: how can we study the uses of Islamic themes in US hip-hop in a way that will further the understanding of the semiotic associations and the functions of these Islamic themes? (2) Much of the research on African American hip-hop has successfully addressed the political dimensions of hip-hop, often in relation to race and identity politics. But there exist surprisingly few studies that have analysed the political aspects related to Islamic themes in hip-hop. Thus, a second important question emerges: how can we analyse the political dimensions of these Islamic themes? (3) Noting that the literature often erroneously presumes that only Muslims partake in the creation of Islamic themes in hip-hop, a third research question arises: who is active and has a say in the production of Islamic themes in hip-hop?

[70] '#BlackIslamSyllabus', https://docs.google.com/document/d/1avhgPrW30AFjegzV9X5aPqkZUA3uGd0-BZr9_zhArtQ/edit (accessed 1 December 2023).

Overview of the Book

Chapter 2 will introduce the theoretical framework used to analyse the empirical material, taking its departure from an analytical assessment by Monica R. Miller of the previous scholarly literature on religion and hip-hop. This chapter will suggest new perspectives and introduce theoretical tools from the field of social semiotics, which in turn will be operationalised and used as an interpretative framework for the empirical chapters. The chapter will outline my arguments and explain how this study offers new ways of approaching Islamic themes in hip-hop and provide novel theoretical insights to the larger field of Islamic studies.

Chapters 3 and 4 will contextualise hip-hop historically, while Chapters 5, 6 and 7 will offer three in-depth case studies of hip-hop and Islamic themes. The topics of the latter three chapters illustrate and offer alternative analyses; they do not present an exhaustive account of Islamic themes in US hip-hop. Chapter 3 will argue that African American religious culture has a long and complex relationship with Islam, which finds various expressions from music-making during the transatlantic slave trade to the birth of hip-hop. This relationship unfolds over centuries of African American music-making. The chapter will discuss a wide array of musical genres in brief, but it does not aspire to paint a full picture. Nevertheless, this chapter will serve as an important contextual backdrop to the main topic of this book: the manifold uses of Islamic themes in hip-hop music. Chapter 3 is mainly based on existing scholarship, but some new findings based on archival sources and music will also be presented. There, I will point to the fact that music has been a prominent arena where Muslims as well as non-Muslims have used Islamic themes in their artistic productions, even before the birth of hip-hop music.

Chapter 4 will examines Islamic themes as social constructions produced by Muslims as well as non-Muslims, as they mobilise semiotic resources understood as 'Islamic' by connecting these to a perceived Islamic past. The chapter will focus on two organisations that have been crucial in extending earlier efforts to combine semiotic resources perceived as Islamic with music: The Universal Zulu Nation and The Nation of Gods and Earths (or the Five Percenters). Both organisations, so I argue, are of utmost importance for understanding how semiotic resources from the cognitive universe of Islam have been used within US hip-hop culture – and this despite the fact that neither of the organisations describes or considers itself as Muslim.

Chapter 5 will illustrate the complexities – and serendipities – of visual, textual and aural hip-hop culture by analysing one single song and its accompanying music video, namely 'Paid in Full (Mini Madness: The Coldcut Remix)' (1987) performed by Eric B. & Rakim, remixed by the British electronic music duo Coldcut and directed by British music video director Bruno Tilley. This chapter recognises the individual efforts made by different actors involved in the production of the music video and shows how they, together and in different intertwined ways, have shaped what has been perceived as Islam or Islamic by many commentators.

Chapter 6 centres on Malcolm X, one of the most visible figures in US popular culture. Malcolm X and his legacy will be analytically dissected as semiotic resources. The chapter will scrutinise how Malcolm X and his legacy have triggered the imaginations of US hip-hop artists since the early days of the genre, and how this has been used in different ways by hip-hop artists, including those stressing the Muslim and Islamic side of Malcolm X. The existing research has addressed the importance of Malcolm X as important either for African American politics or for his connections to Islam. This chapter will argue that his politics and his Islamic beliefs are intertwined, and that one cannot be understood without the other.

Chapter 7 will discuss representations of 9/11 in US hip-hop by providing selected readings of how 9/11 and its legacy have been used by US hip-hop artists. 9/11 is particularly important in the context of my argument since Islamic semiotic resources are placed in a variety of semiotic regimes by a large variety of hip-hop artists with very different agendas. This chapter will show how semiotic resources generally not understood as Islamic can become coded as Islamic through a new contextualisation. The chapter registers shifts in the semiotic articulations over time and in the fact that 9/11 and narratives of the 'War on Terror' have become crucial if we wish to understand the relationship between Islam and hip-hop.

Finally, Chapter 8 will provide a conclusion with suggestions for future avenues of study.

2

THE STUDY OF RELIGION AND HIP-HOP

This chapter will discuss some of the theoretical vantage points and key concepts used to analyse the empirical material. First, I will examine the study of religion and hip-hop, focusing on Monica R. Miller's recent work, then present the theoretical underpinnings of this book: these include my own theoretical background within Islamic studies as well as social semiotics. Key terms in social semiotics – *multimodal*, *semiotic resource*, *affordance* and *semiotic regime* – will be introduced and discussed in the context of Islamic studies. I will also discuss the material of the study and the limits thereof.

Religion and Hip-Hop

Apart from the literature on Islam and hip-hop reviewed in the previous chapter, there exists a burgeoning research field that examines the relationship between religion and hip-hop. The contours of this field have been delineated by academics such as Michael Eric Dyson, Cornel West and Anthony B. Pinn. In 1991, Jon Michael Spencer edited a special issue of *Black Sacred Music: A Journal of Theomusicology*, titled 'The Emergency of Black and the Emergence of Rap', which has contained contributions by Michael Eric Dyson, William Eric Perkins and Angela M. Nelson. It has examined hip-hop culture, theology, spirituality and religion from different academic perspectives. In the middle of the 1990s, Dyson published *Between God and Gangsta Rap: Bearing Witness to Black Popular Culture* (1995), while Pinn published *Why, Lord? Suffering and Evil in Black Theology* (1995). Both books have shone light on hip-hop as source material for theology and religious studies and paved the way for several other studies in the early 2000s, not least the previously mentioned *Noise and Spirit: The Religious and Spiritual Sensibilities of Rap Music* (2003), edited by Pinn, and *Shamanism, Racism, and Hip-Hop Culture* (2005) by James W. Perkinson. The latter book has put race and religion at the centre of its examination of hip-hop. These studies have offered fine descriptions of hip-hop's religious dimensions. However, they have not presented analyses that are sufficiently informed by theory.

In 2013, Monica R. Miller published the book *Religion and Hip Hop* (2013). This work has departed from much of the prior scholarship on religion and hip-hop and marked a significant theoretical turn within the field. Miller's book has presented a theoretically driven approach, coupled with an ambition to 'refashion' the study of hip-hop and religion.[1] In doing so, Miller has relied on a wide range of approaches from constructivist social and cultural theory. With the help of scholars such as Russell T. McCutcheon and Talal Asad, Miller has critically argued that the category 'religion' is a result of 'disciplinary manufacturing' constructed by scholars who for a variety of reasons have had an interest in preserving the idea of religion as a unique phenomenon.[2] She has argued:

> There is no need here to ask the question: 'What is religious?' Rather, as scholars of religious studies we can approach cultural practices with the understanding that there is nothing in and of itself unique about religion. Of greater interest is the exploration of *why* certain social processes come to be understood and classified *as* religious, and furthermore what these classifications accomplish among particular groups across time and space.[3]

According to Miller, there has been a lot of wasted scholarly effort put into describing what is religious within and about hip-hop culture. Less attention has been directed towards investigating the *uses* of what are perceived to be religious manifestations. When assessing earlier research, Miller has noted

[1] Miller 2013: 178.

[2] Ibid. p. 8.

[3] Ibid. p. 178.

that the pioneering works in the field, 'the first wave', as she has called it, were primarily concerned with proving the 'academic legitimacy and religious "merit" of Hip-Hop culture, more specifically rap music'.[4] She has continued: 'The more common religious and theological approach to exploring Hip-Hop culture is erroneously occupied with preserving truth claims of what counts *as* religious among Hip-Hop source material'.[5]

Since the publication of *Religion and Hip Hop*, Miller has been involved in two other important books that have helped solidify religion and hip-hop studies, *The Hip Hop and Religion Reader* (2015), co-edited with Anthony B. Pinn, and *Religion in Hip Hop: Mapping the New Terrain in the US* (2015), co-edited with Anthony B. Pinn and Bernard 'Bun B' Freeman. *The Hip Hop and Religion Reader* has brought together some of the most significant contributions to the field in one volume, in an attempt to frame and capture the multi-disciplinarity and depth of the field. The aim of *Religion in Hip Hop: Mapping the New Terrain in the US* has been to 'advance a methodological and theoretical housing for the study of hip-hop and religion'.[6] Both books have served as important milestones on the path to defining the still emerging field of religion and hip-hop.

My book takes its cue from Miller's core ideas and aims to contribute to the sub-field of Islam and hip-hop. It attempts to move away from essentialist claims about 'true', 'purposeful' or 'sincere' religion within US hip-hop culture and to shift towards a form of inquiry that looks at how Islamic themes in US hip-hop can be and have been used in contingent social, cultural, religious, musical and political contexts. This way of reasoning chimes with my own background in Islamic studies, which I will discuss next.

An Islamic Studies Perspective on Islam and Hip-Hop

One common definition, used in various phrasings by different scholars to define the field of Islamic studies, has been provided by Edward E. Curtis IV: 'I would argue that the student of Islam should not even insist on using a person's identification with the Qur'an as a kind of minimal definition of what it means to be a Muslim. Instead, wherever and whenever a person calls himself or herself

[4] Miller, Pinn and Bun B 2015: 4.

[5] Miller 2013: 12.

[6] Miller, Pinn, and Bun B 2015: 4.

Muslim, scholars should include this person's voice in their understanding of what constitutes Islam'.[7] Further, Curtis has suggested:

> If one's goal is to avoid such essentialism in Islamic studies, there is not and cannot be any one normative definition of Islamic tradition or its boundaries and limits. But scholars can identify competing definitions of Islam by examining the historical interpretations of Muslims themselves.[8]

In his more recent essay, 'Ode to Islamic Studies: Its Allure, Its Danger, Its Power', Curtis has reflected on the state of Islamic studies and somewhat modified his position from the above-quoted work.[9] 'The study of Islam', so Curtis has argued, 'has outgrown its orientalist roots'. For Curtis, Islamic studies 'has become indispensable to the study of what it means to be human', and he has acknowledged the immense power and cultural influence that 'Islam' has on today's world:

> Islam as a semiotic sign is simply too important for any one party to define or control it. Its role in global politics, ethics, and culture insures its contestability. Put too simply, Islam – again, as a sign – is everywhere. From D.C. think-tanks to the Myanmar countryside, from intimate, private interactions to public displays, it is ubiquitous in modern life.[10]

Curtis's position is, of course, not unique; it is similar to the stance taken by several leading Islamic studies scholars. Curtis is somewhat ambiguous about the role of non-Muslims (in this case, perhaps, illustrated by 'DC think-tanks') in the (political, moral and so on) production of Islam. In this study, by contrast, Muslims as well as non-Muslims have been acknowledged as potential and actual producers of Islam. These non-Muslim actors could, for example, be pundits, politicians, academics or musicians who write and talk about Islam in the public sphere.

[7] Curtis 2002: 6.

[8] Ibid. p. 5.

[9] 'Ode to Islamic Studies: Its Allure, Its Danger, Its Power', https://www.meforum.org/campus-watch/21420/ode-to-islamic-studies-its-allure-its-danger-its (accessed 6 May 2023).

[10] Ibid.

The fact that actors who do not identify themselves as Muslims participate in the process of shaping what is perceived as Islam is an overlooked aspect in the field of Islamic studies – one that only recently has begun to draw attention. A small but growing number of scholars have sought to map how non-Muslims construct and relate to 'Islam'. Armando Salvatore's *Islam and the Political Discourse of Modernity* (1997) has touched on this subject. Salvatore has recognised that 'political Islam' is manufactured with interference from a global political discourse of modernity and Islam. This non-Islamic discourse affects, according to Salvatore, all interpretations of Islam and helps to shape what is perceived as Islamic.[11]

Another good example of a recent scholarly work within the field of Islamic studies that has taken an interest in non-Muslims' understanding of Islam is Johan Cato's PhD dissertation *När islam blev svenskt: Föreställningar om islam och muslimer i svensk offentlig politik, 1975–2010* (*When Islam Became Swedish: Representations of Islam and Muslims in Swedish Public Policy, 1975–2010*) (2012). Cato has described how Islam and Muslims were portrayed in Swedish public policy debates in that thirty-five-year period, arguing that from 1989 onwards the Swedish state and parliamentary parties tried to construct, administer and channel an 'acceptable' version of Islam (and simultaneously a non-acceptable one) that encompasses what is perceived as moderate Islamic values. Thus, Cato has studied how non-Muslims also contribute to the processes that shape what is perceived as Islam. However, the consequences of this novel approach have not been theorised. Likewise, studies on Islamophobia often touch upon this issue, but seldom develop a theoretical understanding of the significance for Islamic studies.[12]

This is something that I have developed with my colleague Jesper Petersen in the article 'The Case for Studying Non-Muslim Islams' (2022). This article was partly the result of the empirical findings in the present study.[13] In light of the discussion above, I suggest that Islamic studies – as well as hip-hop and religious studies – need to develop theoretically, and I will now suggest a way forward for doing precisely that.

[11] Salvatore 1997.

[12] See, for example, Bevelander and Otterbeck 2010.

[13] Petersen and Ackfeldt 2022.

A Social Semiotic Approach to Islam

Social semiotics is a sub-field of semiotics that discards the structural determinism of Ferdinand de Saussure, Claude Levi-Strauss and Marcel Mauss, finding fresh inspiration in theorists such as Charles Sanders Peirce, Mikhail Bakhtin and Michael Halliday.[14] Central to the field of social semiotics is the assertion that language is not seen 'as a set of rules but as a resource', as Halliday has stated in his classic work *Language as Social Semiotics* (1978).[15] The emphasis here is on the 'human processes of interaction' and on the constant changes to and reworkings of the meaning of these resources.[16]

In recent years, scholars in the field have extended the linguistic origins of social semiotics to include other ways of communicating, such as gesticulations, pictures, layout, sound and motion. A central concept in the field is *semiotic resources*, defined by Theo van Leeuwen as follows:

> the actions and artefacts we use to communicate, whether they are produced physiologically – with our vocal apparatus; with the muscles we use to create facial expressions and gestures, etc – or by means of technologies – with pen, ink and paper; with computer hardware and software; with fabrics, scissors and sewing machines, etc.[17]

According to van Leeuwen, semiotic resources have a meaning potential, based on their past uses, along with a set of affordances (the prospective use of a given object). Affordances are not static: 'Because perception is selective, depending on the needs and interests of the perceivers, different perceivers will notice different affordances. But those that remain unnoticed continue to exist objectively, latent in the object, waiting to be discovered'.[18] Semiotic resources are governed by *semiotic regimes* – that is, the specific ways in which the uses of semiotic resources are ordered in specific contexts. Each context has its own role models, personal authorities and conformities, and an inner logic that helps to shape the use of semiotic resources. Further, these semiotic resources

[14] Vannini 2007: 115.

[15] Halliday 1978: 192.

[16] Ibid.

[17] Leeuwen 2005: 3.

[18] Leeuwen 2005: 273.

(actions and artefacts) are channelled and shaped through the medium of the *communicative act* or *mode*. Examples of different kinds of modes include images, music, moving images and gestures.[19] Most communicative acts do not involve one mode (*monomodal*) but operate over two or more modes (*multimodal*), all of which contribute to the creation of meaning.

As mentioned above, my understanding of Islam and the idea of being Muslim is informed by scholars who view Islam not as a static, monolithic construction but rather as multiple, dynamic traditions shaped during particular times and in particular socio-geographic spaces; in other words, as a product of 'human processes of interaction'.[20] The Saudi anthropologist Talal Asad's view of Islam as a *tradition* has provided an especially useful vantage point here since a tradition can be viewed as historical processes of interaction between individuals.[21] Describing the concept, Asad has written:

> A tradition consists essentially of discourses that seek to instruct practitioners regarding the correct form and purpose of a given practice that, precisely because it is established, has a history. These discourses relate conceptually to *a past* (when the practice was instituted, and from which the knowledge of its point and proper performance has been transmitted) and *a future* (how the point of that practice can best be secured in the short or long term, or why it should be modified or abandoned), through *a present* (how it is linked to other practices, institutions, and social conditions). An Islamic discursive tradition is simply a tradition of Muslim discourse that addresses itself to conceptions of the Islamic past and future, with reference to a particular Islamic practice in the present. Clearly, not everything Muslims say and do belongs to an Islamic discursive tradition. Nor is an Islamic tradition in this sense necessarily imitative of what was done in the past.[22]

In this book, I focus on the products and actions (in other words, the semiotic resources) of these 'human processes of interaction'. Like Asad, I recognise

[19] Kress 2010: 79.

[20] See, for example, Stenberg 1996; Hjärpe 1997; Otterbeck 2000; Stjernholm 2011.

[21] Since the publication of Asad's highly influential text 'Idea of an Anthropology of Islam' (1986), an ever-growing body of anthropological work within the field of Islamic studies (and outside of it) has turned to studying Islam as a tradition.

[22] Asad 2009: 14f.

that 'Islam' cannot be studied independently of perception, and that there is nothing that is inherently 'Islamic'. There are only actions, concepts and appearances that are perceived and conceptualised as 'Islamic' by being indirectly connected to ideas of an Islamic discursive tradition with a past, present and future. These semiotic resources can be said to be organised by semiotic regimes that can potentially be Islamic through their relation to the Islamic discursive tradition.

A positional stance follows from my reading of Asad (a position not taken or possibly not considered by Asad himself): one does not have to consider oneself Muslim in order to produce Islam – in other words, to mobilise *semiotic resources* understood as Islamic by being part of a perceived Islamic past. This position is, as I will demonstrate, crucial for the interpretation of the empirical material in this book. This study is therefore not necessarily about Muslims who make hip-hop or Islamic hip-hop; rather, the focus is on how artists (Muslims as well as non-Muslims) have utilised *semiotic resources* understood as Islamic within hip-hop culture. Islam is not viewed as a structure of rules or symbols, but as a discursive tradition manifested in semiotic resources – the uses and meanings of which are negotiated by individuals. But these semiotic resources are always subject to repetition, which strengthens expected future use. However, they can be put in new contexts and relatedly, actively (and occasionally subversively) renegotiated. As discourses are not contained systems, unexpected semiotic resources may be introduced into the discourse, and its regimes may awaken the potentiality of being perceived as Islamic. Hip-hop culture, in my view, with its broad variety of Islamic interpretive traditions, provides an excellent arena for the study of Islamic semiotic resources.

For Halliday, whom some view as the father of social semiotics, the building blocks of languages – sentences and words – carry 'meaning potential' rather than specific meanings. This potential, according to Halliday, needs to be studied in a social context. Within the field of social semiotics, and in close relationship to 'meaning potential', the concept of semiotic potential or affordance is crucial. As soon as an object, or a concept, has been defined as a semiotic resource, it becomes possible to identify its potential for different kinds of meaning – the semiotic potential of any given semiotic resource.[23] The meanings of semiotic

[23] Vannini 2007: 127.

resources are intimately connected to our comprehension of the conventions and practices that are present in the social context in which specific resources are used.[24] A semiotic resource can be understood in different, sometimes competing and sometimes completing ways. Some semiotic resources are likely to be interpreted in a certain way, in a specific context, more so than others.

The Empirical Material

To advance an understanding of how semiotic resources are shaped and developed in US hip-hop culture, the interplay between textual, aural and visual resources must be taken into consideration. This raises a set of methodical concerns which I will now address.

The bulk of the empirical material for this study is comprised of a bricolage of lyrics, songs, music videos, album covers, flyers, magazines and other manifestations of US hip-hop culture which I have collated over the years. This material was first collected out of both personal and academic interest in the relationship between Islam and hip-hop, an interest that sprung from my background in Islamic studies, as well as the fact that I have been an active listener of US hip-hop music since my early adolescence. Over time, this interest turned into a methodical endeavour, as I began to assemble a comprehensive compilation of references to Islam within hip-hop culture. This systematic collection transcended mere casual observation, turning into a scholarly pursuit, where each reference to Islamic theology, culture or practice in lyrics, videos and artist personas was catalogued. This aggregation of Islamic references in hip-hop has laid the groundwork for the examples used in this present study: the examples and case-studies included in this book are carefully selected from this collection to represent broader tendencies and patterns within the intersection of Islam and hip-hop culture.

In this context, it is important to acknowledge the emergence of a distinct sub-genre within hip-hop culture over the past two decades, a sub-genre that exhibits a more pronounced Sunni Muslim identity among its artists. This genre seeks to appeal to a Muslim audience and is characterised by artists who overtly place Islam at the heart of their creative expression, similar to how Christian rock artists integrate their faith into their music. Prominent artists

[24] Ibid. p. 133.

within this sphere, both in the US and internationally, include Native Deen, Deen Squad, Sista Keilana, Poetic Pilgrimage and Baraka Blue. Although this 'Muslim and/or Islamic' hip-hop scene has attracted significant scholarly interest, it remains outside the scope of the present study.[25]

This project has afforded me further potential to critically engage with questions concerning Islam and hip-hop culture. While doing so, I have become involved in the ongoing academic dialogue and collaboration between academics and hip-hop artists. For example, I have participated in 'Tawasul', a Swedish/Lebanese hip-hop project spearheaded by Hanna Cinthio, a Swedish artist, activist and scholar who brought together Middle Eastern artists and their Swedish counterparts to record music and share experiences. This was financed by the Swedish Institute, a public agency that promotes Swedish cultural interests around the world, organising seminars, programmes and cultural events, both in Sweden and internationally.

I also arranged several seminars and concerts with hip-hop artists and activists at Lund University and elsewhere. It is not uncommon that hip-hop scholars co-author books with practitioners or invite practitioners to be keynote speakers at academic conferences. I personally consider such collaborations to be crucial and fruitful, provided they do not compromise the scholarly analysis or lead to mere veneration of hip-hop. I recognise the possibility of potential conflicts concerning the 'insider-outsider debate', as well as the connected discussion concerning the debate between 'critics' and 'caretakers'. These debates are central to the academic study of Islam and indeed the study of religion in general, but they also need to be taken into consideration when it comes to the academic study of hip-hop, since many scholars in the field are invested in the culture as practitioners or through close relationships with practitioners.[26] In this study, I engage the empirical material with a critical eye, and not as a fan or activist.

According to cultural geographer Gillian Rose, semiotic studies require extensive knowledge about the empirical material analysed as well as about the social conditions that surround that material.[27] My own background as

[25] See, for example, Miah and Kalara 2008; Rantakallio 2013.

[26] For a discussion of this insider/outsider debate within Islamic studies in the US, see, for example, Hughes 2014.

[27] Rose 2001: 73.

an academic analysing hip-hop and as a consumer of hip-hop culture has given me wide-ranging knowledge and made it possible for me to understand a variety of textual, aural and visual expressions of hip-hop culture – similar to the way in which an anthropologist draws from fieldwork and participant observation.

The disparate empirical material may seem incoherent and difficult to handle, yet its composition represents my goal to go beyond merely analysing lyrical content and words. Most acts of communication are multimodal in their nature, and the interaction between the textual, aural and visual changes how people make sense of the images, texts and sounds that they encounter. Rose has noted:

> Even the most abstract painting in a gallery will have a written label on the wall giving certain information about its making, and in certain sorts of galleries there'll be a sheet of paper giving a price too, and these make a difference to how spectators will see that painting.[28]

This study is not a reception study. It is not concerned with how listeners-watchers-readers interpret the material at hand. Instead, it investigates how semiotic resources are used and developed in the specific context of US hip-hop culture. To effectively navigate and structure the diverse material, I have made specific demarcations, selected my empirical examples based on the literature review and identified three key areas for investigation. These areas provide distinct and crucial instances of how Islamic semiotic resources are alternately negotiated and challenged. Furthermore, these empirical examples can be viewed as gateways to a deeper understanding of the subject. The examples included have been selected because they are conceptually interesting and because they clearly illustrate a range of uses of Islamic semiotic resources.

Chapter 5 will investigate the first site of semiotic contestation, namely the use of Islamic semiotic resources in the music video 'Paid in Full (Mini Madness: The Coldcut Remix)' (1987) from the hip-hop duo Erik B. & Rakim. The primary empirical material analysed in this chapter is the music, lyrics, cover art and music video. The chapter will also draw on secondary material: earlier scholarly work on the video and music, correspondence with

[28] Ibid. p. 10.

the video's director Bruno Tilley, and journalistic articles such as reviews and other features concerning the video. The reason for choosing this video is that earlier scholarship discussing it has largely neglected to engage with its use of Islamic semiotic resources, even though the music video is one of the first commercially successful crossover hip-hop hits to include such semiotic resources. I have studied the video, lyrics and sounds in detail, following every possible inter-textual lead to be able to contextualise 'Paid in Full' as systematically as possible.

Chapter 6 will analyse the second site of semiotic contestation: the ways in which US hip-hop artists have made use of Malcolm X and his legacy as Islamic semiotic resources. The chapter will not make a complete inventory of the use of Malcolm X in hip-hop; rather, it points to the large variety of different uses. It will draw on examples ranging from samples of Malcolm X's voice to cover artwork and tattoos. Several of the examples have been described in the literature, but this chapter will contribute previously overlooked material. To gain more information about the song 'Let's Vote', previously not described in the literature and most likely the first hip-hop song to namecheck Malcolm X, I conducted an interview with the former hip-hop artist (now record producer) Erik Nuri and with Taharqa Aleem of the early electro group The Fantastic Aleems. Both interviews lasted approximately two hours and were conducted in New York in May 2015. The two interviews were semi-structured and recorded.

Chapter 7 will examine the third and final site of semiotic contestation by delving into the ways in which 9/11 and its legacy have been articulated by US hip-hop artists. It will stress the shifts in the nature of the multimodal articulations over time and the fact that 9/11 – and the subsequent narratives of the 'War on Terror' – has become crucial to the framing and understanding of the use of Islamic semiotic resources within American hip-hop music. This chapter is based on a variety of examples of how 9/11 has been depicted within US hip-hop. The profound importance and influence of 9/11 in American popular culture is reflected in the growing number of scholarly works produced on the topic; academic articles and edited volumes have looked at literature, TV, films, music and the visual arts in relation to the tragic events of 9/11.[29] Although hip-hop songs are often mentioned in connection to music and 9/11, few systematic studies on

[29] Bragard, Dony and Rosenberg 2011; Melnick 2009; Melnick 2011.

the topic exist. This is surprising since the events have had a long-standing influence on hip-hop culture in the US and beyond.

In addition to these three sites of semiotic contestation, the book contains two background chapters (Chapters 3 and 4) that are intended to familiarise the reader with the relationship between Islam and African American music-making, from the time of the transatlantic slave trade to the present day. These chapters should be viewed as a backdrop to Chapters 6 and 7, and they point to a continuous practice of incorporating semiotic resources perceived as Islamic among African American artists and music makers. The material for these chapters draws mainly on scholarly books and articles on Islam and hip-hop, as well as scholarly works on Islam in the African American experience. To a lesser extent, Chapter 3 draws on my own archival research at the Schomburg Center for Research in Black Culture in Harlem, New York City.

While writing this book, I visited the US four times for research purposes (New York in 2012, 2013, and 2015; Los Angeles in 2014), for a total of eight weeks. My research trips afforded me the privilege of visiting many of the historically significant places about which I write, and among these a few stand out: the site of Malcolm X's assassination (the Audubon Ballroom located in the Washington Heights neighbourhood of Manhattan, today the location of the Malcolm X and Dr Betty Shabazz Memorial), and the Allah school in Mecca – the world headquarters of the Five Percent Nation – located in the heart of Harlem. Furthermore, I interviewed and had informal conversations with artists and others active in the US hip-hop community. These interviews consisted of informal meetings and interviews without protocol. These more casual conversations were carried out in record stores, mosques and cafés. Most of these interviews are not directly reported in the text, but they have granted me important insights into my material, opened up new angles and given rise to new ideas.

This project also gave me the opportunity to visit two exhibitions examining the relationship between Islam and hip-hop. In the fall of 2014, I visited Sohail Daulatzai's impressive exhibition 'Return of the Mecca: The Art of Islam and Hip-Hop' at the William Grant Still Arts Center in Los Angeles. The exhibition showcased the diversity of cultural expressions perceived as Islamic in hip-hop through jazz, spoken word, hip-hop record covers, historical newspaper articles, flyers, fine art photographs, miscellaneous items such as a handwritten letter by Malcolm X to his biographer Alex Haley, video installations and books. In 2015, I was given the opportunity to visit and contribute to the French exhibition 'HIP-HOP, du Bronx aux rues arabes' at the Institut du Monde Arabe in Paris. The massive multimedia exhibition was curated by French hip-hop legend Akhenaton and told the history of hip-hop in the US, connecting it to the 2011 Arab Spring. The two exhibitions manifested a popular interest in the relationship between Islam and hip-hop. Both made a strong and inspiring case for the need for more scholarship on Islam and hip-hop around the globe.

In summary, to meet the aims of this study, I have employed concepts and insights from social semiotics and taken inspiration from this field's methodology to analyse the use of Islamic themes in US hip-hop culture. I am aware of the risks taken when analysing material as varied and vast as the one studied here, but I take inspiration from the literary scholar Jonathan Culler, who has suggested that scholarly work should be daring, rather than wary.[30]

[30] Culler 1992.

3

ISLAM IN AFRICAN AMERICAN MUSIC-MAKING

This chapter outlines the ways in which Islamic semiotic resources have been used in African American music-making – by Muslims as well as non-Muslims – from the transatlantic slave trade until the birth of hip-hop culture in the early 1970s. While covering more than a century of African American music-making and discussing a broad palette of musical genres as well as organisations, the chapter in no way aims to paint the full picture. Rather, using mainly secondary sources from different fields, it serves as an important contextual backdrop to the empirical material analysed in the subsequent chapters. My aim is to introduce the reader to organisations, developments and key actors, as it is necessary to be aware of this history in order to understand the use of Islamic semiotic resources in present-day hip-hop. They have become important reference points and therefore Islamic semiotic resources on their own, not only in hip-hop – they have also triggered the imagination of other types of artists considering African American history or trying to shape its future.

Islam on New Shores

The first large numbers of Muslims to arrive on the shores of present-day America were brought as enslaved people.[1] Scholars estimate that between

[1] Some scholars have argued that the first Muslims on US soil sailed with the Spanish explorers of the New World. Others have suggested that Muslims set foot on the New Land prior to Columbus. See, for example, Van Sertima 2003; Dirks 2006. Even if these claims were correct,

1525 and 1866 12.5 million Africans were forcefully shipped to the New World. Of these, 10.7 million survived the deadly crossing to reach the shores of North America, the Caribbean and South America. Of the approximately 455,000 enslaved Africans who were transported to North America, 389,000 came directly from West Africa and 66,000 from the Caribbean.[2]

There is no scholarly consensus on the exact number of enslaved Muslims that arrived during the transatlantic slave trade. In the first comprehensive investigation devoted to the topic of enslaved African Muslims in North America, *African Muslims in Antebellum America: A Sourcebook* (1984), Allan D. Austin has assessed the total percentage of Muslims to 7 or 8 per cent of all Africans enslaved in North America.[3] Michael A. Gomez has suggested that 'at least 200,000 came from areas influenced by Islam to varying degrees. Muslims may have come to America by the thousands, if not tens of thousands'. Furthermore, he has pointed out that. . .

> it would be a mistake to focus simply on the Muslim population, for Islam's impact in West Africa was not confined to the converted, practicing community. On the contrary, many non-Muslims were acquainted with some portion of its tenets through the activities of Muslim traders and clerics.[4]

The prominent historian Sylviane A. Diouf has estimated that Muslims 'probably represented from 10 to 15 per cent' of the total number of people shipped to North America, the Caribbean and South America. She has also noted that the percentage could be higher if one only counted enslaved people in North America, since the second-largest group directly brought to the US came from the Muslim-dominated area of Senegambia.[5]

Although, or perhaps because, scholars know less than they would like about the early Muslim presence in North America, interest in the topic continues to grow. A series of newly discovered written sources has recently appeared,

they would not alter the history of African American music and the Islamic semiotic resources that I am sketching out in this chapter.

[2] Gates 2012: 145.

[3] Austin 1984: 29.

[4] Gomez 1994: 682.

[5] Diouf 2004: 77.

and once researchers will have finished evaluating these texts, we will most likely achieve a more complete picture of the lives of enslaved Muslims.[6]

Some general patterns have emerged from the research about enslaved Muslims and how Islam was practiced among enslaved Africans in North America: dietary laws were observed, Muslim names were used, and religious rituals were practiced. Enslaved Muslims dressed in what was perceived as Islamic garb.[7] Some converted to Christianity, or married non-Muslims, but kept their faith in private. Muslims were often working in leading positions at the plantations, and some had knowledge of Arabic.[8] However, whether and how these first-generation enslaved African American Muslims passed on their traditions to later generations is difficult to know.

Some of the strongest evidence for the survival of Muslim traditions among later generations of African Americans comes from interviews conducted in the coastal region of Georgia among the descendants of enslaved Muslims. These interviews were part of the Works Progress Administration programme (WPA) in the 1930s. In these conversations, several of the interviewees accounted for what arguably were Islamic practices among grandparents and great-grandparents. For example, the interviewees described the hijab, religious rituals and the practices of 'pray on duh [Du'a] bead', interpreted as a reference to the Islamic rosary (*tasbih*). Muslim names, such as Fatima and Medina, were also common among the descendants in the region.[9]

The West African Blue Note

Scholars from fields including musicology, history, Islamic studies, anthropology and African American studies have argued that Islamic themes have made their way into African American music-making and practices. Diouf has written: 'In the cultural area, the blues may be counted as a legacy of the African Muslims'.[10] The musicologist Fatima El Shibli has noted: '[E]arly blues contains

[6] Recent discoveries include the narratives of Omar bin Said's Arabic text, 'The Panama Manuscript of Sheikh Sana See', found in 1999, and 'The Autobiography of Nicholas Said', discovered in 2000. For more information on these sources, see Marable and Aidi 2009: 11.

[7] Diouf 1998: 72–82.

[8] Turner 2013: 32.

[9] Gomez 2005: 155.

[10] Diouf 2004: 85.

musical characteristics that strikingly resemble Islamic practices, in particular the recitation of the Koran and the call to prayer'.[11] Both Diouf and El Shibli have presented several examples of how Islam may have influenced both the tonal expression and the lyrical content of early African American music.[12]

One significant example is the field holler 'Levee Camp Holler', recorded by Alan Lomax, an ethnomusicologist and collector of North American folk music. Lomax and his father recorded the song at a prison farm in the middle of the twentieth century. In his book *The Land Where the Blues Began* (1993), Lomax has connected the song with West Africa and the larger Muslim world and pointed out its relationship with the voice of the *muezzin* and the *adhan*.[13] Lomax has gone on to connect this musical tradition to the rise of blues music in the Americas. He has written:

> A broader look finds that such ornamented, unaccompanied singing is commonplace in the kingdoms and empires of North Africa of the southern Mediterranean and of the Middle East. It seems, in fact, that this song type, which we might call the high, lonesome complaint, is one undercurrent of music in the whole of civilised Eurasia – the ancient world of caste, empire, exploited peasantry, harem-bound women, and absolute power – from the Far East to Ireland. A related and ultimately derivative string-accompanied solo style is also present in this same region. It turns up in West Africa, and in the Americas gave rise to the blues.[14]

The musical traditions of West Africa are rich and multifaceted. In the pre-Islamic era, religious music revolved around the devotion of spirits of animals and ancestors. The Muslim presence in the region dates back to the eighth century, and this gradually changed the soundscape of the area's musical traditions. The characteristic and frequent sliding between notes (*melisma*), used, for example, in the Islamic call to prayer (*adhan*), was introduced, as were religious restrictions on, for instance, dancing and certain musical instruments that were considered *haram* or *halal* according to different Islamic interpretive traditions.[15]

[11] Shibli 2007: 8.

[12] Diouf 1998: 194–98.

[13] Lomax 2002: 233–34.

[14] Ibid. pp. 233–34.

[15] Peretti 2009: 10–11.

Musicologists and anthropologists such as Gerhard Kubik, author of *Africa and the Blues* (1999), and Lomax have argued that some of the characteristics of blues music can be traced back to Central and West Africa.[16] Kubik has offered a persuasive and well-developed argument for how musical traditions, particularly among the Hausa people, in what he has called the 'West Central Sudanic Belt' (an area stretching approximately from Mali across northern Ghana and northern Nigeria into northern and central Cameroon), shaped the tonal expressions of African American delta blues. The music of this region is uniquely influenced by an 'Arabic-Islamic song style' that is recognised by 'melisma, wavy intonation, pitch instabilities within a pentatonic framework and a declamatory voice production. All this behaviour develops over a central reference tone, sometimes like a bourdon'.[17] According to Kubik, these distinctive musical scales explain the usage, frequency and placement of the so-called 'blue notes' often found in blues and jazz music.[18]

Scholars do not know exactly how this music tradition from the West Central Sudanic Belt was transmitted to African American music in the nineteenth-century US. As noted above, Lomax has pointed out that it probably took only one skilled singer among the enslaved Africans in order for the tradition to be transmitted to North America.[19] Kubik has echoed Lomax's argument: 'One charismatic personality will suffice to release a chain reaction. One virtuoso musician can end up being imitated by hundreds'.[20]

Whether other Islamic semiotic resources beside tonal expressions – such as images and words – were transmitted from Africa to the US is still unclear, although some researchers have assumed that the tonal expressions carried other aspects of Islam with them into the US.

[16] Kubik's book has built on and cultivated an argument first proffered by the blues authority Paul Oliver. See Oliver 1970. However, while Kubik's findings and those of others have clearly attested to the West African roots of blues music, there exist other, competing theories. The ethno-musicologist and acclaimed musician Willie Ruff, for example, has suggested that the origins of the blues are to be found in the Scottish Highlands. Per Ruff's theory, this music spread to the enslaved African Americans due to exposure from the slave owners' Hebridean (a widespread archipelago off the west coast of mainland Scotland) gospel songs. However, this theory is highly contested. See, for example, Miller 2009.

[17] Kubik 1999: 94.

[18] Ibid. p. 118.

[19] Lomax 2002: 334.

[20] Kubik 1999: 13.

The Great Migration

World War I put a halt to the flow of European labour migrants to the developing industrial hubs in the Northeast and the Midwest.[21] The northern industrialists were consequently forced to look for cheap labour elsewhere; therefore, many companies sent agents to the Southern States to persuade African Americans to move north for work.[22] Before the Civil War and the abolition of slavery in the 1860s, there was practically no African American migration to the Northern States.

A boll weevil infestation of the cotton fields of the South in the late 1910s also contributed to a migration outflow, forcing many sharecroppers to look for employment opportunities elsewhere. This development was intensified by a decrease in cotton prices, which meant that landowners could no longer afford to hire outside workers, and tenant farmers could no longer afford to

Figure 3.1 Group of Florida migrants on their way to Cranberry, New Jersey, to pick potatoes. Near Shawboro, North Carolina, 1940. Source: Library of Congress, Prints & Photographs Division, FSA/OWI Collection, LC-USF34- 040820-D.

[21] Sernett 1997: 38.

[22] Ibid. p. 40.

pay their rent. As a result, many African Americans were more than ready to accept the free train rides taking them to new job opportunities in the North.[23]

Between 1916 and 1919, an estimated 500,000 African Americans left the South for the Northern cities. This wave was followed by another million people in 1920s. In New York, the African American population grew from 91,000 in 1910 to 152,000 in 1920, and in Chicago it more than doubled during the same period.[24] This migration might seem insignificant when compared to the migration in the 1940s and the 1960s, when millions of African Americans left the South. Culturally, however, the first migration was of greater importance, because it created the urban African American working or lower class. It was also the Great Migration that brought traditional jazz and blues music to the Northern cities. Musicians left for the North for the same reasons as others: failing crops, demand for workers and racial discrimination. The flourishing entertainment industry in the Northern and Midwestern cities promised fame, money and cultural influence for the newly urbanised African Americans.[25]

The Great Migration gave rise to and nurtured a blossoming and creative religious landscape in the African American inner-city neighbourhoods of New York, Chicago and Detroit.[26] Pentecostal preachers, African American fraternal lodges, soapbox orators, a wide array of Islamic movements and esoteric or occult traditions were all part of African American urban religious culture.[27] Black women in particular were associated with occult powers; often dressed up in 'oriental' costumes, including a veil and 'oriental' signs and symbols, they earned a living as fortune-tellers or healers.[28] All of these movements and traditions competed for the souls and minds of the Southern African Americans who arrived in the cities. Many musicians came to be influenced by or even influenced the religious imagery and beliefs of the diverse Islamic milieu that was spawned by the Great Migration in the first decades of the twentieth century.

[23] For a thorough investigation of the impact of the boll weevil on the Great Migration, see Higgs 1976.

[24] d'Eramo 2004: 250.

[25] Hennessey 1994: 30.

[26] Turner 2003: 73.

[27] For an intriguing introduction to the importance of esoteric traditions in the African American religious experience, see Finley 2015. See also Bakker 2015 for a study of the importance of esoteric traditions in the teachings of NOI.

[28] Curtis 2002b: 57.

One Aim! One God! One Destiny!

> Whenever and wherever it has been necessary, great Negro warriors have arisen from the ranks of Islam, and inspired by the teachings of the new faith, which merges all distinctions in one great brotherhood.
>
> Edward W. Blyden[29]

Even though Islam had existed in the 'New World' since the days of the transatlantic slave trade, it is impossible to understand the African American Islamic interpretive traditions without paying attention to the Pan-Africanism of Edward W. Blyden (1832–1912), which forms an ideological bridge between 'old Islam' and 'new American Islam'.[30] Blyden was a leading African American intellectual and political figure. He was the first English-speaking African American to depict Islam in a positive light in published writing, although his relationship to Islam was multifaceted and changed over time. He argued that Islam was the natural religion for African Americans and a far better 'medium' for Black self-determination than Christianity. Islam, according to Blyden, encouraged the growth of African nationalism and the development of an African American nation in West Africa.[31]

At the time of his death in 1912, Blyden's Pan-Africanism was mainly the preoccupation of African American intellectual elites. It was not until the political breakthrough of Marcus Garvey (1887–1940) and his organisation, the Universal Negro Improvement Association (UNIA), founded in Jamaica in 1914, that these thoughts would reach larger groups of African Americans. The first American branch of UNIA was founded in Harlem in 1917.[32] UNIA became the first nationalist racial mass movement in the history of Black culture. Under the motto 'One God! One Aim! One Destiny!' Garvey organised Black people all over the world. At its peak, UNIA represented the largest mass movement in African American history, and it is beyond dispute that millions were directly affected by Garvey and his message and globally involved in his movement.[33]

[29] Blyden 1994: 141. This book was first published in 1888.

[30] Turner 2003: 47.

[31] Curtis 2002b: 21.

[32] Martin 1983: 2. According to Martin, UNIA had 1,100 branches in over forty countries in South, North and Central America, as well as in Africa, Europe and Australia.

[33] Gates and Higginbotham 2004.

Figure 3.2 Marcus Garvey, 1924. Source: Library of Congress, Prints & Photographs Division, LC-USZ61-1854.

Even if religion played an important role in Garvey's political mission, it was not the main feature of the movement. Like Blyden before him, Garvey had an eclectic relationship to Islam, and it is fair to say that Garvey's approach came from his studies of Blyden's writings. Although Blyden's advocacy of Islam never became a central part of Garvey's political thought, he had great appreciation for Blyden's legacy.[34] In 1915, Garvey considered Blyden to be someone who had '[d]one so much to retrieve the lost prestige of the race, and to undo the selfishness of alien historians and their history which has said so little and painted us so unfairly'.[35]

Garvey's movement rested on what Edward E. Curtis IV has named 'Abrahamic universalism'. However, race always came first; UNIA's ultimate goal was to unify the 'Negro race' all over the world, despite its religious diversity.[36] Garvey fostered what Mattia Gardell has called 'the ground myth of black nationalism', the idea of Black chosenness, which states that Black people are God's chosen people and the original people of planet Earth.[37] This idea echoes in many African American Islamic movements even today. Music and poetry were essential for Garvey and his movement's aesthetics. Art served as a way to unify the African diaspora and as a tool for furthering African progress.[38] UNIA often used rhetoric and themes generally associated with Islam in speeches, songs and writings when it suited its political agenda. Garvey himself was, for example, often compared to the Prophet Muhammad or the child of Allah in poems composed by his adherents.[39]

Music in particular was used in order to reinforce the message of UNIA. The fact that the organisation had its own musical director underscores the central role of music in the organisation.[40] The musical director, Arnold Josiah Ford (1877–1935), also served as the choirmaster of the Universal Choir in the Liberty Hall in Harlem (the world headquarters of the UNIA) and was the bandleader of the UNIA band and orchestra. Ford had a deep musical background and was a multi-instrumentalist; before joining UNIA in 1917, he had

[34] Curtis 2002b: 50.

[35] Marcus Garvey, citied in Martin 1983: 164.

[36] Curtis 2002b: 23.

[37] Gardell 1996: 42.

[38] Martin 1983: 8.

[39] Turner 2003: 88.

[40] Redmond 2013: 54.

performed jazz at Harlem's Clef Club, a popular entertainment venue and society for African American musicians. Ford was also the bandmaster for the New Amsterdam Musical Association, which today stands as the oldest African American musical organisation in the US.[41] The Liberty Hall in Harlem also hosted the Black Star Line Band under the leadership of William Isles.[42]

The fact that music played a key role in shaping the message of UNIA is reinforced by a series of six in-depth articles on the topic of music published in *The Negro World* in 1922.[43] The series, entitled 'The Negro and Music', was written by William Isles. Isles was presented as an 'indefatigable student' of music and as someone who 'is able to combine art and propaganda'.[44]

As the musical director of UNIA, Ford was the main architect and promoter of its religious component. His musical compositions drew on the harmony of 'Abrahamic universalism' and incorporated religious themes from Christianity and Judaism as well as Islam. Shana L. Redmond has written in her book *Anthem: Social Movements and the Sound of Solidarity in the African Diaspora*:

> It was not necessary for Garvey to preach a conventional religious message – he had others to do that work for him. Ford enters into this discussion as one of the primary architects for the UNIA's faith program. His songs brought into harmony religious traditions and Garvey's secular vision of redemption from the quotidian racism of Black life.[45]

The main musical compositions used by UNIA are found in 'The Universal Ethiopian Hymnal', compiled and partly composed and written by Ford.[46] The 1922 reprint of the compilation includes eighteen compositions and one

[41] Wintz and Finkelman 2004: 400.

[42] Martin 1983: 106.

[43] *The Negro World* was the main mouthpiece of the UNIA. Published weekly, it reached 200,000 readers at its peak in the mid-1920s. The newspaper often included advertisements with Islamic connotations – for example, 'The Ancient Moorish Secret' and 'Zura Shampoo', used by 'Zura, famous Queen of the Moors'. The advertisement promised users 'long hair which shone like the Raven's wing'. Another advertisement promoted 'James' Temple of Allah Oriental Incense' for use in 'places of worship' as well as at 'house parties'. On such marketing, see Edwards 2000.

[44] Ford 1922a.

[45] Redmond 2013: 53.

[46] See Ford 1922b. 'The universal Ethiopian hymnal' was reprinted at least three times, in 1920, 1921 and 1922.

Figure 3.3 Front cover of *The Universal Ethiopian Hymnal*, compiled by Arnold J. Ford, 1922.

prayer. Four of the arrangements include the mention of 'Allah'.[47] For example, in 'Potentate's Hymn', one can read: 'God bless our Potentate / Long live our Potentate / Our chief to be. / May he our rights proclaim / In the Name of the most sacred name / 'Allah' – One God, One Aim, / One Destiny'.[48] Further, in the composition 'God Bless our President', Ford's opening stanza mentions: 'Father of all Creation, / Allah Omnipotent, / Supreme O'er every Nation / God bless our President'.[49]

Scholars have tended to disagree over the extent and nature of the influence that Garvey and UNIA had on early African American Islamic movements such as the Moorish Science Temple and NOI.[50] However, it is clear that Garvey and his organisation introduced and helped to normalise Islam, thus introducing semiotic resources associated with the Islamic discursive tradition to broad layers of African Americans through poetry, speeches and music. UNIA was not only the first African American organisation that selectively introduced Islamic semiotic resources to the African American general public in order to achieve political goals, but it also stands as one of the first non-Muslim African American organisations using Islamic semiotic resources. As we will see below, other movements and persons would, deliberately or not, use the same strategy.

The Moorish Science Temple of America

The development of 'homegrown' African American Islamic organisations was the main source of the growth of Islamic movements among newly urbanised African Americans in the first decades of the twentieth century, while more traditional Sunni and Shia movements became established later on.

[47] The included compositions are: 'Shine on, Eternal Light', 'God is Love', 'Missionary Chant', 'Blest Be the Tie', 'Allah-hu-ak Bar', 'One God, One Aim, One Destiny', 'Oh Africa Awaken', 'God Bless Our Native Country', 'Awake! Behold the Morning', 'Potentate's Hymn', 'Africa', 'God Bless our President', 'Ethiopia's Children', 'The Password', 'Prayer for Peace', 'Adon Olam', 'The Mercy Seat', 'Rock of Ages' and 'Atonement'. The Hymnal also includes one prayer. The four hymnals that refer to Islam are 'Allah-hu-ak Bar', 'Potentate's Hymn', 'God Bless our President' and 'The Password'.

[48] Ford 1922b: 9.

[49] Ibid. p. 11.

[50] Curtis 2002b: 48–49.

The Moorish Science Temple of America (MST) was probably the first of these homegrown organisations. The early history of the MST is still debated by scholars, and until very recently the origins of the founder Noble Drew Ali were hidden in the fog of hagiographical accounts.[51] However, recent research has presented compelling evidence that Noble Drew Ali was born on 8 January 1886 in Virginia and that his birth name was Thomas Drew.[52] In 1913, Drew Ali formed the Canaanite Temple in Newark, New Jersey, which later became the MST. MST skilfully crafted a message aspiring to be perceived as Islamic, by including practices and semiotic resources such as dietary laws, the Qur'an and Allah, blending them with African American popular religious beliefs and mystic traditions. By doing so, the MST fashioned an Islamic message in tune with the needs of African American inner-city communities.[53]

Figure 3.4 Attendees of the 1928 Moorish Science Temple of America Convention in Chicago. Noble Drew Ali is in white, front row centre.

[51] See, for example, Curtis 2009.

[52] See Abdat 2014.

[53] Nance 2002: 125.

MST members refused to call themselves Coloured, Black or Negro. According to Drew Ali, the slave owners had given these labels to them. Instead, he introduced the concept of 'Moorish Americans', supposed descendants to the Moabites who were part of the great 'Asiatic nation' and the original people of planet Earth. In 1927, Noble Drew Ali presented the *Holy Koran of the Moorish Science Temple of America*, not to be confused with the Holy Qur'an of mainstream Muslims. This MST sacred text borrowed its content generously from esoteric texts that were circulated in the first decades of the twentieth century, among them *The Aquarian Gospel of Jesus the Christ* (1908) and the Rosicrucian book *Unto Thee I Grant* (1925). Curtis has summarised the message in *The Holy Koran of the MST* as follows: 'Blacks must separate from whites, reclaim their original group identity, understand their own divine origins, meditate upon the true spiritual nature of all being, and follow a strict moral code'.[54]

To mark their new Moorish identity, members of the MST dressed in Islamic or Middle Eastern-influenced garbs: long white robes and red fezzes for men, and veils for women. For the purpose of promoting their new selves, they added 'El' or 'Bey' to their names. A 'Moorish passport' was issued to all members, and the Moorish flag was introduced in addition to the American flag.[55] At the end of the 1920s, the MST founded the Moorish Industrial Group. They operated various small business establishments, restaurants, barbershops and stores selling a variety of religious relics, charms and magical potions. Drew Ali, the self-titled 'second prophet of Islam', died on 20 July 1929, but the MST continued to both grow and fracture after his death. At its peak in the 1920s and 1930s, the MST factions had major congregations in many American cities, including Philadelphia, Detroit and Chicago.

Very little has been written about the relationship between music and the MST. Still, it seems that music, at least in some temples, was a crucial part of MST meetings. In a 1935 advertisement in the Kansas City newspaper *Plaindealer*, solo singing by Sister Clay Bey and a duet performance of Sister Duncan and Father was advertised in connection with a Sunday afternoon service.[56] Also,

[54] Curtis 2002b: 61.

[55] Gardell 1996: 43.

[56] See Ahmed A. Bey/Moorish Temple Collection and the Moorish Temple Collections, Schomburg Center for Research in Black Culture, Manuscripts, Archives and Rare Books Division (Call number Sc MG 435).

the official records of the MST support the notion that music played a vital role in connection to services, national conventions and festivities. For example, on one occasion, celebrating the successful election campaign of a congressman supported by the MST, the movement organised 'an outstanding parade through Chicago's residential district with Temple officials dressed in full Moorish-regalia' and a 'musical concert featuring the Moorish Chorus'.[57]

In 1928, the MST also organised a 'Big Mid-Summer Dance', which included 'Good Music' as well as 'Refreshments of all Kinds'. Accounts of the MST's religious services show that singing was an integral part of the programme: hymns and popular gospels – 'He Promised Never to Leave Me Alone', 'Don't Turn Back', 'Great Judgment Morning' and 'Tell the Truth Always', to name a few – were sung as a part of the service programme.[58] Whether MST's music in rituals and festivities included Islamic semiotic resources or not is hard to tell as previous research has not addressed the issue, and since my archival studies have not yielded any significant facts to help us decide.[59]

However, several musicians were notably influenced by MST. One prominent figure among them was Warren Tartaglia, also known as Walid al-Taha (1944–65). Al-Taha, a jazz musician and poet of Jewish descent, was introduced to the teachings of MST by Sultan Rafi Sharif-Bey in Baltimore during the late 1950s. Sultan Rafi Sharif-Bey had served as the head of Moorish Science Temple #13 in Baltimore before he founded the Noble Order of Moorish Sufis as an outgrowth of the MST. Together with members of the Moorish Sufis, al-Taha went on to form the Moorish Orthodox Church of America (MOCA). MOCA was established in order to apply esoteric readings to the teachings of Noble Drew Ali. After moving to New York for university studies in 1962, al-Taha continued to spread his Moorish science among jazz musicians and Beat poets. He proclaimed himself the Moorish Governor over the Orissa Province (New York), and a new temple was established in a basement on 103rd street off Broadway. It was during this time that al-Taha came to meet and introduce Islam to a young Peter Lamborn Wilson (also known as Hakim Bey). Lamborn Wilson (1945–2022) was an American anarchist author, primarily known for introducing the concept of Temporary

[57] Ibid.

[58] Ibid.

[59] Ibid.

Autonomous Zones (TAZ), but he also wrote extensively on Islam, primarily Sufism and mysticism.[60] Lamborn Wilson left MOCA in 1971 and went on to pursue other mystic Islamic traditions. Al-Taha died of a heroin overdose in Central Park. He was only twenty-one years old.[61]

Noble Drew Ali's Moorish Science Temple was among the first of the homegrown Muslim organisations to popularise 'Moorishness' and other concepts perceived as Islamic among the newly urbanised African Americans. With the help of the semiotic resource 'Moorish identity', Drew Ali created and revitalised ideas of moral self-determination among this group. Drew Ali's strategy is crucial in decoding the success of the most famous African American Islamic organisation that sprung from the unique religious milieu created by the Great Migration, namely NOI.

The Birth of a Nation: Nation of Islam

There is no scholarly consensus concerning the true identity of the founder of NOI, W. D. Fard (also known as Wallace D. Fard Muhammad or Fard Muhammad). He appeared in Paradise Valley, a predominantly African American district in Detroit, during the summer of 1930.[62] Fard made his living as a street peddler selling everything from raincoats to silk garbs and artefacts to newcomers from the South. While selling his merchandise, he also told his potential customers stories about a glorious past. The African Americans, he said, belonged to the lost but newly found Tribe of Shabazz, descending from the holy city of Mecca. The divine tribe had been stolen from its home country by the 'Caucasian devil'. Tribal members had been enslaved and brought to 'the Wilderness of North America'. Fard's godly mission was to teach them that their true religion was Islam and their true language Arabic.

[60] See, for example, Wilson 1988, 1993.

[61] One of the few authors who have written about the life of al-Taha is Michael Muhammad Knight. See Knight 2006, 2012.

[62] All works on Fard have relied either on an article by the American sociologist Erdmann Beynon (see Beynon 1938), interviews with members of NOI, or FBI files. Beynon's article was written four years after the disappearance of Fard in 1934, a point at which the story could have turned hagiographic. FBI memos have suggested that there was an intense campaign by the agency to discredit Fard. With this background there is a great number of competing stories concerning Fard's identity and history. For a presentation of some of the more popular theories, see Gardell 1996 or Gibson 2012.

This man, who many believed to have hailed from the Arabian Peninsula, piqued urban African Americans' interest. Some wanted to know more about their 'home country' and started to invite Fard to informal meetings in their homes. The former street peddler now took on the role of a prophet sent from God. Word of the prophet spread quickly in the African American inner-city neighbourhoods of Detroit, and the number of Fard's followers grew rapidly. Fard's prophetic message worked so well that he rented public halls for his orations, and his 'Nation of Islam', as the new movement was called, began to take a more formal shape.

One of the workers attracted by Fard's message was Elijah Poole. He joined the organisation in 1931 and took the name Elijah Muhammad, very soon becoming a central part of NOI. Fard personally mentored Elijah, who was promoted to the position of Supreme Minister. Elijah was a capable coordinator and established several religious centres of worship. The movement began to set up African American-owned businesses, with the goal of promoting self-sufficiency and African American economic independence. After Fard's puzzling disappearance in 1934, Elijah revealed to the followers of NOI that Fard was God (Allah) and that he had left Elijah as his messenger to guide the lost-but-found Tribe of Shabazz in the wilderness of the North. Under Elijah's leadership, NOI's influence on African Americans grew in practically every major city in the country.

In the early 1950s, NOI attracted a convicted street hustler named Malcolm Little (1925–65). He had encountered Elijah's teachings while serving time in Charlestown State Prison, Massachusetts, for having committed burglary. It was while being incarcerated that Little converted to Islam and took the name Malcolm X. After he was paroled in 1952, he quickly rose in the ranks of NOI, and Malcolm X led and organised temples in Boston, Philadelphia and New York. In 1959, the WCBS-TV news reporter Mike Wallace helped to give both Malcolm X and NOI national exposure in the five-part series 'The Hate That Hate Produced'. Even though the series portrayed NOI as an anti-American supremacist organisation, Malcolm X became a sought-after commentator on US race relations on radio and TV shows. He was often controversial, but always eloquent and charismatic.

In 1964, Malcolm X broke with NOI and started Muslim Mosque, Inc., a more mainstream Sunni organisation. After extensive travels in Africa and the Middle East, where he also performed the *hajj* (the pilgrimage to Mecca), Malcolm X renounced the teachings of NOI. On 21 February 1965, Malcolm X was assassinated while giving a speech at the Audubon Ballroom in Harlem, New York. Three members of NOI were convicted for the shooting in 1966, but the exact circumstances surrounding his death are still debated.[63] Arguably, Malcolm X stands as one of the most important and best-known Muslim leaders in the history of the US. His life and legacy (mainly in the form of his autobiography) keep inspiring new generations of readers. In 1992, Spike Lee's skilfully marketed biographical movie about Malcolm X triggered a renewed interested in his life and political endeavours. This interest also reinforced Malcolm X's status as a radical political icon among many hip-hop artists.[64]

While there exist plenty of academic accounts of the use of Malcolm X in modern popular music, only a few discuss Malcolm X's own musical preferences. Judging from his autobiography, music played a significant role in his life. When the young Malcolm Little worked as a shoeshine boy at the Roseland Ballroom, he encountered some of the major musical stars of the time as customers. While peddling reefers at the nightclubs and speakeasies in Harlem, Malcolm X (then known as Detroit Red) rubbed shoulders with some of the most important artists of the time, among them Dizzy Gillespie, Billy Eckstine, Billie Holiday, Ella Fitzgerald and Dinah Washington. 'In every band, at least half of the musicians smoked reefers', he stated in his autobiography. 'I'm not going to list names; I'd have to include some of those most prominent then in popular music'. He further wrote: 'We had wild times backstage with the musicians [. . .] I was known to almost every popular Negro musician around New York in 1944–1945'. In his book *Malcolm X: A Life of Reinvention*, Manning Marable has revealed that Malcolm X himself performed as an entertainer in bars under the name Jack Carlton, dancing and sometimes playing the drums.[65]

Malcolm X seems to have picked up a thing or two about self-presentation and a longing for fame during these years. Marable has written: 'One major lesson Malcolm absorbed from the jazz artists' performances in the forties was

[63] See, for example, Marable 2011. Marable has given an extensive account of the life of Malcolm X and revisited the murder, where he has named a new alleged killer.

[64] This topic will be explored in Chapter 5.

[65] Marable 2011: 63.

the power of black art to convey celebrity status. Young Malcolm wistfully dreamt about the adoration of the crowd'.[66] Marable has argued that Malcolm X's entanglement with the New York jazz scene in the 1940s provided him with unique insights into the radical new sound coming out of Harlem and its potential for shaking the very foundation of US mainstream culture. Not surprisingly, so Marable has noted, many of the jazz artists 'became avid supporters [of Malcolm X] in the 1960s'.[67]

A letter dated 9 March 1950 and sold at auction in January 2015[68] has provided further insight into Malcolm X's view on music:

> Music, Brother, is ours [. . .] it is us [. . .] and like us it is always here [. . .] surrounding us [. . .] like the infinite particles that make up Life, it cannot be seen [. . .] but can only be felt [. . .] Like Life!!! No, it is not created [. . .] but like the never-dying Soul [. . .] eternally permeates the atmosphere with its Presence [. . .] ever-waiting for its Master [. . .] the Lordly Musician [. . .] the Wielder of Souls [. . .] to come and give it a Temple [. . .] mould it into a Song. Music without the Musician is like Life without Allah [. . .] both being in need of the house [. . .] a home [. . .] The Temple [. . .] the Complete Song and its Creator. Yes, Brother, Allah is Truly God!![69]

Later in the letter, Malcolm X wrote that he heard that 'Diz' (Dizzy Gillespie) was a Muslim and that he knew that many jazz musicians had converted to 'the Ahmadiyya Movement'.[70] In the letter, he also asked the unknown recipient to send him a list of all the jazz artists that he knew to adhere to Islam, specifically 'which ones that are in show Biz belong to ours, under Mr Elijah Mohammed'.

The letter shows that after his conversion to Islam Malcolm X had an eclectic relationship to music, recognising its beauty and potential for channelling ideas. But he also confessed that he dreaded 'the temptations of that life and

[66] Ibid.

[67] Ibid. pp. 62–63.

[68] RR Auction in Boston auctioned the letter in January 2015. A scanned copy of the complete six-pages-long letter is published online: https://www.rrauction.com/auctions/lot-detail/345605706310161-malcolm-x-autograph-letter-signed (accessed 6 May 2024)

[69] Ibid.

[70] See the section 'The Moslem Sunrise' for a brief discussion of Dizzy Gillespie and his relationship to Islam.

its memories', adding: 'I steer as far clear from the subject as possible unless I know the fellows are brothers [Muslims]'.[71]

When Elijah Muhammad died in 1975, his son Warith Deen Mohammed took over as national leader (Supreme Minister). He left his father's controversial teachings behind and transformed NOI into a Sunni-oriented organisation. The new direction of NOI did not please all of its members. In 1978, the former calypso singer and violinist Louis X rejected the changes of Warith Deen Mohammed and founded a new Nation of Islam, based on the original teachings of Elijah Muhammad. Louis X is today known as Louis Farrakhan; as of 2024, he still serves as the leader of NOI.

Farrakhan (born Louis Eugene Walcott on 11 May 1933) had a genuine musical background. He learned the violin at a young age and in his early teens played with the Boston College Orchestra and the Boston Civic Symphony. As a young musician, he performed on radio and TV shows and won the popular music competition Ted Mack's Original Amateur Hour.[72] After dropping out of college in North Carolina, he began a career as a calypso singer, performing at nightclubs in Boston, touring and releasing records. The first calypso song he wrote was titled 'Why America is No Democracy'.[73] Despite earning good money and having a respectable career under the stage name The Charmer, his career never really took off.

It was in connection to one of his shows at the Chicago nightclub The Blue Angel in 1955 that the then Louis Walcott was first invited to attend the annual Saviours' Day Convention. Not long after the convention he became Louis X, a bestowed follower of Elijah Muhammad and a member of Temple #7 in New York under the leadership of Malcolm X, whom he had already met,

[71] Hisham Aidi has argued along the same lines in an article published in *The New Yorker* (28 February 2015), titled 'The Music of Malcolm X'. He wrote: 'For the rest of his life, Malcolm X would try to balance his love of music with his political and religious commitments. In a speech in 1964, he underscored the importance of music to black liberation, stating that music was "the only area on the American scene where the black man has been free to create. And he has mastered it"'. The speech was given by Malcolm X on 28 June 1964 at the founding rally for the Organization of Afro-American Unity (OAAU). It has been published in full in Breitman 1992. Aidi's article is available online: http://www.newyorker.com/culture/culture-desk/the-music-of-malcolm-x?mbid=social_twitter (accessed 10 September 2023)

[72] Gardell 1996: 120.

[73] Gates and West 2000: 349.

Figure 3.5 Yearbook photo of Louis Farrakhan playing the violin, Winston-Salem State University, 1953. Source: Winston-Salem State University.

unsurprisingly, in a Boston nightclub in 1953.[74] Even though Farrakhan left his career as a nightclub performer shortly after joining NOI, he never stopped singing, playing and recording. For example, in 1960 he recorded the 7-inch single 'A White Man's Heaven is a Black Man's Hell' under the name Louis X, and in 1984 he released the song 'Let Us Unite' under the name Louis Farrakhan.[75]

Farrakhan's musical past is likely to have influenced his interest in combining music and politics in more recent years. For example, during much of the 1990s, US hip-hop was consumed by the so-called 'East Coast-West Coast Beef' between artists and fans of East Coast hip-hop and West Coast hip-hop. The rivalry culminated with the murders of Tupac '2Pac' Shakur in September 1996 and Christopher 'The Notorious B. I. G.' Wallace in March 1997.[76] As a

[74] Gardell 1996: 120.

[75] Louis X, 'A White Man's Heaven is a Black Man's Hell' (A Moslem Sings © 1960); Louis Farrakhan, 'Let Us Unite' (A. V. C. Records © 1984).

[76] Peter Spirer's documentary *Beef* (Image Entertainment © 2003), on the historical evolution of hip-hop feuds, has presented a good account of the 'East Coast-West Coast Beef'. In the film, artists from both sides are interviewed, as well as journalists and other actors of the music industry.

direct reaction to these tragic deaths, Def Jam Records founder and rap mogul Russell Simmons encouraged Farrakhan to host a hip-hop peace summit at the headquarters of NOI in Chicago. The meeting was held in April and preceded by preliminary meetings in New York, Atlanta and Los Angeles.[77] The meeting gathered an impressive list of participants: Snoop Dogg, Tha Dogg Pound, Ice Cube, Bone Thugs-n-Harmony, Channel Live, Nate Dogg, Mack 10, WC, Too Short, Willie D, The Goodie Mob, Fat Joe and Chuck D.[78] At the concluding 'rappers' unity' press conference held on 3 April 1997 in Chicago, Farrakhan, surrounded by the participants, called an end to the rivalry. Artists including Snoop Dogg, Willie D and Doug E. Doug all pledged to honour the agreement.[79] The summit helped to reinforce Farrakhan's reputation as a trusted personality in the hip-hop community.[80] In September 1997, the hip-hop magazine *Vibe* published a four-page interview with Farrakhan, titled 'The Charmer' (calling attention to Farrakhan's former stage name as a calypso singer).[81] In the article, Farrakhan spoke about the state of hip-hop and why he had made the decision to leave his music career, while also answering questions concerning his alleged anti-Semitic views and statements.

In another attempt to combine his love for music and to score political points, in April 1993 Farrakhan appeared in a symposium in Winston-Salem, North Carolina, called 'Gateways: Classical Music and the Black Musician'. During the symposium, he performed Felix Mendelssohn's Violin Concerto, Op. 64. The symbolic choice of Mendelssohn did not escape the chief music

[77] The meeting in Mosque #7 in Harlem was hosted by Conrad Muhammad, who had styled himself as 'Hip-hop Minister'. East-Coast rappers such as Notorious B. I. G., A Tribe Called Quest, Chuck D and Sean 'Puffy' Combs attended the meeting. 'Nation of Islam Plans Rap Summit', https://lasvegassun.com/news/1996/sep/17/nation-of-islam-plans-rap-summit/ (accessed 6 May 2024).

[78] For a personal first-hand account of the meeting, see hip-hop journalist Davey D's article 'Nation of Islam Hip Hop Peace Summit', http://www.daveyd.com/peacesummit.html (accessed 14 September 2023).

[79] A video recording of the full preconference is available online: '1997 Hip Hop Summit' (3 parts), https://www.youtube.com/watch?v=C7deHBTofks (accessed 14 September 2023).

[80] The 1997 summit was not the only time when Farrakhan was personally involved in the hip-hop community. For example, in 2001 Russell Simons invited him as a keynote speaker to the hip-hop summit in New York, and in 2003 Farrakhan sat down with rapper Ja Rule in an interview broadcast on MTV, where he talked about his ongoing feud with rapper 50 Cent.

[81] 'The Charmer', *Vibe*, September 1997: 132–36.

critic of the *New York Times*, Bernard Holland. In his review of the performance, he has noted:

> Mr. Farrakhan acknowledged the symbolism in his playing of music by a European Jew, although he also said he had not known Mendelssohn was Jewish until two years ago. (The Mendelssohn family converted to Christianity.) He plans to repeat the Mendelssohn performance on May 17 in Chicago, both to acknowledge his 60th birthday and to send out more ecumenical messages.[82]

When Farrakhan repeated the performance (accompanied by the New World Orchestra conducted by Michael Morgan) in front of a Chicago audience at Christ Universal Temple, almost 3,000 people attended the event, which was meant to celebrate Farrakhan's sixtieth birthday. His performance was followed by a press conference where Farrakhan was quoted as saying: 'Let us hope the music will open a way to dialogue and erase the bitterness and misunderstandings between the communities [Muslim and Jewish]'. Farrakhan also envisioned an ecumenical musical performance where Judaism, Christianity and Islam would come together with the help of the 'universal language of music'.[83]

He is often seen in photos with hip-hop celebrities, and during his annual 2015 Saviours' Day address, he mentioned meeting with Kanye West and West's former wife Kim Kardashian. After the speech, Kanye West revealed that he and Farrakhan were working on a film project together, a documentary on Farrakhan's lifelong love of music.[84] Even today, although Farrakhan has passed his ninetieth birthday and maybe lost some of his former sway within the hip-hop community, he maintains an association with artists and the hip-hop community in general.

[82] Bernard Holland, 'Sending a Message, Louis Farrakhan Plays Mendelssohn', http://www.nytimes.com/1993/04/19/arts/sending-a-message-louis-farrakhan-plays-mendelssohn.html (accessed 14 September 2023).

[83] 'Minister Farrakhan Celebrates 60th Birthday Performing Violin Concert', *Jet*, 7 June 1993. A video-recording of the Chicago performance is available online: 'Mastering the Mendelssohn: Minister Farrakhan's Stunning Performance of Violin Concerto 2nd Movement', https://www.youtube.com/watch?v=u1mzLsU5hLI (accessed 12 September 2023).

[84] 'Kanye West Interview at The Breakfast Club Power 105.1 (02/20/2015)', https://www.youtube.com/watch?v=toWk6mybzVE&spfreload=10 (accessed 14 September 2023).

The Moslem Sunrise

Islamic movements founded outside the US have also had a profound influence on African American music-making. The Ahmadiyya Muslim Community was founded in 1889 by Mirza Ghulam Ahmad Qadiani (1835–1908) in the Punjab province of India. Mirza Ghulam proclaimed that he was a *mujaddid*, a renewer of Islam. He also declared himself to be the *Mahdi*, the guided one, who will come at the end of time as Jesus incarnate. His claim was that all religions constituted a unity and that the message of this unity issued from Allah. Therefore, followers of the main branch of the Ahmadiyya movement do not believe that the Prophet Muhammad was the final prophet (although he is understood as the last law-bringing prophet). In stating this belief, they have received substantial critique from Sunni Muslims. Even so, the movement has become famous for its *dawa* (missionary work). Ahmadiyyas were among the first Muslims to translate the Qur'an into English: in 1917, a Lahori Ahmadiyya named Muhammad Ali translated the Qur'an, a translation that has been distributed widely.[85] The movement started its missionary work in the US in 1920, when Mufti Muhammad Sadiq was sent to the US in response to the inroads of Christian missionaries in India. The stated goal was to convert Americans to Islam.[86] Sadiq arrived in New York, but quickly relocated his mission to Chicago.

At that time, Chicago had small but significant Muslim communities that originated from different countries in the Middle East. Sadiq quickly became respected among these Muslim communities and cultivated good relations with them. Several African Americans were attracted to the Ahmadiyya message of unity and equality over ethnic and racial barriers, and many assumed leading roles within the movement.[87] The Ahmadiyya organisation published the widely circulated newsletter *Moslem Sunrise* to disseminate its message. The sprawling activities of the Ahmadiyya movement are often considered to be one of the sources of inspiration for early African American Islam.[88] And even though music was not central to Ahmadiyya missionary strategies or its

[85] The Lahori Ahmadiyya is a group separate from the main branch of the Ahmadiyya. But there is consensus between the two about the excellence of the translation.

[86] Safi and Hammer 2013: 52.

[87] Schmidt 1998: 49–50. Most of the 200 members of the Ahmadiyya mosque in the early 1950s were African American.

[88] McAlister 1999: 624.

rituals, there was a particular music scene that came to be interconnected with the Ahmadiyya faith: jazz.

Scholars have demonstrated how Islamic semiotic resources have coloured the fabric of jazz music and given jazz musicians an alternative to Christianity. For example, Christopher W. Chase has claimed that '[i]n a larger sense, Islamic sacred history has provided opportunities to sidestep the entire Christian socio-colonial *habitus*, whether in the form of "Moorishness", or an anti-Apartheid musical *ummah* of resistance'.[89] The message of unity and equality between races apparently attracted jazz musicians to Islam. An often-cited article published in *Ebony* in 1953 pointed to the 'trend among Negro musicians [. . .] during the last ten years to convert to Islam'.[90] The article portrayed two jazz musicians – Sahib Shihab (Eddie Gregory) and Al Hajj Abdullah Rasheed Ahmad (Lynn Hope). They were attracted to and joined the Ahmadiyya in the late 1940s. Al Hajj Abdullah Rasheed Ahmad is pictured as one of the most learned members of the Moslem Faith in America.[91] Photos accompanying the article show him teaching Arabic to youngsters, as well as leading other Muslims in prayer, and it describes him as being an aspiring *Hafiz*, having 'committed 31 chapters of the Koran, Moselm [sic] bible, to memory in Arabic'.[92]

Another aspect stressed in the article is the fact that these musicians' new faith enabled them to travel freely in the racially segregated Jim Crow South:

> 'We are recognized as whites in the South and are not Jim Crowed', Hope says. 'We do not accept Jim Crow laws or regulations'. Hope and his all-Moslem orchestra have been served in white restaurants in Atlanta, Birmingham, New Orleans, Nashville, Louisville, Charleston, W. Va., and Gadsden, Ala. Hope and his men, wearing their turbans, enter a restaurant with superb aplomb, and are usually told very quickly, 'We don't serve colored people here'. Hope's answer is swift, calm and always the same: 'We are not Negroes but members of the Moslem faith. Our customs are Eastern. We claim the nationality of our Arabic ancestors as well as their culture'. Almost invariably, they receive courteous treatment.[93]

[89] Chase 2010: 180.

[90] 'Moslem Musicians', *Ebony Magazine*, April, 1953: 104. This article is often cited by scholars writing about the subject Islam and jazz. See, for example, Porter 2002; Nash 2008; Chase 2010; Bivins 2015.

[91] Ibid. p. 108.

[92] Ibid. p. 104.

[93] Ibid. p. 107.

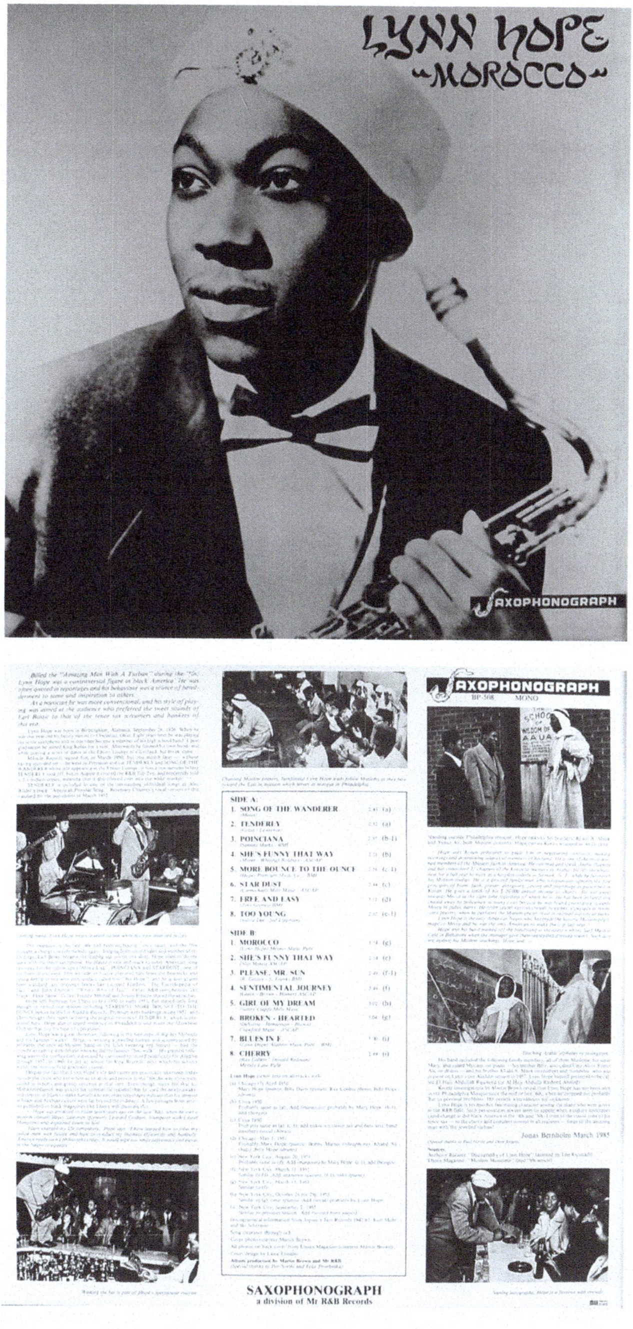

Figure 3.6 Album cover (LP; front and back) of Lynn Hope's *Morocco* (1985), with images on the back showing Hope (aka Al Hajj Abdullah Rasheed Ahmad) teaching Arabic to young students in 1953.

The article claimed that around 200 jazz musicians had converted to Islam because 'Islam breaks down racial barriers and endows its followers with purpose and dignity'.[94] Interestingly, some observers today have pointed to a similar trend within the hip-hop community and are intrigued by white rappers converting to Islam in order to gain access to spaces that would otherwise be inaccessible to them. Hisham Aidi has written:

> For many white hip-hoppers in the US, the sought-after 'ghetto pass' – acceptance in the hip-hop community – comes only with conversion to Islam, which is seen as a rejection of being white. The white rapper Everlast, formerly Erik Schrody of House of Pain, claims that conversion to Islam and mosque attendance allow him to visit ghetto neighborhoods he could never enter as a non-Muslim white.[95]

Another musician attracted to Islam was the American Grammy Award-winning jazz musician Yusef Lateef (William Emanuel Huddleston). After a meeting with trumpet player Talib Dawud in 1946 during a jam session at a club on Chicago's West Side, Lateef started to explore Islam. He converted in 1948 and until his death in 2013 was a member of the Ahmadiyya Muslim Community.[96] When Yusef Lateef died, the Ahmadiyya community in the US put out a press release mourning his passing. The press release underscored the important role that Lateef had played within the movement and pictured him as 'a groundbreaking musician and a passionate Ahmadi Muslim brother'. Lateef was further described as a devout Muslim who did not perform his music in venues that served alcohol, 'because he came to believe music shouldn't be presented in alcohol-and-smoke cellars'.[97]

Sahib Shihab, Al Hajj Abdullah Rasheed Ahmad, Talib Dawud and Yusef Lateef all belonged to the first wave of jazz musicians incorporating Islamic semiotic resources into their music-making. During the following decades

[94] Ibid. p. 104.

[95] Aidi 2003: 50.

[96] Lateef 2006: 56.

[97] 'Press Release: Dr Yusef Lateef, American Muslim Icon and Grammy Award-Winning Musician Dies at 93', 24 December 2013, http://www.ahmadiyya.us/documents/doc_view/1069-release-20131225-yusuflateef (accessed 22 September 2023).

many other jazz musicians converted and followed different Islamic interpretive traditions, including guitarist Grant Green (NOI), drummer Idris Muhammad (Sunni Islam) and pianist Ahmad Jamal (Sunni Islam), to name a few. Jazz musicians have given a variety of reasons for converting to Islam, but social pride and spiritual dedication appear to be most common.

Interestingly, some artists seem to have felt external social pressure, from the media in particular, to convert to Islam. For example, in October 1948 *Life* magazine ran a six-page story on Dizzy Gillespie and the emergence of 'the new school' of jazz: bebop. The story is richly illustrated with photos, and in one Dizzy is posing on the floor, shirtless, in something resembling a Muslim prayer posture. The text beneath the photo reads: 'MOHAMMEDAN LEANINGS are shown by many bebop musicians, some of whom have actually turned Mohammedan, interrupting rehearsals at sunset to bow to the east. Here Dizzy bows to Mecca from his Hollywood apartment'.[98]

In his biography, Gillespie retold this story. He claimed that he had been tricked into posing in a Muslim prayer posture for the photo shoot, saying: 'They tricked me into committing a sacrilege. The newspapers figured that if the "king of bebop" converted, thousands of beboppers would follow suit'.[99] Gillespie described taking an interest in and studying Islam, but never actually converted.[100] He recognised the fact that Muslim identity provided a sanctuary from racial prejudice against and discrimination of African Americans, but that Muslim identity could also trigger other prejudices:

> [. . .] sometimes in Europe I'd wear a turban. People would see me on the streets and think of me as an Arab or a Hindu. They didn't know what to think, really, because I'd pretend I didn't speak English and listen to them talk about me. Sometimes Americans would think I was some kind of 'Mohammedan' nobleman. You wouldn't believe some of the things they say in ignorance.[101]

[98] 'Bebop – New Jazz School is Led by Trumpeter Who is Hot, Cool and Gone', *Life Magazine*, 11 October 1948: 142.

[99] Gillespie 2009: 293.

[100] Dizzy Gillespie was clearly a spiritual man. When the 1960s ended, he converted to the Bahá'í Faith. He was an adherent of the religion until his death in 1993. The New York Bahá'í Center still pays tribute to Gillespie with weekly jazz sessions on Tuesday evenings.

[101] Gillespie 2009: 293.

Figure 3.7 'Bebop king, Dizzy Gillespie, a Mohammedan, is bowing to Mecca from his Hollywood apartment', *Life Magazine*, 11 October 1948. Source: Allan Grant/The LIFE Picture Collection/Shutterstock.

Other artists came in contact with Islam through people who had converted, even though they themselves never did so. Scholars have argued that their music has been influenced by Islamic semiotic resources, one noteworthy example being John Coltrane. Christopher W. Chase has suggested that Islam was a crucial part of the milieu that influenced the famous jazz saxophonist.[102] Not only did Coltrane's influences derive from relationships with fellow jazz musicians who had converted to Islam, but he was also, during the mid-1950s, married to Juanita 'Naima' Austin, a Muslim convert.[103] Chase has argued that this influence can be found in biographical statements, liner notes and Coltrane's musical expressions. He has also suggested that the message was 'coded' to be 'compatible with both his black Gospel heritage and the Islam of

[102] Chase 2010: 175.

[103] His marriage to Naima inspired Coltrane to write the ballad 'Naima'. The song first appeared on the LP album *Giant Steps* (Atlantic Records © 1960).

his jazz community'.[104] Chase has used Coltrane's famous 'A Love Supreme' as an illustration:

> The prophetic promise of Coltrane's religious conversion and its most famous musical example could not be lost on his fans, and its full context should suggest a pluralist ecstatic prophetics of which Islam was a significant part. There may be additional coding in the body of the performance itself that was purposefully meaningful to Muslim fans and Coltrane's own loved ones and colleagues. In the first part, Coltrane's famous four-note repetition blends into voices chanting 'A Love Supreme'. At times these words blend, and at least one scholar has heard this blending as 'Allah Supreme'. As Moustafa Bayoumi points out, this phrasing and interpretation would be easily recognizable to all English-speaking Muslims as 'Allahu Akbar' ('God Is the Greatest'), the beginning of the adhan.[105]

On one level, then, the use of Islamic semiotic resources provided a way for jazz musicians to escape racial discrimination. However, on another level, it gave them the means to explore the universal aspects of the imagined community of Muslim believers. It connected them, on a third level, with their own perceived roots. And finally, on a fourth level, Islamic semiotic resources provided these musicians with the means to explore other musical traditions and new soundscapes, Muslim and non-Muslim alike.

Islam and the Black Arts Movement

The Black Arts Movement (BAM) in the 1960s and early 1970s was as an artistic extension of the Black Power movement's confrontation with what it perceived as white notions and conventions regarding art, literature and aesthetics. In this confrontation, BAM sought to distance itself from previous African American creative traditions and movements.[106] The movement did so by embracing a radical political stance. Amiri Baraka, discussed previously, has often been accredited as the driving force behind BAM, with its epicentre in Harlem. BAM attracted a wide variety of African American writers, musicians

[104] Chase 2010: 180.

[105] Ibid. p. 177.

[106] Daulatzai 2012: 106.

and intellectuals. Poets and musicians issuing from the ranks of BAM, such as Gil Scott-Heron and the Last Poets, are often cited as sources of inspiration by early hip-hop MCs such as DJ Kool Herc and Coke La Rock.

But the relationship between BAM and hip-hop culture is not confined to perceived musical similarities. It extends to the use of Islamic semiotic resources in the construction of a new radical African American identity. As stated in the quote in the introduction to this book, Islam was in many ways embedded in the DNA of the movement. The use of Islamic semiotic resources went beyond Baraka. The author and academic Melani McAlister has written:

> The influence of Islam and Islamic symbolism went well beyond Baraka; it was highly visible in general in the Black Arts movement, acknowledged, and often supported, even by those who didn't share its presumptions. Members of the Nation of Islam and orthodox African American Sunni Muslims were active in political and cultural organizations all over the country.[107]

For example, the previously mentioned group of the Last Poets was symbolically formed on Malcolm X's birthday (19 May) in 1968, in Marcus Garvey Park in Harlem. This Spoken Word collective would evolve over time, with members joining and departing, but at all times was it clearly influenced by the cognitive universe of Islam, something repeatedly displayed in lyrics and on album covers. For example, on the cover art of the album *At Last* (1973), Jalaluddin Mansur Nuriddin, Umar Bin Hassan and Suliaman El-Hadi are seen wearing Muslim-style garb and appear to carry prayer marks (*zebiba)* on their foreheads.[108] The album also contains lyrical reference to the cognitive universe of Islam. For example, the track 'This is Madness' contains references to Malcolm X as well as to Allah, and the phrase 'Bismillahi ar-Rahman ar-Rahim' (In the name of Allah, the beneficent, the merciful) is chanted over the intense drums.[109]

[107] McAlister 1999: 640.

[108] Prayer marks commonly serve as a public demonstration of piety. Muslims have cultivated techniques to deliberately develop the mark in order to promote the appearance of devoutness.

[109] The Last Poets, *At Last*, 'This is Madness', LP album (Blue Thumb Records Inc. © 1973).

Countless other musicians and writers explored and invoked Islamic semiotic resources. Former airman Henry Dumas was inspired by Sufi Islam and Arab culture after having been stationed in Saudi Arabia.[110] The essayist and poet Marvin X, sometimes called the Rumi of the US, and by many considered the father of Muslim literature in the US, wrote poems and plays with Islamic themes.[111] The poet Sonia Sanchez joined NOI for several years in the early 1970s, before she left the organisation because her views on women's rights did not correspond with those of NOI. During her time in NOI, she kept a recurring column of poetry in *Muhammed Speaks*, the official newspaper of NOI. She also published poems celebrating the movement and its message in, for example, *Negro Digest* (later *Black World*).[112]

Baraka founded the record label Jihad Productions in the 1960s. The label only released three records: Sunny Murray's *Sonny's Time Now* (1965), The Jihad's *Black and Beautiful . . . Soul and Madness* (1968) and *The Black Mass (a Play by Imamu Baraka)* (1968). The first two records are best described as experimental and influenced by free jazz. Baraka appears on both of them, reading highly political poems. *The Black Mass*, probably the most famous of the three records, contains a play that retells NOI's creation myth in which the evil and mad scientist Yakub crafted the 'white devil' (in NOI mythology, this process is known as *grafting*). The play is set to music performed by Sun Ra, considered to be one of the early pioneers of the Afrofuturist movement, and his Myth-Science Arkestra.[113]

At the time of BAM, the use of Islamic semiotic resources reached far outside Muslim circles, as broader layers of US society were exposed to Islam. Melani McAlister has written:

> In the 1960s, this [Islamic] influence was significant. By 1965 or 1966, one need not have ever entered a Muslim temple nor read a Nation of Islam newspaper to know that, within the African American community, Islam had moved far beyond the sectarian curiosity it had been just ten years earlier. In a cultural

[110] Womack 2013: 172.

[111] Safi and Hammer 2013: 289.

[112] See, for example, Sanchez 1974.

[113] For an intriguing account of the aural aspects of the Afrofuturist movement, see Steinskog 2018.

> field that ranged from poetry and plays to highly charged sports matches, from local community theaters to the boxing ring, Islam was a significant presence. In various manifestations, Islam – and the Nation of Islam in particular – played a central role in reconfigurations of black radicalism, challenging both the hegemony of black Christianity's religious values and the politics of integration associated with it.[114]

In the mid-1970s Baraka started to distance himself from African American nationalism and the Islamic interpretive traditions promoted by NOI. Instead, he turned to Marxist-Leninism and became involved in the struggles of Third World liberation movements. As Baraka turned to the Third World, the cultural momentum of the movement had simultaneously begun to fade away at home. But the exploration and use of Islamic semiotic resources would soon reappear in another cultural arena in the US: hip-hop music.

[114] McAlister 1999: 624f.

4

FROM PLANET ROCK TO INDIGOISM

This chapter begins by looking at the scene in the South Bronx at the time of the birth of hip-hop culture. The South Bronx has since become a site of pilgrimage for hip-hop fans from around the world, occupying a special place in hip-hop lore.[1] While there may be some disagreement within the scholarship and criticism as to when hip-hop culture originated, there also exists a consensus on the importance of the South Bronx as the area of New York where youths laid the foundation of what today is known as hip-hop. However, the creative activities and cultural impulses behind hip-hop were not exclusive to the South Bronx: the DJing, rapping, break dancing and graffiti culture were found in other boroughs of New York, as well as in cities such as Philadelphia and Detroit.[2]

I will focus here on two organisations that have been crucial in extending earlier efforts to fuse Islamic semiotic resources with music: The Universal Zulu Nation and The Nation of Gods and Earths (the Five Percenters). Both are of the utmost importance, I believe, for understanding how semiotic resources from the cognitive universe of Islam have been used within US hip-hop culture – even though neither organisation describes or considers itself as Muslim. Given such a seemingly surprising use of Islamic resources, this

[1] For example, the tour company Hush Hip Hop Tours offers daily tours with early hip-hop pioneers as guides.

[2] Rivera 2003: 50–51.

chapter will conclude with a discussion of different ways of understanding the use of Islamic semiotic themes.

Afrika Bambaataa and the Universal Zulu Nation

> You go back to when the slaves came to these shores, to be-bop and the poetry of Sonya Sanchez, the Last Poets. Then you go into James Brown when he used to do his call-and-response rap, the Revolutionary Rap of Malcolm X, the honorable Minister Louis Farrakhan, Barry White's style of rap, Isaac Hayes, Millie Jackson. Pigmeat Markham did 'Here Comes the Judge' which had the rhymes and the funky breakbeat behind it. It's always been there but once we came around, we named the whole hip-hop culture. Even when we're talking to each other, we're rapping to each other. It might not be in synch but we're rapping.
>
> Afrika Bambaataa[3]

As the 1960s gave way to the 1970s, the cultural energy created by the Last Poets, Baraka and other artists from BAM dissipated. But, in modified form, this culture re-emerged within the burgeoning hip-hop culture in the South Bronx.[4] New York City in the early 1970s was on the verge of bankruptcy, and the South Bronx lay in ruins. Berman has provided one telling description of the situation in the Bronx during the first half of the 1970s:

> The deindustrialization of America wiped out the blue-collar jobs that had kept generations of Bronxites alive. Drugs and arson are the biggest local industries now. The most striking visual feature, by the mid-1970s, was miles and miles of ruins. Dozens of blocks, blocks that for decades had been the densest and most crowded in the city, now were suddenly as open as the deserts. Within a decade the South Bronx lost half its population, as hundreds of thousands of peoples fled the fires. (Population loss then became the pretext for closing the firehouses.) This was the decade when New York nearly went bankrupt, and *The Daily Mail* summed up very aptly the federal government's role in the story: FORD TO CITY: DROP DEAD.[5]

The Bronx was a burning wasteland that epitomised urban decay. On top off this deterioration, gangs such as the Glory Stompers, the Ministers and the

[3] 'Afrika Bambaataa Article/interview by Jason Gross (February/June 1999)', http://www.furious.com/perfect/afrikabambaataa.html (accessed 22 September 2023).

[4] Daulatzai 2012: 113.

[5] Berman 1996: 166.

Black Spades controlled micro-neighbourhoods in the borough, and turf wars between them plagued local neighbourhoods. The gang leaders were rarely older than twenty, and members could be as young as eight.[6] Along with the gangs and fires, heroin addiction among adolescents had been on the rise since the late 1950s.[7]

It was against this backdrop that DJs such as Kool Herc, Disco King Mario, Disco Wiz and Grandmaster Caz laid the foundation for hip-hop, by isolating and looping the drum beat – the break – in disco songs played at block parties, school parties, park jams and, when hip-hop grew in popularity, nightclubs. Another key figure in the early hip-hop scene was Afrika Bambaataa (born Lance Taylor on 19 April 1957), who in 1969 had joined a local division of the Black Spades, the largest gang in New York at the time. In the early 1970s, he drifted away from the gang.[8] Through his mother he had acquired a keen interest in music, but he had also cultivated an awareness of African American politics. Bambaataa took his artist name from the Zulu Chief Bambatha kaMancinza, often credited as an inspiration to and precursor of the anti-apartheid movement in South Africa. In an interview with music journalist David Toop, Bambaataa elaborated on his background:

> In the '60s that's when I was young and I was seeing a lot of things that was happening around the world. What got me excited first was when James Brown came out with 'Say it Loud, I'm Black and I'm Proud', that's when we transcended from negro to black [. . .]. Black was evil, turn the other cheek, believe all the stuff that the Bible is telling you. The Bible contradicts itself. So Martin Luther King was the thing happening because he was fighting for civil rights, but Malcolm X was more on the aggressive side. Myself, I was more on the Malcolm X way of thinking.[9]

Aged twelve, Bambaataa started to frequent the Black Panther Information Center on Burton Road. Clearly, he was trying to get in tune with the radical politics of the time.[10] Confronted by the despicable conditions of the South Bronx and its gang violence, Bambaataa joined NOI, mainly, so he claims,

[6] Jonnes 2002: 237–40.

[7] Schneider 2008: 137–40.

[8] Keyes 2004: 47.

[9] Toop 2000: 58.

[10] Hager 2004: 14.

because he respected the organisation's social work and how they attempted to clean up the community.[11] Bambaataa came from a family with several NOI members, and already as a child he had heard Elijah Muhammad speak at a rally.[12]

Bambaataa's efforts to combine self-improvement, transcendence and social mobility with music to positively influence and educate the youth of the South Bronx was manifested in his musical career. When Bambaataa performed as DJ at hip-hop block parties in the late 1970s, he was known for superimposing the voices of Malcolm X and other NOI ministers over the electro-pop outfit Kraftwerk's eerie *Trans-Europe Express* (1977).[13] When Bambaataa made his record debut in 1980, he was already a well-known DJ in New York. He recorded the album *Zulu Nation Throw Down* (1980) together with Cosmic Force. In 1982, Bambaataa and the Soulsonic Force released the commercially successful and hugely influential *Planet Rock* (1982). The song's idealistic message and electro-sound gained both grassroots hip-hop and mainstream pop credibility. The growth of the Universal Zulu Nation was elevated by the success of *Planet Rock*, which made not only hip-hop but also the Zulu Nation known worldwide.[14] By the early 1980s, the Zulu Nation had thousands of followers around the globe.[15]

Significantly, the Zulu Nation provided hip-hop with an ideological foundation. Members of the Zulu Nation were asked to follow forty-six bylaws collected in the 'Laws and Regulations of the Universal Zulu Nation'. Members were, for instance, not allowed to be affiliated with gangs, and they had to commit to a life free of violence, drugs and alcohol. Members were also encouraged to pray daily, speak the truth and participate in Zulu Nation meetings.[16]

The Zulu Nation does not self-identify as a religious organisation or a 'cult'. It presents itself as being on a mission to gather truths and facts from all religions and beliefs. A religion, according to the Zulu Nation, implies a belief system, a structure; the Zulu Nation 'do not have a belief structure', and all

[11] Toop 2000: 59.

[12] Keyes 2004: 48.

[13] Toop 2000: 130.

[14] Daulatzai 2012: 113. Bambaataa used record sleeves to spread and promote the message of the Zulu Nation. See, for example, the 12-inch single Afrika Bambaataa and Family, 'Bambaataa's Theme' (1986).

[15] Hebdige 2004: 226.

[16] Saphire [n. d.], vol. #1: 4–7.

religions are part of the Zulu Nation if they are positive in nature.[17] The Zulu Nation also takes a stand against racism and discrimination and decrees that it 'is for all people of any colour, age, culture or gender. As long as you have an open mind and are really ready to better yourself'.[18] This attitude clearly separates the Zulu Nation from predecessors such as NOI and Marcus Garvey, since it lacks the component of African American nationalism and Black chosenness. In fact, the organisation extends its message to 'Aliens' and 'life forms of all forms' on all planets of the universe.[19] But the Zulu Nation shares with all African American movements, Islamic as well as non-Islamic, the injunction of self-improvement. This injunction is also vital, as we will see, to many hip-hop artists influenced by different Islamic interpretive traditions.

The teachings of the Zulu Nation, or 'infinity lessons', as they are called inside the organisation, are mainly collected in two books: *The Green Book* (n. d.) and *The Black Book* (n. d.). The *Green Book* is intended for a general audience, while *The Black Book* is for members only. Members are encouraged to study and memorise the lessons in these books. There are at least two *Gold Books* (n. d.), which include what are considered to be more advanced infinity lessons (so called 'infinity plus lessons'). In the *Gold Books*, the members are encouraged to send their own infinity lessons to the organisation, after the principle 'Each one Teach one'. It is not easy to summarise the lessons since they include everything from how to prepare for earthquakes and what food to eat (eating pork is strongly discouraged), to hip-hop and Zulu Nation history, rules and regulations of the organisation and quotes from the Bible and the Qur'an. The content of these books taken together constitutes 'Zulu Knowledge', which in turn is the key tool for improving the 'knowledge of self' and becoming a 'Zulu Master'.

Some of the core beliefs (or, as they are called within the organisation, *factology*) are found in the manifesto 'The Beliefs of the Universal Zulu Nation'. The first tenet of the manifesto states:

> We believe in one God, who is called by many names – Allah, Jehovah, Yahweh, RA, Eloahim, Jah, God, The Most High, The Creator, The Supreme One. We believe as Amazulu, we will not fight or kill other human beings over which

[17] Ibid., vol. #1, p. 2.

[18] Ibid.

[19] Ibid., vol. #1, p. 16.

> proper name to call God. We will recognise them all to be the same one God. We believe God will come to be seen to the human eye and will straighten out the problems that Human Beings brought upon this planet so-called Earth.[20]

The tenet reverberates the Abrahamic universalism of ideological predecessors such as Marcus Garvey. Abrahamic universalism is further stressed in 'The Universal Prayer of the Universal Zulu Nation of This Planet So Called Earth'. The beginning of the prayer reads:

> In the Name of The Force, who is The Source, whom is called, by many names, ALLAH, JEHOVAH, YAHWEH, JAH, GOD, EL KULUWM, AMEN RA, THE ALL, THE SUPREME ONE FORCE. We Amazulus (The Peoples of The Heavens), bear witness to our way of life (Religion) which is Truth, backed by facts of the known and not just beliefs although we do have beliefs, we are always seeking, Truth of the Known and the Unseen, which is yet Known. We Amazulus respect The Scriptures of The Force, Who is The Source of us all, who sent down words and written words to all the Prophets, Messengers and Warner's of The Creator, The Supreme One. We Amazulus call on The Spirits of all our Ancestors from the past, whom did righteousness, in the Name of The Force, who is The Source, the Angels and other Life Forms, who do righteousness, In The Name of The Force, to watch over all of Amazulus and all Human Beings on this planet so called Earth.[21]

The Universal Zulu Nation's manifesto is clearly also influenced by Bambaataa's background in NOI. It borrows, sometimes verbatim, from NOI's widely circulated pamphlet 'What the Muslims Believe'. The third bylaw in 'The Beliefs of the Universal Zulu Nation' states: 'We believe that the Bible has been tampered with and must be reinterpreted, so that mankind will not be snared by the falsehoods that have been added to it'. This passage is taken directly from NOI's 'What the Muslims Believe'.[22] The influence of NOI and

[20] 'The Beliefs of the Universal Zulu Nation', http://new.zulunation.com/zulu-beliefs/ (accessed 16 September 2023).

[21] 'Zulu Prayers the Universal Prayer of the Universal Zulu Nation of This Planet So Called Earth', http://new.zulunation.com/zulu-prayer/ (accessed 22 September 2017).

[22] 'What the Muslims Believe', https://www.noi.org/muslim-program/ (accessed 22 September 2023).

other Muslim movements such as the Ansuru Allah Community has been recognised by Bambaataa in interviews.[23]

As part of the infinity lessons, members are encouraged to study and learn Arabic along with Islamic vocabulary and names such as *abu* (father); *bab* (door, in this context probably a reference to a metaphorical door that opens up to spiritual knowledge); Bilal (after Bilal ibn Rabah who, according to Sunni traditions, was an enslaved Abyssinian and one of the earliest converts to Islam, and believed to have been the first *muezzin*, the one who recites the call to prayer; because of his dark complexion, many African American Muslims see Bilal as an important symbol); *haram* (in Islamic jurisprudence, *haram* refers to conduct forbidden by Allah); *jinn* (spiritual beings described in the Qur'an); and *kafir* (unbeliever, or disbeliever). Many of the concepts and practices of the Zulu Nation reverberate in traditions found within the Nation of Gods and Earths (to be discussed below). These similarities led to conflicts between the two organisations throughout the 1970s and 1980s. The Nation of Gods and Earths accused the Zulu Nation of stealing their concepts and traditions. The Zulu Nation, in response, felt compelled to organise its own security force, Zulu War Security.[24]

The Zulu Nation's message and influence over hip-hop culture might have peaked in the late 1980s and early 1990s, but as Sohail Daulatzai has explained: 'This early and influential blue print for hip-hop was deeply informed by Islam and Black Nationalism, and it created an ideological paradigm out of which hip-hop and its relationship to Islam would continue to flourish'.[25] Today, over a half century after its founding, the Zulu Nation stands as the first and longest-lasting hip-hop organisation. It remains active with chapters across the US and around the globe. Bambaataa himself spearheaded the organisation until 2016, when Ronald Savage, a political activist and Bronx native, went public with allegations that Bambaataa had sexually molested him as a youth. Following Savage's allegations, three more men accused Bambaataa of sexual abuse. In a statement in the music magazine *Rolling Stone*, Bambaataa vehemently denied the claims and characterised the allegations as 'baseless' and a

[23] Alim 2006: 26.

[24] 'Zulu King Mark Luv Officially Resigns from Zulu Nation after 26 Years', https://www.youtube.com/watch?v=pkWtykolE9Y (accessed 22 September 2023).

[25] Daulatzai 2012: 113.

'cowardly attempt to tarnish' his reputation and legacy within the hip-hop community.[26] Several weeks after Bambaataa's statement, the Zulu Nation issued an apology to multiple alleged victims who came forward with similar stories and changed the leadership of the organisation.[27] In 2017, numerous chapters separated from the Zulu Nation, driven by infrastructure challenges and divergent ideological and moral perspectives, to form and establish a new organisation, the Zulu Union.[28]

It remains to be seen what will happen to the Zulu Nation. Nevertheless, the Zulu Nation and Bambaataa constituted important actors in extending the use of Islamic semiotic resources from earlier generations and bringing them to the attention of the hip-hop generation. Through literary reproduction and 'remixing' the Zulu Nation message with Islamic semiotic resources, the Nation created a new sound, much like generations of jazz musicians and artists of BAM had done before the Nation.

In God We Trust: The Five Percent Nation of Gods and Earths

The Nation of Gods and Earths (NGE), also known as the Five Percenters, was established by Clarence 13X (born Clarence Edward Smith in 1928 in Danville, Virginia) in Harlem in the mid-1960s, as an offshoot of NOI. Clarence 13X proclaimed himself to be 'Allah'. Adherents of the teachings of the Five Percenters do not consider themselves to be Muslims (why they do not do so is explained below), but they nonetheless make use of Islamic semiotic resources.

The Five Percenters were already an integral part of hip-hop culture at the time of the first parties in the Bronx. In an interview, DJ Kool Herc recalled their presence:

> So even the gang members loved us because they didn't want to mess with what was happening. You know? They come in, keep to themselves. Not only that,

[26] 'Afrika Bambaataa Calls Sexual Abuse Claims "Baseless and Cowardly"', http://www.rollingstone.com/music/news/afrika-bambaataa-calls-sexual-abuse-claims-baseless-and-cowardly-20160412 (accessed September 16, 2023).

[27] 'Afrika Bambaataa's Universal Zulu Nation Changes Leadership', http://pitchfork.com/news/65314-afrika-bambaataas-universal-zulu-nation-changes-leadership/ (accessed 22 September 2023).

[28] 'Our Mission', https://www.thezuluunion.com/about/about-us (accessed 22 December 2023).

> a lot of Five-Percenters (a splinter group of the Nation of Islam) used to come to my party [. . .] you might call them 'peace guards', and they used to hold me down: 'Yo Herc, don't worry about it'. So we was just havin' a good time.[29]

The role of NGE in hip-hop can be linked to that of the Rastafari movement within reggae and dancehall culture. The concepts and the vocabulary of the movement are so incorporated in hip-hop culture that it is impossible to tell if artists using them actually are members of the organisation, sympathisers, or just inspired by the dazzling speaking patterns and the philosophy of the movement. As Sunez Allah, a long-time NGE member, has said:

> Many MCs are posers; they just snatch bits and pieces of the truth, without knowing what really goes down. They just copying our way of speaking cause it sounds dope. Others like RZA in Wu-tang really know what's going on. I know many people who say 'peace' and it means peace; a lot of people in the rap game use that word but they don't give a fuck about peace.[30]

Adherents or not, the importance of NGE's influence on hip-hop music goes deep and is beyond dispute, and I will give ample evidence of this in the coming chapters.

The core teachings and ideology of NGE deviate substantially from mainstream Sunni Muslim interpretive traditions as well as from interpretations by NOI. NGE ideology revolves around 'The Lessons' (commonly known as the 'One Twenties', or '120' in written text). Members often learn these teachings by heart.[31] 'The Lessons' are taught via catechisation and, as the title implies, there are 120 questions and answers. According to NGE lore, W. D. Fard, the mysterious founder of NOI, gave the Lessons to Elijah Muhammad, the leader of NOI from 1934 until his death in 1975. The Lessons are interpreted and understood through an esoteric usage of the so-called 'Supreme Mathematics' and the 'Supreme Alphabet', as developed by the founder, Allah. In his seminal article on the Five Percenters, scholar Yusuf Nuruddin has compared their

[29] Interview with DJ Kool Herc, in Knight 2007: 177.

[30] Author's interview with Sunez Allah, 23 June 2006.

[31] For a personal and extensive account of the history as well as the ideology of the movement, see Knight 2007.

esoteric method to the numerology found in various mystic traditions within Islam.[32] In these traditions, letters and numbers are believed to harbour hidden meanings. For example, the number 1 symbolises 'Knowledge', 2 symbolises 'Wisdom', and 3 represents 'Understanding'; the first letter 'A' stands for 'Allah', and the seventh letter 'G', to give one more example, stands for 'God'.

According to 'the 120', the world is divided into three categories of people: 85 per cent of people are characterised as 'deaf, dumb and blind'; these people are considered to be ignorant and self-destructive people who do not have true knowledge of the self. Another 10 per cent of the population is characterised as 'the skunk of the planet Earth'; these individuals teach the lie that there is a mysterious God 'up in the sky'. These 10 percent are perceived to actually have knowledge, but to use that knowledge to perpetrate wickedness and to deceive the 85 'deaf, dumb and blind' per cent of the population. Members of NGE consider themselves as the 'Poor Righteous Teachers', the 5 per cent of the population that has knowledge of their true divine or godly identity. The musical group Poor Righteous Teachers has addressed this categorisation:

> Yo, where the teachers went, with all that pro-black shit?
> Where all the conscious niggas that used to chat like this?
> See, I remember yesterday when ya'll was Gods and Earths
> Egyptians and metaphysicists on the verge of giving birth
> To understanding, and planting seeds that grow
> Now everybody's on that bullshit about killing and so
> Eat my pussy, suck my dick, well that's the size of the shit
> So in the head of ignorance, I rip some conscious clip
> Niggas is small, my task is educate ya'll.[33]

A Poor Righteous Teacher has the potential to civilise the uncivilised by teaching them about their true nature. Members of the movement take great care in separating Islam as a science, 'a way of life', as they say, and Islam as a religion. Members are believed to be Gods (or Earths); hence, they do not see themselves

[32] Nuruddin 1994: 122.

[33] Poor Righteous Teachers, *The New World Order*, 'Conscious Style', CD album (Profile Records © 1996).

as Muslims, whom they define as people who submit to the will of God. Male members of NGE acquire 'godly names', including Divine Cee Allah or Um Allah. In the context of NGE, Allah is an acronym for 'Arm, Leg, Leg, Arm, Head', signifying the (male) human body. Women within the movement are commonly known as Earths or Moons. Common names for women can be, for example, Afrocentric names such as Arabia, Be-Asia, Shauqan or Shatike; instead of adding Allah in their names, they often add Earth or Queen, like Queen Latifa. This mirrors the belief within NGE that the Moon (female) reflects the Sun (male). The Earth metaphor symbolises women's role as the mothers of the Black and original nation 'Mother Earth'. An Earth should typically be dutiful as a wife to a 'God', thus reflecting his skills as a provider and protector over the family, much like the Moon reflects the light of the Sun.

From the beginning of its history, NGE has maintained the practice of renaming towns and areas where, as one member says, 'knowledge has been founded' – that is, places where NGE branches have been established. This theo-geographical project is sometimes called 'Allah's Atlas'. It started with the five boroughs of New York, or 'Now Why' as the members call it: Manhattan/Harlem is commonly known as Mecca, Brooklyn is Medina, Bronx is Pelan, Long Island is Lord's Island, and Staten Island is Savior's Island. When the movement spread across the country, US states were also

Figure 4.1 The Allah School in Mecca (Harlem). Source: Photo courtesy of the author.

given 'Godly names'.[34] Cee Allah is California (Los Angeles is Love Allah); Kansas is Kabba; Missouri is Arabia. In Canada, Toronto is known as True Cipher, and in England London is Love Divine.

The teachings of NGE revolve around a distinct oral tradition and a way of speaking that Nuruddin has called 'street corner philosophical dialogue'. NGE members have their own names for it: 'dropping science' or 'building'.[35] The power of the spoken word is one of the cornerstones in the teachings of NGE. Words are broken down with the help of the Supreme Alphabet and the Mathematics in order to find their 'true' or 'divine' meaning. This practice is often used in daily conversations, where words replace numbers – for instance, seven o'clock is commonly referred to as 'God hour', since seven is represented by 'God' in the Supreme Alphabet, and the year 2017 is expressed as 'Wisdom Cipher Knowledge God', where each numeral is represented by a word.

NGE does not practice services or prayer meetings. Instead, members gather for special assemblies, family days, rallies and the Universal Parliaments which are held once a month. The movement also arranges so-called 'Civilization Classes', where members congregate to learn the foundations of the movement's teachings. NGE has its own national anthem, 'The Enlightener', and its own flag, 'The Universal Flag', displaying a large number seven in the centre of a stylised sun, with the crescent moon and a star in the background. This composition is in turn encircled by the words 'In the name of Allah'.

Clarence 13X was shot and killed in June 1969 by an unknown assassin. However, his passing did not mark the end of NGE. After the death of Allah the Father, a leader of the movement could not be agreed upon; therefore, at the end of 1970 NGE reorganised under a shared leadership and started to arrange several activities for members. Allah's teachings continued to spread by word of mouth throughout New York and, with the help of hip-hop music, to the rest of the world.

NGE's influence on hip-hop runs deep and has been widely discussed by scholars.[36] NGE has influenced not only the vernacular of hip-hop, but it has

[34] Pelan (or Patmos) is the island in NOI mythology where the white race was created by an evil scientist named Yakub. Yakub set out to create a group of people in direct opposition to his own. According to the story of Yakub, the first white man appeared only about 6,000 years ago, on the island in the Aegean Sea following a 600-year-long breeding process called 'grafting'.

[35] Nuruddin 1994: 121.

[36] For a thorough scholarly account of NGE's influence on hip-hop music, see Miyakawa 2005.

also shaped the culture of visual and aural aesthetics with the assistance of a wide range of influential artists – among them Rakim, Big Daddy Kane, Brand Nubian, Wu-Tang Clan and Poor Righteous Teachers. Regardless of whether they are active members, NGE's rhetoric and teachings have had a noteworthy and visible impact on outsiders. As stated above, many NGE words that circulate in the world of hip-hop have become an essential part of the culture – for example, 'Word is Bond', an abbreviation of 'My word is my bond', meaning that what one is saying is true and without reproach. Another example is the phrase 'Wassup G?' This was originally a salutation between male members of NGE, with the 'G' standing for God. Nowadays the 'G' is commonly interpreted as being short for 'Gangster', while the original meaning is long forgotten within general popular culture. In the same way, the expression 'Word!' has become an integrated part of hip-hop jargon; originally it was a shout of affirmation that a statement by another God was spot on or insightful.

Hip-hop lyrics inspired by NGE's oral traditions are filled with references to NGE philosophy and verbal mannerisms. Common motifs in hip-hop music in relation to NGE are Black pride, calls for positive behaviour and coded references to the beliefs of the movement. Also, the notion of 'the Black man' being God is a common theme in lyrics inspired by the philosophy of NGE. Acronyms like C. R. I. M. E. (Criminals Robbing Innocent Muthafuckas Everytime), or C. R. E. A. M. (Cash Rules Everything Around Me) are frequently heard in the lyrics. Words like 'Old Earth', meaning mother, or 'Seeds', meaning children, can also be found in hip-hop lyrics. In addition to acronyms, 'backronyms' – such as I Self Lord and Master (I. S. L. A. M.) and Arm Leg Leg Arm Head (Allah) – are common in hip-hop lyrics influenced by the teachings of NGE.

One of the more influential hip-hop acts in recent years is the hip-hop collective Wu-Tang Clan.[37] Since their debut album *Enter the Wu-Tang (36 Chambers)* (1993), the group has displayed a strong commitment to the teachings of NGE. One of the more outspoken exponents of the ideas of NGE within the hip-hop

[37] The Wu-Tang Clan was originally composed of the rappers RZA, GZA, Method Man, Raekwon, Ghostface Killah, Inspectah Deck, U-God, Masta Killa, Cappadonna and the late Ol' Dirty Bastard. In addition to seven studio albums, members have released several studio albums as individual artists. Furthermore, they have introduced or launched the careers of numerous other artists and groups, as well as ventured into a multitude of ambitious side projects and business ventures: clothing lines, comics and computer games being a few examples.

collective is the Clan's principal producer and de facto spearhead, RZA. In the book *The Wu-Tang Manual* (2005), RZA has discussed the importance of the teachings of NGE for both his music-making and his own spiritual journey:

> In 1981, when I was eleven, the same year Grandmaster Flash's *Adventures on the Wheels of Steel* came out, GZA [another member of the Clan] began teaching me about two things: MCing and Supreme Mathematics. GZA was the first one that I heard talk about God inside, instead of looking up into the sky for God. That snapped a revelation inside my head.[38]

For RZA, the interaction with NGE was the beginning of a long spiritual journey combining the teachings of NGE with Eastern religions such as Taoism and Buddhism, Hong Kong movies and chess into the potent blend that sits as the spiritual and philosophical core under the commercial and creative surface of the Wu-Tang Clan.[39]

The frequent use of Islamic semiotic resources among NGE-affiliated artists has unquestionably helped to expose other hip-hop artists and consumers to the culture and cognitive universe of Islam.[40] Nation of Gods and Earths sells its own apparel through the website www.merchantgods.com. The website sells urban garments with NGE logos, pictures of Clarence 13X and messages such as the

[38] RZA and Norris 2005: 41.

[39] For further information on this, see RZA and Norris 2009.

[40] Sometimes this popularity leads to misunderstandings. For example, in 2005 the right-wing news site CNSnews.com reported that US military veterans and active soldiers were upset over the fact that the Post Exchange (PX) System on US military bases sold T-shirts with the logo and slogan 'Mecca: Since Day One' which, on top of the supposedly inappropriate text, were made in Pakistan: '"What in the hell is going on here?" asked one active duty soldier about to be deployed to Iraq, after seeing the name of Mecca and the slogan "Since Day One" on numerous pants and shirts at a US Army base inside the US. "Guys are getting shot at in the Middle East, and the wives and kids of the military veterans have to come to the base and buy this stuff?" explained the army soldier, who did not want to be identified for this article. He also noted that he believed the military would probably not sell any clothing lines that could be construed to be Christian-themed'. The brand name 'Mecca' in this context derives its meaning from the teachings of NGE and not the holy city of mainstream Muslims. Mecca refers to the nickname of Harlem, or Manhattan in general. 'Since Day One' simply means that Mecca clothes were one of the first brands 'since day one' to come out with urban hip-hop garments. Mecca probably has no connection to NGE, apart from the name.

'Blackman is God' or 'No Pork on my Fork'. The apparel is widely circulated alongside newspapers and literature with links to the movement.

Hip-hop artists are frequently seen sporting medallions, jackets and T-shirts with symbols and messages connected to NGE. These references sometimes stir controversies far outside the hip-hop community. When Jay-Z, the self-proclaimed 'CEO of hip-hop' and, according to business magazine *Forbes*, one of the wealthiest hip-hop artists in the world, was photographed sporting a Five Percenter pendant sitting courtside at a Brooklyn Nets game with his wife Beyoncé in 2014,[41] several media outlets reported on the 'incident'.[42] When asked about his affiliation to the movement and if the eight-pointed sun with the number seven in the middle meant anything to him, Jay-Z reportedly answered 'a little bit'. The cryptic answer sparked a vivid online debate as to whether Jay-Z had any formal affiliation to the movement, or whether he was just making a fashion statement, showing his engagement with the more political and religious aspects of hip-hop. In the darker corners of the Internet, it was speculated whether Jay-Z's wearing of the Universal Flag of the Five Percenters signalled an attempt to distract his fans from his long-rumoured affiliation to the Illuminati, a secret society commonly believed by modern conspiracy theorists to control and manipulate the world for sinister reasons.[43]

Today, a new generation of artists, such as The Underachievers and the Pro Era collective, are consciously or unconsciously re-inventing the sound of the Golden Era.[44] Accompanying this revitalisation is increased social engagement and a will to educate the listeners about alternative spiritual discourses. On

[41] '#36 Jay Z', http://www.forbes.com/profile/jay-z/ (accessed 22 September 2023).

[42] 'Jay-Z Causes Outrage by Wearing Gaudy Medallion of "Five Percent Nation" Group Who Believe Whites are "Wicked and Weak"', http://www.dailymail.co.uk/news/article-2598174/Jay-Z-causes-controversy-wearing-medallion-group-believe-whites-wicked-weak.html; 'Jay Z's Bling from "Whites are Devils' Group", http://nypost.com/2014/04/06/jay-zs-medallion-bears-logo-of-five-percent-radical-group/; 'Jay Z Sparks Controversy with Five Percent Nation Bling', http://www.huffingtonpost.com/2014/04/07/jay-z-five-percent-nation_n_5107180.html (all accessed 22 September 2023).

[43] For example: 'JAY Z ILLUMINATI Rare Interview & Time Travel Photo Found of Jay Z In 1939', https://www.youtube.com/watch?v=-lf4zco47Gc (accessed 22 September 2023).

[44] The so-called 'Golden Era' of hip-hop is considered to have lasted between 1986 and 1993 and is often said to be characterised by its diversity, high quality and innovation.

'95 'til infinity' (2013), Joey Bada$$, a member of the Pro Era collective, makes a reference to the Five Percenters:

> I combine yours with mine quake, and make the earth shake
> Supernatural disaster on you half-ass rappers
> Pass the herb to an actual pastor, word to the black lip bastard
> I drop knowledge like a Five Percenter
> Every time I drop a line, it touch like five placentas.[45]

This seemingly casual reference did not go unnoticed among fans. In a video interview, Joey Bada$$ explained the line:

> So, what I meant by that, you know every time I come across an older god, he drops knowledge on me, he opens my eyes to something new... So that all it is [...]. Drop knowledge like a Five Percenter [...] like [...] it's self-explanatory [...].[46]

He went on to break down his birth date in relation to the 'The Lessons' (the One Twenties):

> I mean, you know, I was given a very [...] extraordinary and an immense number [...]. You know [...] it's my birthday which is One Twenty, you know when I came across [...]. You know when I started to get knowledge [...] of myself and I thought I came across supreme laws and mathematics. I realized how sacred the number One Twenty was [...]. You know that what it was [...] peace to the Gods and Earths! Knowledge of self [...]. Serious!

In the interview, Joey Bada$$ clearly showed familiarity with the teachings and concepts of the Five Percenters. His use of these semiotic resources is testament that the movement still serves as an important reference point for many hip-hop artists.

Another example of references to the Five Percenter movement is in the lyrical production of the duo The Underachievers, formed in the Flatbush neighbourhood of Brooklyn in 2011, by Issa Gold and AKTHESAVIOR. On

45 Joey Bada$$, *Summer Knights*, '95 Till Infinity', CD album (Cinematic Music Group © 2013).

46 'Ab-Soul & Joey Bada$$ "Smokers Club 2013" in Toronto (Hitstape.com & Knowledge of Self Video)', https://www.youtube.com/watch?v=asM78TS5Vds&feature=youtu.be&t=41s (accessed 22 September 2023).

their acclaimed mixtape *Indigoism* (2013), the duo draws inspiration from the pseudo-scientific New Age discourse of the Indigo Child, blended with an affection for psychedelic drugs and spiritual contemplations. The concept of the Indigo Child was first introduced by Nancy Ann Tappe in her book *Understanding Your Life thru Color* (1986). The concept was later developed by self-styled 'self-help professionals' such as Lee Carroll and Jan Tober. According to the Indigo Child movement, Indigos are believed to possess extraordinary and sometimes mystic qualities and abilities. The researcher Daniel Kline has described the Indigo Child movement as a reaction to diagnoses such as ADD and ADHD:

> The Indigo Child movement is a discourse of critique, revaluing children who are being diagnosed with attention deficit disorder (ADD), attention deficit with hyperactivity disorder (ADHD), or other conditions such as autism spectrum disorders. A diagnosis like ADHD will mean that a child will probably receive pharmaceuticals such as Ritalin to calm them down; in the case of autism spectrum disorders, even stronger medication and constant therapy may be prescribed. These children will be pathologized and their identity will probably be partially defined by their mental illness diagnosis. The Indigo discourse recasts these children as spiritual healers and leaders specially sent to aid in the coming 'new age'. This recasting is a manifestation of New Age rejection of 'materialist' pathologizing definitions and an attempt to re-envision 'problem children'.[47]

The idea of a special, chosen group resonates well with the belief within NGE that 5 per cent of the population is divine. And some fans have made precisely this connection. In an interview with the Austrian musical webzine *The Message*, Issa Gold, one half of hip-hop duo The Underachievers, elaborated on the connection:

> In the past the theory was, that only five percent of society has that certain kind of knowledge and has their third eye open. But I think that as we evolve, the third eye opens automatically for kids who are being born now.[48]

[47] Kline 2013: 353.

[48] 'The Third Eye is a Compass', https://themessagemagazine.at/the-underachievers-interview/ (accessed 6 May 2024).

Gold has thereby reinterpreted the message of NGE: for him, all children born today are chosen ones, Indigo Children, with the third eye, their inner compass, open.[49] This re-interpretation can be understood as a generational shift. The older generation, so he has claimed, 'are what the Five Percenters said couldn't understand the knowledge' (in other words, the 85 per cent). In the same interview, Gold used the belief in an anthropomorphic god as an example:

> They are still trapped in beliefs of – for example – religious morals, like God is sitting in front of the hall and you go either to heaven or to hell. These people [the older generations] still believe that, but I think our generation really kind of knows that there is no guy with a white beard in heaven.[50]

This way of reasoning echoes NGE's message of the 'deaf, dumb and blind' that believe and preach about a 'Mystery God in the Sky'. The influence of NGE is also visible in the lyrical production of The Underachievers. Their first two songs on *Indigoism*, 'So Devilish' (2012) and 'Gold Soul Theory' (2012), contain their trademark psychedelic lyrics combined with allusions to the third eye and spirituality. But these songs also contain several direct references to the teachings of NGE. Issa Gold has stated: 'The Most High, why lie, nigga / I'm on my Jesus shit / As-Salaam-Alaikum my Gods'.[51] 'The Most High' could be interpreted as reference to one of God's (Allah's) 99 names according to mainstream Islamic interpretive traditions (both the Arabic *al-muta'ali* or *al-'ali* are at times translated as 'the most high'). The line 'why lie, nigga' could be understood as a question, implying that the oneness (*Tawhid*) of god is incorrect, which is in line with the NGE concept of a 'Mystery God'. The second line is most likely a wordplay on Issa's own name (Jesus in Arabic). Issa greets all Gods with the universal Islamic greeting 'As-Salaam-Alaikum', meaning everyone in his generation are Gods or Indigo Children.

Another example suggesting influences from the teachings of NGE derives from the song 'The Gold Soul Theory', where AKTHESAVIOR states: 'Generation of generals, keep my word in my genitals / Gender roles, nigga I'm

[49] Ibid.

[50] Ibid.

[51] The Underachievers, *Indigoism*, 'So Devilish', CD album (Brainfeeder © 2013).

God as far as gender goes'.[52] 'Generation of generals' could be understood as a reference to what AKTHESAVIOR believes to be the new generation of leaders (generals), the Indigos, with their third eye open, leading the way into the future. 'Keep my word in my genitals' is a wordplay on the idiom 'breaking balls' – meaning, if I break my word, I am breaking my balls; in other words, I give myself a hard time. AKTHESAVIOR's promises (that is, words) are sacred, an attitude that can be compared to NGE's expression 'Word is Bond', meaning that his words are true and beyond reproach. The second part can be understood as alluding to the teaching of the Five Percenters that every African American man is a God and that every African American woman is an Earth. Consequently, AKTHESAVIOR views himself a God.[53] A final example of a hip-hop act that consciously or unconsciously echoes the NGE belief that African American men are Gods is SpaceGhostPurrp from Miami, Florida. The hook of the dark and gritty track 'The Black God' states: 'The Black God / I got to have the world in my hands I'm a God / I'm no longer a black man / The Black God [. . .]'.[54]

Both the teachings of NGE and references to the movement within hip-hop culture have waned in recent years. This development can partly be explained by the mid-1990s' rise in the popularity of gangsta rap and so-called bling-bling hip-hop, with its fascination with ostentatious materialistic attributes such as gold tooth caps, diamond jewellery and pimped-out cars. It remains to be seen if NGE will regain the cultural position of prominence that it has lost within the US hip-hop of today, but it is clear that the movement's zenith still provides hip-hop with a nostalgic reference point, while re-interpretations of NGE teachings are not uncommon.

Scholar Michael Muhammad Knight, who for a period was affiliated with NGE, has aptly summarised how NGE-inspired hip-hop speaks to two audiences:

> Between rap's worldwide popularity and the Five Percenters' insider language and folklore, outright proselytism like Brand Nubian's 'Ain't No Mystery' and

[52] The Underachievers, *Indigoism*, 'The Gold Soul Theory', CD album (Brainfeeder © 2013).

[53] Several other songs from the *Indigoism* mixtape make similar allusions. For example, in 'Herb Shuttle' (2013): 'Goddammit, I'm free I be GOD, please you are not in my league', or in 'Revelations' (2013): 'I'm a fucking living god, find a truth deep inside'.

[54] SpaceGhostPurrp, *Mysterious Phonk: The Chronicles of SpaceGhostPurrp*, 'The Black God', CD album (4AD Records © 2012).

the esotericism of Rakim's 'The Mystery', a God emcee can have it both ways. He can use the medium to teach the world, but while millions listen, he can also engage his Five Percenter family in a private conversation.[55]

Understanding Islamic Semiotic Resources and Music in the African American Experience

In their book *Music and Social Movements* (1998), Ron Eyerman and Andrew Jamison have explored music's ability to act as the memory of social movements. They have argued that music can resurrect dead political themes and bring them back to life in new forms. 'Many social movements', so they have argued, 'bring older movements back to life by remembering the songs that were sung and the images that were drawn by giving them new meaning'.[56] However briefly, what I have illustrated in this and the preceding chapter is that the relationship between different Islamic interpretive traditions and African American music-making can be viewed as reciprocal and mutually bolstering. Throughout the history of African American music-making, Islamic semiotic resources have been used by both Muslims and non-Muslims, for a myriad of reasons. These synergetic interactions have contributed to changing both the connotations of Islamic semiotic resources and artistic output.

With their roots in African American Islam-inspired spirituality in general, and in BAM and NOI in particular, the Universal Zulu Nation and NGE have been key actors in creating and inspiring a paradigm within hip-hop culture where Islamic semiotic resources, used and interpreted in wildly competing and collaborating ways, have become an integral part of the culture. These resources act as links between the movements and the actors presented and discussed in Chapter 3, as well as the hip-hop artists active over the last few decades.

The history of Islam in the African American experience has been described from a variety of perspectives in the academic literature. Richard Brent Turner has described this experience in relation to 'old Islam' (the Islam of the enslaved peoples), which according to Turner played a key role in inspiring resistance to slavery, and, conversely, to what he calls 'new Islam', with its roots in Pan-African nationalism and the Ahmadiyya movement.[57] Edward E. Curtis IV has discussed differences in African American Islamic thought in light of

[55] Knight 2007: 186.

[56] Eyerman and Jamison 1998: 42.

[57] Turner 2003.

the tensions between 'the idea, on the one hand, that a religious tradition is *universally* applicable to the experience of all human beings and the idea, on the other hand, that a religious tradition is applicable to the experience of one *particular* group of human beings'.[58]

Both these perspectives on the history of African American Islam are valuable and provide important insight into our understanding of the development described in Chapters 2 and 3. Jacques Waardenburg, the seminal scholar of Islamic studies, has noted in his essay titled 'Islam as a Vehicle of Protest' (1985) that 'Islam' since its establishment has had a 'marked reform and protest character'.[59] He has also hinted at the possibility of 'Islam' as a framework for 'Third World' protest against 'Western imperialism' somewhat better suited than other religions and ideologies. According to Waardenburg, 'Islam [. . .] lends itself to use as a symbol of protest by evoking greatness' and provides a wider spiritual framework for a struggle that has consequences extending beyond the grave. He has gone on to write: 'Islam's symbolic function is apparently activated in the community at the moment when essential aspects of life are at stake or elements of it are felt to be threatened'. This reasoning implies that the various shifts in the articulations of 'Islamic protest' are not independent from the pressure of outside forces. In a more recent text, Peter Mandaville has argued that one crucial characteristic of political 'Islam' is its 'capacity to tap into transhistorical discourses of resistance to colonialism, racism, geopolitical hegemony and – more recently – neoliberal globalisation'.[60] Waardenburg's and Mandaville's insights become particularly relevant when trying to understand the, not least political, appropriations of Islamic semiotic resources in hip-hop culture.

In recent years, scholars of esotericism have noted the connection between freemasonry and theosophy in movements such as the Moorish Science Temple, NOI and the Five Percenters. These perspectives are also useful when attempting to understand the use of Islamic semiotic resources in hip-hop. There is one concept from the field of esoteric studies that I have found of interpretive value when understanding and framing both the historical developments of African American Islam and the uses of Islamic semiotic resources in hip-hop:

[58] Curtis 2002b: 1.

[59] Waardenburg 1985: 22.

[60] Mandaville forthcoming: 2.

this is occulture, as developed by religious scholar Christopher Partridge in his two-volume work *The Re-Enchantment of the West: Alternative Spiritualities, Sacralization, Popular Culture, and Occulture* (2004, 2005). Since the publication of this book, Partridge has developed the concept in a series of lectures and articles. His concept has attracted increasing interest from scholars in the fields of religious studies and esotericism. Partridge has described occulture in the following way:

> [O]cculture itself is not a worldview, but rather a resource on which people draw, a reservoir of ideas, beliefs, practices, and symbols. Consumers of occulture may be witting or unwitting; they may engage with it at a relatively superficial level or they may have strong religious commitments; they may themselves contribute to the pool of occultural knowledge or they may simply drink from it. Occulture is the spiritual *bricoleur*'s Internet from which to download whatever appeals or inspires; it is the sacralizing air that many of our contemporaries breathe; it is the well from which the serious occultist draws; it is the varied landscape the New Age nomad explores; it is the cluttered warehouse frequently plundered by producers of popular culture searching for ideas, images and symbols.[61]

Partridge has suggested that these alternative spiritual and religious traditions, developed in opposition to the secular, constitute 'the new spiritual atmosphere of the West'.[62] Partridge has seen occulture as an effect of the critique against organised religion in modern society. Even though the word occulture is a combination of 'occult' and 'culture', Partridge has proposed that occulture is an everyday occurrence in the lives of ordinary people:

> Occulture is not occult culture, in the sense that it is not a milieu of the esoteric and the hidden (although it certainly includes that which is esoteric and hidden); nor is it a site of the exotic and the forbidden (although it certainly includes the exotic and the forbidden). Rather, like culture – which, of course, it is – it is ordinary and everyday. As such, occulture, as culture, is an explanation for Western re-enchantment rather than jargon for occult culture.[63]

Of additional interpretive significance for my study is the emphasis on the lead role that popular culture – in particular music – plays in the efficacy of

[61] Partridge 2004: 84–85.
[62] Partridge 2005: 2.
[63] Partridge 2013: 132–33.

occulture. Occulture is 'both resources and is resourced by popular culture'. This interdependence between music and religion, as I have set out to illustrate in the two preceding chapters, is central when it comes to unearthing the use of Islamic semiotics in hip-hop.

One essential aspect of occulture is the 'cut-up method', used to produce new ideas and concepts:

> The point is that cut-up or remix is central to occulture. It is not simply that particular ideas and signifiers are disseminated within an occultural environment, but rather that in the process they are cut-up, remixed, deconstructed and reconstructed. New synergies are formed, which are then, in a dialectic process, cut-up and remixed, the results of which then attach to other ideas and signifiers and so on.[64]

These processes of cut-up and remix are, as revealed in the following chapters, central to hip-hop culture. It is somewhat surprising that Partridge – who has touched on a variety of different music genres, among them dub, trance, post-punk, industrial and metal – has failed to mention hip-hop when discussing occulture. Hip-hop culture is a prominent global arena where Islamic semiotic resources are creatively reshaped to form new methods and strategies of political protest, liberation and resistance to unjust and oppressive societies.

In what follows, I will demonstrate how the history presented in the last two chapters has been put to use by hip-hop artists in their artistic productions to form these new methods and strategies. Movements, personas, historical events and even sounds have become important reference points in the output of hip-hop artists. They can therefore be viewed as Islamic semiotic resources used to express pride, resistance and rejection of social orders such as white supremacy. However, I will also argue that it would be a mistake to understand the use of Islamic semiotic resources in hip-hop *solely* as a means for political resistance and protest. To some degree, they are also used in reaction to materialism, egoism and a general lack of spirituality; this, in turn, is a symptom of the re-enchantment of popular culture, characterised by a spiritual re-awakening that emphasises personal development and well-being rather than institutional worship. Such use can of course be political as well.

[64] Ibid. p. 130.

5

PAID IN FULL: THE SERENDIPITY OF ISLAMIC SEMIOTICS IN HIP-HOP

This chapter examines the complex multimodal processes of meaning-making from the perspective of visual, textual, aural and cultural studies. These processes are illustrated with my reading of a single hip-hop song, 'Paid in Full' (1987) from Eric B. & Rakim's album of the same name. There follows an analysis of the remix of the song and the accompanying music video, demonstrating that this song must be understood as the outcome of individual efforts and contributions made by multiple actors involved in its production: Eric B. & Rakim, Coldcut – the DJ duo that made the remix of the song – and Bruno Tilley, who directed the video. The music video is titled 'Paid in Full (Mini Madness: The Coldcut Remix)' (1987) and presents a shorter version of Coldcut's longer 'Paid in Full (Seven Minutes of Madness: The Coldcut Remix)' (1987).[1] My argument is that it is crucial to keep in mind the interplay between the visual, textual and aural components in the music video in order to understand the ways in which US hip-hop artists have made use of Islamic semiotic resources in their artistic productions.

Rakim came to influence fellow hip-hop artists with his rhyming technique and linguistic style, but he also influenced other artists to make use of Islamic semiotic resources. 'Paid in Full' and the accompanying music video played an

[1] Since the longer version is a prolonged version without additions of interest to this study, I will limit the analysis to the shorter and more commonly known version of the song.

Figure 5.1 Album cover (LP) for Eric B & Rakim's *Paid in Full*, 1987.

important role in this development, since it was the first global mainstream hip-hop hit that made use of Islamic semiotic resources. Yet, none of the key figures involved in the making of the song, the remix or the video considered themselves Muslims. The cultural production of Islam by non-Muslims is therefore eminently showcased by the making, content and impact of the song.

Another major reason for dedicating this chapter solely to 'Paid in Full' consists of the importance that the song and the video have been allotted in the literature. In 1989, the American sociologist and author Tricia Rose provided an interpretation of the song and its 'technologically sophisticated and complex urban sound'.[2] For Rose, the song is a demonstration of the power of technology in the making of hip-hop music and the artistic ambition to take control over the means of production – the recording studio. She has written:

> This rap's acknowledgment of the presence of the recording studio juxtaposed against Rakim's rhyme about life on the street without money, demystifies

[2] Rose 1989: 43.

> technology and its production. [. . .] Eric B. and Rakim's manipulation of Ely is to be understood as symbolic control over the process of technological reproduction.[3]

Rose has made these claims in order to contrast and nuance claims that hip-hop music should primarily be seen as an outgrowth of earlier African American oral traditions. For Rose, acknowledgement of the importance of technology is key in order to understand remix hip-hop.[4]

Several interpreters of 'Paid in Full' have observed what has been described as a 'Lutheran work ethic' in the song.[5] These interpretations often view the song as an account on how Eric B. & Rakim seek to turn their skills as musicians into money and fame. As hip-hop scholar James Peterson has written, . . .

> Paid in Full is the prototypical rap figure at the crossroads of lack and desire. As he contemplates ways to 'get some dead presidents', he remembers when he was a 'stick-up kid' and reaffirms a more righteous present for himself as a 9-to-5 job seeker. Of course, for Rakim and for his narrator, postindustrial urban unemployment rates suggest his penchant for rapping over beats might be the only logical employment option.[6]

In one of the earliest academic books on hip-hop, *Signifying Rappers: Rap and Race in the Urban Present* (1990), the authors Mark Costello and David Foster Wallace have suggested a variation on this interpretation. They have argued that the lyrical content of 'Paid in Full' should be seen as a parody of the fixation on money and material wealth in hip-hop culture. The book also has an appendix containing a transcript of the remix of the song, so as to illustrate how rich and complex hip-hop music can be. Regardless of whether the song is presented as a comment on technology, fame, money or Lutheran work ethics, or is indeed a parody, crucial dimensions of the song have been left out of the analyses: the Islamic semiotic resources saturating the lyrics, the video and the artists' biography. I will now explore these dimensions.

[3] Ibid.

[4] Ibid.

[5] Rehn and Sköld 2005: 13.

[6] Peterson 2006: 895–96.

Approaching the video as a multimodal text, I will go beyond the prevailing dichotomised methodological perspective according to which written and oral texts are seen as separate from image and sound. Instead, I will focus on all the semiotic resources that compose the multimodal text in question: the verbal text, the visual and sound material and – more importantly – the way in which these different semiotic resources interact with each other to produce meaning; in this case to synthesise Islamic semiotic resources and repackage them as part of an Islamic semiotic repertoire that in turn became available for future hip-hop artists to draw from. I will first discuss the religious preferences of Rakim, followed by a presentation of the album Paid in Full and a discussion of the sounds, lyrics and visuals of the song and music video.

Rakim: A God on the Microphone

The hip-hop duo Eric B. & Rakim was formed in Long Island, New York, in 1986, by the DJ Eric B. and the MC Rakim. The duo split up in the early 1990s but later reunited for a concert at the Apollo Theater in New York City in 2017 and for a US tour in 2018. Of the two, Rakim has had the more successful solo career with four albums, and he is a highly acclaimed rapper, often seen as an innovator of rhyming. The headline 'The Microphone God' is the title of an interview with Rakim in the hip-hop magazine *Vibe*: 'Hearing Rakim discuss writing lyrics is akin to hearing Igor Stravinsky discuss composition. It's an honor on par with hearing Thelonious Monk discuss chord changes – all you can really do is sit down, shut up and listen'.[7]

William Michael Griffin (born 28 January 1968), better known by his stage name Rakim Allah, or just Rakim, is often cited by both fellow artists and hip-hop commentators as a source of inspiration and a game-changer when it comes to his lyrical content and complex rhyming style.[8] Rakim's creative and imaginative artistic output has fascinated hip-hop scholarship since its inception. Several scholars have recognised the importance of Rakim's alleged 'Muslim identity', both within hip-hop and beyond. For example,

[7] 'The Microphone God', *Vibe*, December 1997–January 1998, vol. 5, No. 10.

[8] According to Rakim, his name is a construction of two words taken from ancient Egyptian: 'Ra' (meaning the 'sun god') and 'kim', supposedly meaning the 'land of the burned-face people'. See 'The Five Percent Solution', *Spin*, February 1991.

Sohail Daulatzai has compared his importance to that of Malcolm X when discussing the content of his song 'Casualties of War':

> Just as Malcolm X saw Islam as the bridge that connects Black peoples in the United States with those in Africa and Asia, Rakim embraces his Muslim identity to forge a vision of the Muslim international that powerfully and poetically combines the past and present, the local and the global, and slavery and contemporary imperialism into a grammar of resistance the critiques not only the U.S. nation-state but also any bounded sense of Black identity.[9]

Although I believe that Daulatzai is right in his piercing interpretation of the song, it is important to point out that Rakim never considered himself to be a Muslim. This is something that Rakim has discussed in public several times, including in 2011, when he was chosen, not without controversy, as the most influential Muslim MC of all time by the prominent hip-hop WebTV channel VladTV. In an interview on VladTV, Rakim was questioned about the fact that he, as a member of NGE, had been chosen as the number one 'Muslim' MC:

> No, we are not Muslims but we study the same lessons, Muslims have a slightly different belief than the way [. . .] the Nation of Islam [. . .] The Five Percent Nation [. . .] It is similar, but you know, the Muslim submits to the will of Allah, but we come in the divine name of Allah. So it is a little different [. . .].[10]

In an interview with Mats Nileskär on Swedish radio, Rakim retold the story of when he first came in contact with NGE. In his early teens, he met a member of the movement asking for train fare in a station. Rakim reacted to the NGE member's 'gift to gag', the way he spoke,[11] as NGE vernacular is characterised by witty one-liners, mesmerising wordplay and dazzling rhyme patterns. Even though Rakim did not recognise it for what it was during this first encounter, he would let the teachings of NGE influence both the message of his lyrics and his way of rhyming throughout his career, starting with his 1987 debut album.

[9] Daulatzai 2012: 131.

[10] 'Rakim Speaks on VladTV's 50 Best Muslim Rappers of All Time', https://www.youtube.com/watch?v=le100dAW6hY (accessed 14 September 2023).

[11] 'P3 Soul, 'Rakims tårar' [Rakim's Tears]', Swedish National Radio (aired 22 September 2023), https://sverigesradio.se/avsnitt/rakims-tarar (accessed 14 September 2023).

Rakim was not the first rapper to be inspired by the teachings of NGE. One of the more famous early hip-hop groups that paid homage to NGE was the World's Famous Supreme Team, whose members included Just Allah the Superstar, See Divine the Master Mind and Malcolm McLaren (the latter more famous as manager of the punk group The Sex Pistols). In the extended version of their hit song 'Hey DJ' (1984), the group makes what is often considered to be the first NGE reference in hip-hop when it declares: 'Rockin' the house with the greatest of ease for the Gods, Earths, men, women and babies'.[12]

But even if Rakim was not the first MC to be connected to NGE, it can be argued that he was the most influential one. I believe that the remix of 'Paid in Full' played a significant role in establishing him as such. The remix is critically acclaimed and often cited as a landmark remix, and upon its release climbed the charts in the US as well as in several European countries. In New Zealand, the single reached its highest position globally, spending eleven weeks in the Top Forty and peaking at number two in March 1988. *Rolling Stone* magazine has named the original version of the song the tenth-greatest hip-hop song of all time.[13]

Following the success of 'Paid in Full', several other artists started to incorporate Islamic semiotic resources in their songs and music videos. This was something that caught the attention of Charlie Ahearn, the famous hip-hop journalist, filmmaker and author. In an article in the American music magazine *Spin* in 1991, which is one of the first accounts of NGE in hip-hop, he has written:

> I got a question that's bugging me: Why is it that certain white teens across America seem to be craving contact with the metallic powers of Satan while their black brethren are busy digging the prophets of ancient scripture? Rap's got religion and that religion's Islam. The Nation of Islam or, better yet, The Five Percent Nation.

[12] The World's Famous Supreme Team, 'Hey D. J. (Extended Version)', 12-inch single (Charisma Records Ltd. © 1984).

[13] 'The 50 Greatest Hip-Hop Songs of All Time', http://www.rollingstone.com/music/lists/the-50-greatest-hip-hop-songs-of-all-time-20121205/eric-b-and-rakim-paid-in-full-19691231 (accessed 14 September 2023).

Ahearn has also noted that the message of NGE was transmitted by record labels and MTV: 'MTV and major record companies are pipelining Five Percent Nation doctrine all across America'.[14] Ahearn's text has given a detailed account of the teachings of NGE and included a 'Five Percent Glossary'. It has also listed artists such as Rakim, King Sun, Brand Nubian, Lakim Shabazz and Poor Righteous Teachers as prominent examples who advertised their affiliation to NGE in their lyrics.

Paid in Full: 'But Now I Learned to Earn Cause I'm Righteous'

> When we got the deal with 4th & B'way, we got the check and it said PAID IN FULL on it, so we was lookin' at it and Eric said, 'Yo, that's what we're gonna name the album' I wasn't sure about it at first, but that idea definitely worked. It was a statement.[15]

The album *Paid in Full* (1987) was reportedly recorded in less than one week, in the home studio of legendary DJ and record producer Marley Marl. The album reached gold status by the end of 1987, and platinum in 1995, with more than one million copies sold worldwide.[16]

The album represented something new when it arrived. It is regarded by many as one of the most important hip-hop albums ever released, earning its place in the hip-hop canon. The soundscape of the album included some of hip-hop's first James Brown-breaks accompanied by Rakim's complex rhyme patterns, delivered with a laid-back and confident flow inspired by the solos of jazz giants such as Miles Davis, John Coltrane and Dizzy Gillespie. This combination influenced the sound as well as the aesthetics of hip-hop for years after the album's release, thereby expanding hip-hop's mood register from its party-oriented vibe to a darker and more contemplative state of mind. *Paid in Full* contains ten songs and runs slightly over forty-five minutes. It embodies one of the fundamental paradoxes of hip-hop music: it is both a beacon of gold chain-commercialism and an expression of a deep and critical consciousness, often with an Islamic soundboard. The impact wave of the album, as we shall see next, has reached shores beyond those of hip-hop.

[14] 'The Five Percent Solution', *Spin*, February 1991.

[15] Rakim Allah, cited in Coleman 2007: 208.

[16] The Recording Industry Association of America, database, https://www.riaa.com/gold-platinum/?tab_active=default-award&se=Paid+in+full#search_section (accessed 14 September 2023).

Several of the songs on *Paid in Full* contain more or less overt textual references to the teachings of NGE. For example, in the song 'Eric B. is President' Rakim announces, 'No tricks in '86 / it's time to build',[17] a reference to the eighth degree of the Supreme Mathematics' 'Build and Destroy'. The Supreme Mathematics, as one may recall, is an esoteric numeral system designed to assign numbers to concepts and words. 'Build' in this context likely refers to elevating the mind by sharing the knowledge and discussing the teachings of NGE. The term also has a more mundane meaning, as it also could refer to the concept 'Building' – that is, NGE's encouragement to nurture power, status, health and wealth.

At the end of the fifth song on the album, 'Move the Crowd', Rakim is even more explicit in his references to NGE:

> So I'mma let my knowledge be born to a perfection
> All praises due to Allah and that's a blessing
> With knowledge of self, there's nothing I can't solve
> At 360 degrees I revolve
> This is actual fact, it's not an act, it's been proven
> Indeed and I proceed to make the crowd keep moving.[18]

'Knowledge' represents the first degree in the Supreme Mathematics, and 'Born' represents the ninth degree: 1+9 equals 10. The tenth degree or zero ('0') represents the completion of the Cypher,[19] which is 360 degrees. When the Cypher is completed, one can gain knowledge of self: the Black man as God or Allah. Remember that 'Allah' represents 'Arm Leg Leg Arm Head', symbolising that God is manifested in the Black man. The world, from NGE's point of view, is seen as a place where chaos rules. To find one's place amid this chaos and build order, one must gain knowledge about the self and comprehend and apply the 'science' of Islam (meaning 'I Self-Lord Am Master'). Thus, the use of the Supreme Alphabet and the Mathematics is essential for restoring harmony in the universe. And in order to change the universe, one

[17] 'Eric B. is President' was released as the first single from the album, with 'My Melody' as the B-side.

[18] Eric B. & Rakim, *Paid in Full*, 'Move the Crow', 12-inch single (4th & B'way Records © 1987).

[19] The Cypher (sometimes spelled Cipher) represents a perfect circle of 360 degrees, according to the Supreme Alphabet. One's 'Cypher' (represented by the letter 'O') covers the areas in their life over which they have control; or it is one's sphere of influence.

must first change oneself. Islamic semiotic resources are manifested visually, too. In the music video to 'Move the Crowd', Rakim is seen sporting a knitted *kufi* cap and performing in front of the Universal Flag of Islam of NGE.

The original version of the song 'Paid in Full' appears as the sixth track on the album and was released as the album's fifth and final single. The original version was, according to the record sleeve, written and produced by Eric Barrier (Eric B.) and Rakim Allah. However, it was the soundscape of the remix and the visuals of the music video that would give Eric B. & Rakim their global breakthrough. I will next describe and analyse the song 'Paid in Full (Mini Madness: The Coldcut Remix)' and the accompanying music video from a multimodal perspective, looking at the interplay between its aural, textual and visual aspects.

Aural: The Voice of Peace

The aural foundation of the minimalistic soundscape of the original version of 'Paid in Full' consists of a drumbeat and flute loop from the song 'Ashley's Roachclip' (1974) by the Washington DC funk group The Soul Searchers. The hard-hitting bassline is sampled from 'Don't Look Any Further' (1984) by Dennis Edwards and Siedah Garrett. The Coldcut remix is a completely different kind of monster. It has been described as a selective remix and, while adding and subtracting sounds from the original recording, still maintains some of the original's atmosphere and unique expression. This remix technique was very popular among dance DJs in the 1980s.[20]

After a straight thirty-six hours in the New York studio, some thirty-plus samples were added to the remix, including drum loops, basslines and a variety of sound bites.[21] The soundscape created by Coldcut spans the highlands of Yemen, James Brown's funky 'Hot Pants', the voice of Ronald Reagan and classic Saturday Night Live episodes. The original song was extended from three minutes and forty-eight seconds to seven minutes and ten seconds. The shorter music video version based on the remix is three minutes and thirty-five

[20] Navas 2012: 65.

[21] 'Coldcut Deconstruct "Paid in Full" – Eric B. & Rakim (Commentary)', https://www.youtube.com/watch?v=6-EaWqxg7HQ (accessed 14 September 2023).

seconds long. The most striking element of the remix is Coldcut's use of the finely tuned voice of the Israeli singer Ofra Haza (1957–2000) for the hook.

Haza was born in a Yemeni-Jewish family in Hatikva, a working-class neighbourhood in south-eastern Tel Aviv, as the youngest of eight children. Her parents had immigrated to Israel during Operation Magic Carpet.[22] In 1983, she represented Israel in the Eurovision song contest in Munich, with the disco-esque horah dance-inspired song *Hi*.[23] She finished in second place, and the song launched her international career. Following the success in the Eurovision song contest, Haza started to explore her Yemenite heritage through her music. In 1984, the album *Yemenite Songs*, containing traditional renderings of these, was released on the small independent record label Hed Arzi. The album was praised by critics but did not sell very well initially. However, it was soon propelled onto the world stage thanks to a British pirate radio DJ. In

[22] Due to a combination of harsh economic conditions, pogroms, different religious beliefs of an apocalyptic and messianic nature, and rumours about the prospects for a better life in Palestine, the first Yemenite Jews immigrated to Palestine in the late nineteenth century. The migration was initially organised by small groups with no formal connections to the Zionist movement or its ideology. After World War I, the migration took a more organised form. In 1929, a Jewish Agency migration office was established in Aden, and from this point onwards the Zionist movement's involvement in the migration movement increased. In May 1948, the State of Israel was established, and the Yemenite Jewish migration culminated in what has been called Operation Magic Carpet. From 1949–50 onwards, around 50,000 Yemenite Jews were airlifted out of the country by the Israeli government. The body of Jewish inhabitants in Palestine, before the establishment of the State of Israel, was diverse: in addition to the Jewish communities already settled in Palestine, sizeable groups arrived from Eastern Europe, escaping the pogroms in the late nineteenth century, as well as Jewish groups from all over the Middle East (including Yemen). It was not only institutions, ideologies and new settlements that emerged from the influx of new immigrants: new forms of musical expression were also shaped in the meeting of diverse Middle Eastern and Eastern European musical expressions. These hybrid musical expressions still echo in Israel's vivid pop/rock and hip-hop scenes. For a thorough account of Operation Magic Carpet, see Meir-Glitzenstein 2014. For a discussion of the role of music in the construction of Israeli culture in the present, see Halper, Seroussi, and Squires-Kidron 1989.

[23] Haza, 'Hi'. The A-side version is sung in English, the B-side in Hebrew. The Hebrew version should correctly be titled Chai (חַי). Horah is a joyous Jewish circle dance, typically danced at weddings.

January 1985, Grant Goddard arrived outside the shores of Israel in order to broadcast pirate radio from the studio of 'The Voice of Peace', a ship stationed off the coast of Israel but in international waters. During his visit, he was introduced to Haza's mezzo-soprano voice on the single 'Im Nin'alu'. He recalled:

> It was a traditional Yemeni song, re-mixed and cut up into a state-of-the-art club tune that sounded to me like a new, exciting 'Middle East meets West' genre. I wanted to find out more, but the terrible winter storms and shortage of staff meant that I was stuck working on the ship for the next three months. Eventually, during my first shore leave, I visited the Tel Aviv office of the small independent record company, Hed Arzi, that had produced the Ofra Haza single. They were baffled that a British DJ would be so interested in one of their worst selling record releases, and particularly one that seemed to have such minimal mainstream potential.[24]

With the record company's support, he started to send out copies of the song to radio stations around Europe, and when he returned to the UK, he continued to hand out copies to radio DJs. Eventually a copy landed at the pirate station Kiss FM at the London School of Economics. The British DJs Jonathan More and Matt Black (who formed the recording duo Coldcut) apparently liked the song so much that they decided to use a sample of it as a hook in one of their landmark remixes.

Coldcut sampled Haza's adaptation of the famous Hebrew poem 'Im Nin'alu' (1984), originally written by the celebrated Yemeni-Jewish mystic and poet Rabbi Shalom Shabazi in the seventeenth century.[25] Haza's mesmerising

[24] 'Ofra Haza: The Making of World Music's First International Star', https://grantgoddardradioblog.blogspot.com/2010/12/ofra-haza-making-of-world-musics-first.html (accessed 14 September 2023).

[25] The seventeenth-century Yemenite Jewish poet Shalom Shabazi's life is hidden in the fog of legend. Legend holds that he was known for his ability to transport himself over vast distances in the blink of an eye. It has been said that he left Yemen every Friday afternoon for the purpose of observing the Sabbath in Jerusalem, only to return every Saturday evening. Legend also states that Shalom Shabazi predicted the exact time of his passing. In preparation, he dug his own grave, picked out his burial garment and bathed himself. His tomb outside Ta'izz in the central Yemeni Highlands is a place of pilgrimage among Jews as well as Muslims. The few facts of his life rely solely on his own words in the approximately 550 poems written in

voice adds a feeling of otherworldliness and what can best be described as a Middle Eastern vibe to the song. The following transliteration of the Hebrew words sung by Haza is given on the sleeve to the album *Fifty Gates of Wisdom: Yemenite Songs* (1985): 'If there be no mercy left in the world, the doors of heaven will never be barred. The Creator reigns supreme and is higher than the angels'.

Apparently, Haza was not consulted when Coldcut sampled her voice for the song, but when she first heard it, she took it as a compliment: 'a beautiful production, a really good production, and it was a big compliment for me', she stated in an interview.[26] The fact that Haza's adaptation of the poem, as well as Coldcut's remix, has been sampled in recordings by several other hip-hop artists, ranging from Public Enemy and Snoop Dogg to Fabolous and Vanilla Ice, stands as a powerful testament to its aural impact. Outside of hip-hop, Madonna used an adaptation of the poem for her song 'Isaac' on the album *Confession on a Dance Floor* (2005). Also, the Swedish house music crew The C&N Project used 'Im Nin'alu' in their song 'The Queen of Tel Aviv' (1998). Haza herself re-recorded an updated version of the song in 1997 for her eponymous album, which became her last studio recording. Haza died in early 2000.

Eric B. & Rakim were never consulted about the remix. Jonathan More of Coldcut remembers that, despite the successes and influence of the song, Eric B. disliked the remix and referred to it as 'girly disco music'. Rakim, however, really liked it and called it the 'best remix he'd ever heard'. Perhaps it spoke to Rakim's more spiritual side.[27]

Hebrew, Arabic or Aramaic and left for posterity. His poems often deal with the themes of religion, mysticism and the harsh life in Yemen. One peculiar feature of Shabazi's poems is the fact that his name emerges in acrostic form within the poems. Shalom Shabazi has been described as 'the greatest of Yemenite Jewish poets', and one of the most popular and widely known of his poems is arguably 'Im nin'alu daltei nedivim' ('If the doors of the wealthy are locked [. . .]'). It has been sung to many melodies, in different settings, in different times and on different social occasions. Alternate verses exist in Arabic and Hebrew.

26 'Ofra Haza Interview', https://www.youtube.com/watch?v=1QB-Qg00fhU (accessed 14 September 2023).

27 'The Tasteful Turntable', https://www.chicagotribune.com/1997/10/17/the-tasteful-turntable/ (accessed 14 September 2023).

The Words: A Journey into Sound

In a review of the album published in the British music paper the *New Musical Express* (*NME*) (August 1987), its US correspondent Richard Grabel has described the lyrical content of 'Paid in Full' in the following poignant words:

> 'Paid In Full' is a strange mind game in which the boys do a little dialogue about their business arrangements, name checking their booking agents, record companies and managers. Then, the melody switches off leaving the drum machine rocking away, 'and we outta here'. Weird and ingenious.[28]

The song's basic theme, according to Grabel's interpretation, is that Rakim's proficiency as a lyricist and Eric B.'s unique beat-making skills, together with their good connections with the record company, will bring them wealth and fame.

In her pioneering book *Black Noise: Rap Music and Black Culture in Contemporary America* (1994), Tricia Rose has offered an insightful breakdown of the lyrical content of the song:

> Rakim's deep and ominous voice combined with sarcastic references to life on the edge of respectability keep the listener on edge [. . .]. This rap's acknowledgment of the presence of the recording studio juxtaposed against Rakim's rhyme about life on the street without money, demystifies technology and its production and highlights the reality of rap as a means of upward mobility for young blacks for whom meaningful jobs for meaningful pay are scarce.[29]

For Rose, the song represents a manifestation of the marriage between a 'technologically sophisticated and complex urban sound' of hip-hop music and oral African American history. The verbal aspects of hip-hop, so she has argued, 'are not to be understood as primary to the *logic* of rap [. . .]. To interpret rap as a direct or natural outgrowth of oral African American forms is to romanticise and decontextualise rap as a cultural form'.[30]

[28] 'Eric B & Rakim: Paid in Full Review', https://digital.library.cornell.edu/catalog/ss:16057823 (accessed 14 September 2023).

[29] Rose 1994: 140.

[30] Rose 1994: 142.

But what Rose and several others fail to acknowledge when analysing the song are the minor references made to NGE. The lyrics to 'Paid in Full' are not exactly saturated with references to Rakim's beliefs, but a closer reading reveals that the opening bars in the song contain a sentence that reveals a connection to the movement: 'Yo, I'm doing the knowledge, E, man I'm trying to get paid in full'. In the first part of the sentence, Rakim announces his commitment to the teachings of NGE by declaring 'I'm doing the knowledge' – in other words, he is aware that there is no mystery God. E is of course short for Eric B., but it could also be interpreted as a reference to the Supreme Alphabet of Nation of Gods and Earths where E equals 'Equality', which, according to the Supreme Alphabet, means the following:

> to knowledge your knowledge, you will deal with everything within your cipher equally, which gives birth to Wisdom that is showing and proving. Everything is everything, which equals one. Equality gives birth to Wisdom, and Mathematics do not lie.

One reading of this line would be that Rakim is living the NGE life, proclaiming the wisdom of NGE lessons to Eric B., at the same time affirming the importance of Equality in knowledge. For his religious efforts, then, he will be paid in full.

Another line that is revealing of Rakim's beliefs is the following: 'But now I learned to earn cause I'm righteous'. This is a direct reference to the heart of the 'knowledge' from which NGE draws its worldview and concept of self. NGE describes its members as 'the Poor Righteous Teachers', or simply the 'Righteous': the 5 per cent that have knowledge of their true divine identity. A Poor Righteous Teacher could civilise the uncivilised and teach them about their true nature as Gods. In the last lines of the song, Rakim signs off with yet another reference to NGE by saluting 'Peace, Peace, Peace', a common greeting used by NGE members.

If one takes the references to NGE into account when analysing the song, a new avenue of interpretation opens up: that of a moral subtext. With the line 'But now I learned to earn cause I'm righteous', Rakim taps into and replicates a conversion narrative common in the African American Islamic experience. This narrative stresses the transformative power inherent in the individual spiritual encounter, elevating Rakim from his life of sin and ignorance to a life of salvation, enlightenment and ensuing success. This narrative is most famously exemplified and embodied in Malcolm X's spiritual journey from the street hustler Detroit Red to Malcolm X, as presented by the author Alex Haley in *The Autobiography of Malcolm X* and as discussed in the next chapter.

The Visuals: 'I Simply Matched Sound to Vision'

As MTV and similar networks grew in importance at the end of the 1980s, it became increasingly pertinent for artists to record music videos to promote their careers. During the first half of the 1980s, MTV had been accused of racism when largely excluding African American artists from their network. But crossover successes such as Run-DMC/Aerosmith's 'Walk This Way' and Fat Boys/The Beach Boys' 'Wipeout' opened up the network for other African American artists. The popularity of hip-hop music eventually led the network to launch a dedicated hip-hop show in 1988: Yo! MTV Raps. With this, interest in hip-hop culture grew, and hip-hop was suddenly introduced to a bigger and more diverse group of consumers.[31]

Bruno Tilley, at the time the creative director at Island Records in the UK, was assigned to produce the video for 'Paid in Full'. In an interview with Eric Ducker for the music magazine *Wax Poetics*, Tilley described what he wanted to accomplish with the video:

> Because of the nature of the track, I went and shot sections for each sample part. I also got some stock footage of things we couldn't shoot, and we put it all together in the edit. I particularly wanted to use graphics in it, so I used type, which hadn't really been seen before as far as I know. It became this sort of new form of scratch video.[32]

According to Tilley, Eric B. & Rakim did not have a say when it came to the creative decisions made in the video production. The video was shot in the UK, while the group was there on a promotional visit, and apparently Eric B. & Rakim were not familiar with Coldcut's remix of the song when they entered the set:

[31] Forman 2002: 241.

[32] 'On the Job Training: Part Four', http://www.waxpoetics.com/blog/features/articles/on-the-job-training-part-four/ (accessed 14 September 2023).

> They came to the studio and they didn't know anything about the video, it had just been thrown at them. So I was trying to explain what I wanted them to do and they said they'd give me one take. I put the track on for them to hear and they absolutely freaked out because it's got all these samples in it that I didn't realize weren't true to their music.[33]

The video starts with the words 'This is a Journey into $ound' in light blue, flickering over a starry sky. The words match the plummy tones of the British actor Geoffrey Sumner, sampled by Coldcut from a 1958 Decca recording called 'A Journey into Stereo Sound'.[34] Throughout the video a variety of graphics and typefaces are used to reiterate the sampled voices in the remix. When the snippet from 'Im Nin'alu' is played in the hook for the first time, Tilley matches it with the moving pictures of a female oriental dancer in action, and to further accentuate the arabesque or oriental atmosphere an Arabic script scrolls over the footage. The Arabic script consists of passages from Sura *at-Talaq* (Qur'an, Chapter 65). The Qur'anic writings appear one more time towards the end of the video, this time in red. The Qur'anic chapter mainly deals with the topic of divorce between man and woman and seems to have been chosen randomly by Tilley.

Tilley also included footage of Muslims performing *salat* (prayer), crosscut with footage of what seems to be riot police running in the street, a peace sign in black and white and images of the Pope (most likely John Paul II) on the balcony of St Peter's Basilica in the Vatican. These shots are mixed together with images of people dancing to the groove and pictures of Rakim rapping with Eric B. behind the turntables. This section of the video adds to its Middle Eastern aura. In the final sequences, as the sound fades, Tilley returns to the starry sky where the video began.

Tilley has been hesitant to talk about the creative decisions he made in the music video, and he could not see any point in expanding on it with me because, as he wrote in an email, 'I simply matched sound to vision and wasn't

33 '25 Remixes That Made You Forget about The Original', https://www.complex.com/music/2013/02/25-remixes-that-made-you-forget-about-the-original/ (accessed 14 September 2023).

34 Various, *A Journey into Stereo Sound*, LP album (Decca © 1958).

flying any flag for any particular religion'.[35] As with the remix, the music video is made by a non-Muslim white British director. Both the remix and the music video were outside of the creative control of Eric B. & Rakim. The introduction of common Islamic semiotic resources, other resources signalling the Middle East (the belly dancer), and others still would lead to similar uses in multiple subsequent videos by other artists.

Conclusion: The Serendipity of Islamic Semiotic Resources in Hip-Hop

In this chapter, I have illustrated and analysed the complex multimodal processes of meaning-making by using a case-study concerned with a single hip-hop music video. I have emphasised the individual efforts and contributions made by different actors involved in the production of the song and the music video: the artists, the video director and the DJs who made the remix of the song 'Paid in Full' (1987).

Although the song has been analysed by scholars before, its Islamic references have been largely ignored in favour of other interpretations. Yet, as I have demonstrated, the lyrics contain subtle references to the teachings of NGE, the members of which do not consider themselves to be Muslims but nevertheless use Islamic semiotic resources in their teachings. If these NGE references are considered when analysing the song, a new interpretation becomes possible and gives the song a moral subtext in the form of a common conversion narrative: from a thuggish lifestyle to a successful pious life. However, these references do not in any way act as the foundation of the song's popularity. Instead, it is the soundscape and visuals that are important if one wants to understand both the centrality of the song in hip-hop culture and the relationship between hip-hop culture and Islam.

In his book *Remix Theory: The Aesthetics of Sampling* (2012), Eduardo Navas has described three basic types of remixes. The first is the extended remix, a longer version of the original track containing protracted instrumental parts in order to be easier to mix for club DJs. The second is the reflexive remix, described as a remix where the 'spectacular aura', the song's cultural recognition, is challenged 'due to their [the artists'] extensive manipulation in the studio' and '[push] for autonomy'.[36] The last type of remix described by

[35] Bruno Tilley, email correspondence with the author (12 May 2014).

[36] Navas 2012: 66.

Navas is the selective remix; it is within this type that Navas has categorised Coldcut's remix 'Paid in Full'. He has described the selective remix as follows:

> [I]t consists of adding or subtracting material from the original composition. This type of remix, during the 1980s, made DJs popular producers in the music mainstream. One of the most successful selective remixes is Eric B. & Rakim's 'Paid in Full', remixed by Coldcut in 1987. In this case Coldcut produced two remixes, the most popular version not only extends the original recording, following the tradition of the club mix [. . .] but it also contains new sections, as well as new sounds, while others were subtracted, always keeping the 'essence' or 'spectacular aura' of the composition intact.[37]

I would suggest, in friendly disagreement with Navas, that while he is right in that Coldcut added new sections, sounds and vocals, Coldcut did not do so without a fundamental change to the 'spectacular aura' of the song. After Coldcut's thirty-six hours of remix frenzy in the studio, the original song was changed from being a song about Eric B. & Rakim getting 'Paid in Full' for their artistic outputs (and Rakim's spiritual effort) to something completely different.

Rakim's money-making verse became overshadowed by the poetic words of Shabazi in Haza's rendition. Haza's voice, along with the other samples, gives the remix a timeless transcendental aura with a Middle Eastern soundboard. That Haza's voice also added Jewish mystical lyrics to the remix was obviously accidental. The soundscape created by Coldcut produced a different, 'exotic' sound that was new to hip-hop. The Middle Eastern soundboard is completely absent from the original version, and its introduction in the remix gave rise to that 'spectacular aura' of the song which helps us unravel the global resonance of 'Paid in Full'.

What is more, the Coldcut remix grafted what can be perceived as a universal otherworldliness and spirituality onto hip-hop. This element was further enhanced and draped in semiotic resources perceived as Islamic when Bruno Tilley put pictures to the aural landscape created by Coldcut. He 'simply matched sound to vision' and added the visuals of a belly dancer, Qur'anic verses and Muslims in prayer. Although he did so without any intention to promote any specific religion, Tilley's creative decisions and his ideas of the

[37] Ibid.

possible origin of Haza's music further accentuated the Middle Eastern and Islamic soundboard.

Since the remix, countless producers and artists have incorporated Arabic and Indian samples in order to recreate the sound invented by Coldcut. For instance, when Mobb Deep paid Eric B. & Rakim homage in their version of 'Paid in Full', they sampled the Indian singers Alisha Chinai and Ragheb Alameh's 'Laila' in order to recreate the soundscape of the remix of Eric B. & Rakim's, or rather Coldcut's, 'Paid in Full'. The song bridges the heart of the urban marginalised poor in the US and the Muslim world. But it is the Muslim world not as a geographical area; it is the Muslim world as a cognitive universe of ideas, in this case expressed through common concepts, even clichés. Following the commercial success of the video, numerous hip-hop artists have repeated its formula of incorporating semiotic resources perceived as Islamic in their lyrics, record covers and soundscapes. Of course, they have done so for a variety of reasons and with a diversity of inspirations, some of which are Orientalist fantasies. Yet in all this variety, it would be hard to deny the central role played by Coldcut's remix of 'Paid in Full'.

In summary, the moral tale of a conversion to NGE recorded by Eric B. & Rakim became a mega hit in the second reincarnation of the song when other elements, among them Jewish spirituality and orientalised Islamic imagery, were added, and some of the key lyrical elements spoken in the original intro referring to the NGE worldview were deleted. Scholars have often conflated the two different versions and ignored NGE elements in the lyrics.

By approaching the song and music video with a methodology derived from semiotic studies, I have made a semiotic inventory and mapped the origins of the song's aural, visual and textual elements. In doing so, we have arrived at a more complete understanding of the song, in a way that complements the literature about it and opens up new interpretive possibilities for other songs. Especially poignant for scholars of Islamic studies is the significance of Rakim's lyrical narrative about finding a righteous path, built on African American narratives about personal success and frequent references to Islamic semiotic resources. The next chapter will continue to explore this latter aspect by discussing the importance of Malcolm X as an Islamic semiotic resource.

6

SIGHTS AND SOUNDS OF MALCOLM X IN US HIP-HOP

This chapter introduces the ways in which Malcolm X and his legacy have been used within US hip-hop music, using an array of examples. It does not seek to provide a complete semiotic inventory of the uses of Malcolm X in US hip-hop – such an undertaking would most likely necessitate a lengthy volume (or two) of its own. Rather, this chapter aims to contribute to the already available scholarship in the field by building upon existing research and providing original insights.[1]

In the previous chapter, I have argued that the use of Islamic semiotic resources has been treated in a rather simplistic manner, often overlooking the actual ideas and intentions of the sender and the serendipities of the use in parts of the production. Continuing on the path of nuancing this simplification, this chapter sets out to demonstrate how the life and legacy of Malcolm X are integrated in hip-hop culture through artists' frequent invocation of both. My central argument is that US hip-hop artists have been participating in the processes of reinventing Malcolm X and his legacy, not only by casting him as a symbol of local African American resistance against racial inequalities, but also by fashioning him as a global Muslim revolutionary who resonates far beyond hip-hop culture.

[1] See, for example, Abernethy 2013: 209–16; Ackfeldt 2013.

The examples provided are, for the sake of clarity, divided into three time periods. The first period (1980–86) begins with what many consider to be the first commercially released hip-hop song, 'Rapper's Delight', and ends with the dawn of the so-called 'Golden Era' of hip-hop. The second period (1986–93) roughly matches this Golden Era, which older observers of hip-hop culture, somewhat nostalgically, often consider to be when hip-hop peaked both creatively and politically. The Golden Era in this literature is often described as being guided by Afrocentricity and African American nationalism. Geographically, the two first periods are often situated on the US East Coast, more specifically in New York. The final period (1993 to the present) is when hip-hop geographically and stylistically diversified. This phase was also marked by an increased commodification of hip-hop culture. Certainly, these time-periods can be questioned; in reality, no clear lines exist between them. Therefore, I encourage readers to view them as an interpretive temporal map of the development of hip-hop and the use of the semiotics of Malcolm X in hip-hop culture.

'I Don't Come to You to Bang, Bang the Boogie' (1980–86)

1980 was an election year. At the beginning of November, Ronald Reagan and running mate George H. W. Bush won a landslide victory over incumbent President Jimmy Carter. 'Rapper's Delight' by the Sugar Hill Gang was released in September 1979, and the new sights and sounds of hip-hop culture were quickly spreading from New York's inner-city neighbourhoods to the rest of the country.[2]

Earlier in 1979, the aspiring musician and producer Erik Nuri had graduated from Harvard University. Nuri had joined NOI in 1972, the same year that he enrolled at Harvard. His duties in NOI pulled him away from his studies, and during his second year he took a leave of absence from college. Together with his girlfriend and their newborn child, he moved back to his hometown

[2] For written accounts of this development, see, for example, Toop 2000; Ogg and Upshal 2001; Chang 2005. The pictorial accounts of the early years of hip-hop are often forgotten by academics. Photographers such as Martha Cooper, Henry Chalfant, Ernie Paniccioli and Joe Conzo have all made important contributions to our knowledge of early hip-hop history. See Cooper, Zeb.roc.ski and Kramer 2013; Cooper 2015; and Paniccioli and Powell 2014.

of New York City, where his involvement with NOI gained momentum. He worked as a student minister at Temple #7 in Harlem under Louis Farrakhan, and he managed NOI's fruit and vegetable market in Harlem. During this time, Nuri performed as a musician at weddings and other services held by NOI. He performed in different musical line-ups and played mostly jazz and R&B, becoming somewhat famous within the community and appreciated as a musician. When Elijah Muhammed died in 1975, Nuri made the decision to leave the movement and return to Harvard to finish his studies.

Upon his return to Harvard, he started to work as an intern and administrative assistant at the Massachusetts Black and Latino Legislative Caucus. When he graduated, the position of Executive Director became vacant, and Nuri was interviewed and subsequently hired. One of his main duties was to involve young African Americans in the 1980 election. Nuri came up with the idea to create a hip-hop song in order to encourage young African Americans to vote; the song 'Let's Vote' was released during the summer of 1980.[3] It failed to achieve mainstream recognition but was endorsed as the voter registration theme song by both the National Association for the Advancement of Colored People (NAACP) and the National Urban League (NUL). Later, Nuri became the first artist to be signed by Tom Silverman to his newly established hip-hop record label, Tommy Boy Records.[4]

With lines like 'I don't come to you to bang, bang the boogie' and 'So throw your hands in the air / and shake your body like you really don't care but I hear you complaining about your property tax / they pay a little and you pay the max', the song clearly carried a political message, in stark contrast to the party-oriented lyrics of Sugarhill Gang's 1979 mega-hit 'Rapper's Delight', which the first lines of the quote above paraphrase. As such, 'Let's Vote' probably stands as the first political hip-hop song released. The song also contains the lines: 'I love the rap of Brother Malcolm X but what was his plan of success? / He said the ballot or the bullet'. The 'ballot or the bullet' is a reference to Malcolm X's famous 'The Ballot or the Bullet' speech delivered at Cory United Methodist Church in Cleveland, Ohio, in April 1964, which

[3] Erik Nuri, 'Let's Vote', 7-inch single (Tryon Park Records © 1980).

[4] Author's interview with Erik Nuri, New York, 12 May 2015.

makes 'Let's Vote' the first hip-hop song to invoke the name of Malcolm X.[5] This was less than a year after the release of 'Rapper's Delight', the first commercially successful hip-hop song.[6]

It is most likely no coincidence that the first political hip-hop song was introduced by a former NOI member and political organiser. It is also no coincidence that this song contains a reference to Malcolm X. The ethos of NOI encourages political engagement, and within the movement Malcolm X is a symbol of this engagement. From the perspective of Islamic studies, it becomes important to point out that this political engagement is conflated with religious engagement. In fact, it makes no analytical sense to separate politics from religion: 'they' are actually part of the same engagement.

Another early reference to Malcolm X was made in late 1980 (or possible early 1981) by Brother D (Daryl Aamaa Nubyahn), a community activist and mathematics teacher from the Bronx.[7] The song 'How We Gonna Make the

[5] Already in the late 1970s and 1980s, the DJ and hip-hop pioneer Afrika Bambaataa was known to overlay Malcolm X's speeches over the German electro group Kraftwerk's driving and repetitive beats. However, to my knowledge, these sessions were never recorded (Toop 2000: 130). Later, in 1986, Afrika Bambaataa & the Soulsonic Force released the single 'Renegades of Funk' (Tommy Boy Records © 1983), which made reference to Malcolm X in the following section: 'Nothing stayed the same but there were always renegades / Like Chief Sitting Bull / Tom Paine Dr Martin Luther King / Malcolm X / They were renegades of their time and age / So many renegades'. In 2001, the alt rock band Rage Against the Machine released a cover of the song (2001 © Epic). The cover art of the single includes the famous photo from 1964 of Martin Luther King Jr and Malcolm X shaking hands and smiling. The speech can be found in full in Breitman 1989. In this speech, Malcolm X advised his audience to exercise their right to vote, but he also warned that, if the government continued to restrict the rights of African Americans, it might be necessary to take up arms. For background information and an analysis of the speech, see, for example, Jenkins and Tryman 2002: 33; Marable 2011: 303–4.

[6] Nuri started the short-lived record label 'Salaam Records' in 1983, targeting the Muslim community in the US. The record label, named after his mother's surname, only published releases from one group, The Whizdom Kids, consisting of Nuri's two children. The group released songs such as 'Come to Allah', 'My Imam' and 'Elijahville'. The Whizdom Kids made several appearances in events in connection to Muslim gatherings and festivities, primarily in New York. Their curious sound can best be described as electro soul and jazz with some hip-hop elements (author's interview with Erik Nuri, New York, 12 May 2015).

[7] On the sleeve to the cassette-album *Up Against the Beast* (Reachout International Records © 1984), Lister Hewan-Lowe described Brother D as 'the Malcolm X of the 1980s'.

Black Nation Rise?' (1980) was released on Lister Hewan-Lowe's Clappers label, and Brother D was backed by the group the Collective Effort.[8] The song was more explicit in its radical political ambitions than Nuri's 'Let's Vote', and it was recorded to mirror the thinking of National Black Science, a political and educational awareness organisation.[9] Like 'Rapper's Delight', it was crafted around a disco song, Cheryl Lynn's 'Got to be Real' (1978), but the politically charged lyrics are a marked contrast to the joyful disco sound.[10] The song was not only a call for African American solidarity and empowerment at the dawn of the Reagan era, but also a lesson in African American political history. Brother D carefully namechecks prominent African American leaders such as Marcus Garvey, Martin Luther King, Elijah Muhammed and Malcolm X:

> The story might give you stomach cramps
> Like America's got concentration camps
> People like Malcolm lived and died
> Warning us about genocide
> While you're partying on, on, on, on and on
> The ovens may be hot by the break of dawn
> Your party may end one day soon
> When they round the niggers up in the afternoon.[11]

With fiery lyrics such as these, the song was a call for the 'Black Nation' to 'Agitate! Educate! Organize!' Brother D's 'How We Gonna Make the Black Nation Rise?' foreshadows the Afrocentric rhetoric of later hip-hop groups, not least Public Enemy and X-Clan.

Different in tone, the former drummer and staff member of Sugar Hill Records Keith LeBlanc's 'Malcolm X: No Sell Out' (1983) became the first song to sample the spoken word of Malcolm X.[12] Inspired by Alex Haley's

[8] Brother D with Collective Effort, 'How We Gonna Make the Black Nation Rise?', 7-inch single (Clappers Records © 1980). Although the date on the sleeve states that it was released in 1980, Brother D has been quoted as saying that it was actually released in 1981. See Partridge 2004: 84.

[9] Bradley and DuBois 2010: 32.

[10] Cheryl Lynn, 'Got to be Real', 7-inch single (CBS Inc © 1978).

[11] Brother D with Collective Effort, 'How We Gonna Make the Black Nation Rise?', 7-inch single (Clapper Records © 1980).

[12] *Keith LeBlanc, 'Malcolm X: No Sell Out', 12-inch single (Tommy Boy Music © 1983).*

Figure 6.1 Album cover (LP, 12-inch single) for Keith LeBlanc's *Malcolm X: No Sell Out.*

The Autobiography of Malcolm X (1965), LeBlanc decided to sample extracts of Malcolm X's voice from various recordings of his speeches and put them over an early electronic hip-hop beat.[13] LeBlanc was also the first hip-hop artist to use a photo of Malcolm X on a record cover. The cover features the last known photo portrait of Malcolm X, taken by Robert Lee Haggins on 18 February 1965, three days before Malcolm X's assassination.[14] In the photo, Malcolm is wearing a tweed jacket, dark tie, white shirt and his characteristic browline glasses. He thoughtfully looks down, possibly reading something. Red block letters state 'NO SELL OUT' at the top and 'MALCOLM X' at the bottom, surrounding the black-and-white photo. The back cover features a brief biographical text about Malcolm X as well as a short statement from his widow, Dr Betty Shabazz, stressing that Malcolm X was as important now as he was when he was alive.

[13] Charnas 2010: 103.

[14] Robert Lee Haggins was Malcolm X's personal photographer from 1959 to 1965. The cover was designed by Overnight Type & Graphics, who also designed the cover for Afrika Bambaataa & The Soulsonic Force single 'Renegades of Funk' (Tommy Boy Records © 1983).

Critical voices were raised concerning the use of Malcolm X's voice in songs. For example, Paul Winley, CEO of Winley Records, which had released a series of Malcolm X's speeches on vinyl, was quoted as saying: 'It's just like taking one of your idols, one of your heroes and boogie-ing behind em. It's just like taking the Pope's speech and putting some disco music behind it – here's John Paul baby!' Others were concerned by the fact that a white artist and a 'white' record label had released the record.[15] Even so, the recording was cleared by Dr Betty Shabazz. She called LeBlanc a 'wonderful musician', and her only request was that a gunshot echoing at the end of the song be removed.[16]

As described in Chapter 4, different Islamic interpretive traditions have influenced hip-hop's ideological foundation – mainly through Bambaataa's Universal Zulu Nation and NGE. Artists from this time incorporated Islamic semiotic resources from what Partridge has called the pool of occultural knowledge.[17] These resources came from a wide variety of Islamic interpretive traditions, including the writings of the Ansaaru Allah Community, as seen on the back cover of Dr York's single 'Roll-A-Rock' (1980) and the classic instrumental b-boy anthem 'Al-Naafiysh (The Soul)' by Hashim.[18] The latter title alludes to the Qur'anic concept of *nafs*, referring to the soul or ego (the lower self). *Nafs* is an important concept in several Islamic interpretive traditions, not least within Sufism. It is often described as something that should be boxed in and controlled through spiritual training.[19]

Artists also engaged creatively with Islamic traditions by adopting imaginative nomenclatures drawing inspiration from the symbolic repertoire of Islam. To this end, some purposefully utilised names linking to such interpretive

[15] Toop 2000: 124–25.

[16] Charnas 2010: 103.

[17] Partridge 2004: 84.

[18] Dr York, 'Roll-A-Rock', 7-inch single (Passion Music © 1980); Hashim, 'Al-Naafiysh (The Soul)' (Cutting Records © 1983). Dr York is also known as Dwight York (and Malachi Z. York or Issa Al Haadi Al Mahdi). He founded the Ansaaru Allah Community in Brooklyn in the 1970s. The community later developed into the Nuwaubian movement. In 2002, York was arrested for, among other things, over a hundred counts of sexually molesting dozens of children. Dwight York was serving his sentence as late as 2015. For an insightful account of the Ansaaru Allah community and its history, see Palmer 2010.

[19] For more detailed exposition of the concept see E. E. Calverley and I. R. Netton, 'Nafs', *Encyclopaedia of Islam: Second Edition*, http://referenceworks.brillonline.com/entries/encyclopaedia-of-islam-2/nafs-COM_0833 (accessed 14 September 2023).

traditions make it hard not to notice a small but significant trend: for example, the above-mentioned Nuri (from *Nur*, meaning light in Arabic) and *Hashim* (meaning decisive in Arabic). To these, one may add names such as DJ Afrika Islam, T. C. Islam (Bambaataa's son) and Just Allah the Superstar (from the group the World's Famous Supreme Team). This permeation of hip-hop culture with references to Islam was creatively coupled to and inextricably linked with parallel allusions to African American political awareness and expressions of 'Black pride' and strength, as I will next demonstrate.

'Too Black, Too Strong' (1986–93)

In 1986, Run-DMC released the critically acclaimed album *Raising Hell*, which includes well-known hits such as 'Walk This Way' (featuring Steven Tyler and Joe Perry of Aerosmith), 'My Adidas' and 'It's Tricky'.[20] The last track on the album, 'Proud to be Black', is less known to a mainstream audience. In the song, Run-DMC forcefully states: 'Ya know I'm proud to be black ya'll!' Their 'Black and Proud' message was also reinforced with references to Malcolm X. 'Like Malcolm X said I won't turn the right cheek', and 'You read about Malcolm X – in the history text / Jesse Owens broke records, Ali broke necks / What's wrong with ya man? How can you be so dumb? / Like Dr King said, We Shall Overcome!'[21]

For many observers of hip-hop culture, *Raising Hell* marks the beginning of hip-hop's Golden Era, roughly the years 1986–93, when hip-hop culture evolved from a local subculture among predominantly African American and Latino American communities in New York boroughs to one of the fastest-developing sectors of the record industry.[22] These years are also hailed as a time when hip-hop grew more complex and diverse.

[20] Run-DMC, *Raising Hell*, LP album (Profile Records © 1986).

[21] Malcolm X twice alluded to Jesus's 'Sermon on the Mount' in his 'Ballot or the Bullet' speech: 'As they nourish these dissatisfactions, it can only lead to one thing, an explosion; and now we have the type of black man on the scene in America today [. . .] who just doesn't intend to turn the other cheek any longer'. See Breitman 1989: 41. And later on in the same speech: 'And now you're facing a situation where the young Negro's coming up. They don't want to hear that "turn the-other-cheek" stuff, no. In Jacksonville, those were teenagers, they were throwing Molotov cocktails. Negroes have never done that before. But it shows you there's a new deal coming in'. Breitman 1989: 48.

[22] Williams 2015: 301–2. For an important account of Puerto Ricans and other Latino Americans' contribution to early hip-hop culture, see Rivera 2003.

Arguably, no other group has contributed more to the aural and visual articulations of Malcolm X in hip-hop than Public Enemy.[23] Their carefully planned visual and aural agenda not only connected a new generation of hip-hop listeners to his legacy, but they also became an exemplar for other hip-hop acts.[24] Chuck D has repeatedly told the following story:

> One-day Hank [Shocklee] and I was hanging a flyer with Malcolm on the cover of the flyer – of the gig that we were presenting – and this kid comes up and says: 'You know, who's this Malcolm the Tenth?' And you know, we looked at each other, and said 'well, something needs to be done about that!'[25]

While Eric B. & Rakim introduced Islamic semiotic resources found within the teachings of the Five Percenters on their seminal album *Paid in Full* (1987),[26] Public Enemy's sophomore album *It Takes a Nation of Millions to Hold Us Back* (1988) made Malcolm X a hip-hop household name.[27]

The song 'Bring the Noise' was first released on the soundtrack to Marek Kanievska's movie *Less Than Zero* (1987), and it also served as the opening track on *It Takes a Nation of Millions to Hold Us Back*. The soundscape of 'Bring the Noise' consists of an aggressive mix of siren noises, James Brown funk beats, hard-hitting drum machine clatters and wild scratching by the group's DJ Terminator X (another possible Malcolm X reference). At the beginning of the song, Public Enemy's production team, the Bomb Squad, sampled parts of Malcolm X's voice from his speech 'Message to the Grass Roots', delivered at the Northern Negro Grass Roots Leadership Conference

[23] The original members were front man Chuck D, hype man Flavor Flav, DJ Terminator X and Professor Griff. Public Enemy formed in 1982 at Adelphi University on Long Island, New York. Comments by Professor Griff to the *Washington Times* in 1989 brought charges of anti-Semitism, which ultimately resulted in him leaving the group. Today Professor Griff is once again performing with the group.

[24] Alridge 2005: 229–30.

[25] Chuck D, quoted in 'Public Enemy: Prophets of Rage', BBC4 documentary, 2011. This story has been retold by Chuck D on several occasions. It can also be found in the essay 'Malcolm X the Tenth', by Chuck D, published in the commemorative book for the exhibition 'Return of the Mecca: The Art of Islam and Hip-hop' (curated by Sohail Daulatzai).

[26] Eric B. & Rakim, *Paid in Full*, LP album (84th and Broadway © 1987).

[27] Public Enemy, *It Takes a Nation of Millions to Hold Us Back*, LP album (Def Jam Records © 1988).

on 10 November 1963 at King Solomon Baptist Church in Detroit, Michigan. The phrase 'Too black, too strong' is repeated twice.[28] This speech was delivered by Malcolm X just a few weeks before John F. Kennedy was murdered in Dallas and is often considered to be the last great speech that Malcolm X gave as a member of NOI.[29] The speech is forty minutes long and contains some of Malcolm X's most commonly known tropes and metaphors: the house Negro and the field Negro, the difference between the Negro revolution and the revolution, and the difference between black coffee and coffee with white cream. It is also in this speech that Malcolm X started to make his move from local Black nationalism to a more international approach.[30] Moreover, 'Bring the Noise' also contained several lyrical shout-outs to artists such as Rakim and Run-DMC, and it made an often-cited reference to the leader of NOI, Farrakhan: 'Cause a brother like me said, Well Farrakhan's a prophet and I think you ought to listen to / What he can say to you, what you wanna do is follow for now'.[31]

It Takes a Nation of Millions to Hold Us Back is often noted for its strong social commentary and its many references to African American movements, including the Black Panther Party and NOI. A good example of such a reference is the song 'Party for Your Right to Fight',[32] in which the group addresses

[28] The full quote goes: 'It's just like when you've got some coffee that's too black, which means it's too strong. What do you do? You integrate it with cream, you make it weak. But if you pour too much cream in it, you won't even know you ever had coffee. It used to be hot, it becomes cool. It used to be strong, it becomes weak. It used to wake you up, now it puts you to sleep'. See Marable 2011: 264–65. The sample was taken from Malcolm X, *Grass Roots Speech Detroit, Michigan November 1963*, LP album (Winley Records © 1979). Later, the phrase 'Too black, too strong' from 'Bring the Noise' was sampled by the group 2 Black 2 Strong MMG (Mad Motherfucking Gangsters), '2 Black to Strong' (Clapper Records © 1991). The song, which featured Gamilah Shabazz (daughter of Malcolm X), also paid homage to Malcolm X with the lines: 'I'm rated X, like Malcolm / How come the brother wasn't welcome / To tell the knowledge about us?' Gamilah Shabazz also appeared on Big Daddy Kane's 'Who Am I' on the album *Taste of Chocolate* (Cold Chillin' Records © 1990).

[29] Ambar 2014: 32.

[30] Marable 2011: 265.

[31] Public Enemy, 'Bring the Noise', 12-inch single (Def Jam Records © 1987).

[32] The name of the song alludes to Beastie Boys, *Licensed to Ill*, '(You Gotta) Fight for Your Right (To Party!)' (Def Jam © 1987).

the government's attempt to infiltrate and eliminate the Black Panther Party and other radical African American movements through the FBI's Counterintelligence Program (COINTELPRO):

> It was your so-called government
> That made this occur
> Like the grafted devils they were [. . .].
> J. Edgar Hoover, and he coulda proved to you
> He had King and X set up
> Also the party with Newton, Cleaver and Seale
> He ended, so get up
> Time to get em back
> Get back on the track
> Word from the honorable Elijah Muhammed
> Know who you are to be Black.[33]

The song effectively joins together aspects from NOI's creation myth (where the evil Black scientist Yakub, who lived 6,600 years ago, is said to have been responsible for the creation of the white race as a 'race of devils' through the process of 'grafting'), references to prominent radical leaders such as Malcolm X and Elijah Muhammed and actions taken by the FBI to disintegrate African American radical leadership.

Public Enemy's formula for the successful promotion and mobilisation of their ideas cannot be reduced to lyrical quotes and single samples of Malcolm X. The group's entire visual register, including record covers and music videos, signalled a radicalism that accentuated Public Enemy's vision of African American empowerment fuelled by Black Power ideology and the teachings promoted by NOI. In concerts, interviews and promotional pictures, Public Enemy surrounded themselves with NOI's uniformed security force, the S1W (Security of the First World), something that added to the militant aura of the group.[34]

[33] Public Enemy, *It Takes a Nation of Millions to Hold Us Back*, 'Party for Your Right to Fight,' CD album (Def Jam Records © 1988).

[34] Several of these pictures were taken by photographer Ernie Paniccioli.

When MTV launched Yo! MTV Raps in late 1988, Public Enemy successfully made use of music videos in order to disseminate their ideas. Their first real attempt resulted in the video for their third single from *It Takes a Nation of Millions to Hold Us Back*, the track 'Night of the Living Baseheads'. The song addressed the crack epidemic in the US at the time, and in the video, directed by Lionel C. Martin, Chuck D is seen performing in front of the Audubon Ballroom where Malcolm X was assassinated. The visual message is clear: Chuck D picks up the microphone where Malcolm X dropped it twenty-three years prior.

In 1989, Public Enemy wrote the anthem 'Fight the Power' (1989) for Spike Lee's movie *Do the Right Thing* (1989). In the video, directed by Lee, the group is seen performing at a rally in Brooklyn, surrounded by the security organisation S1W in front of a giant Malcolm X photo, with cheering crowds holding pictures of other African American leaders and personages such as Harriet Tubman, Marcus Garvey, Martin Luther King and Jesse Jackson, all symbolising the African American struggle.

The same year that Public Enemy released *It Takes a Nation of Millions to Hold Us Back*, Boogie Down Productions (with rapper KRS-One) released the album *By All Means Necessary* (1988).[35] With its minimalistic soundscape, the album had little to nothing in common with *It Takes a Nation of Millions to Hold Us Back*; yet, the two albums shared similar political concerns. On *By All Means Necessary*, KRS-One assumes the role of Teacher, 'the Edutainer', who takes it upon himself to educate the listeners about such topics as sexually transmitted diseases ('Jimmy'), drug trafficking ('Illegal Business') and street violence ('Stop the Violence'). The title of the album alludes to Malcolm X's famous speech ('By Any Means Necessary') at the Organization of Afro-American Unity's founding rally on 28 June 1964.[36] 'By any means necessary' was also something of a catchphrase invoked by Malcolm X in several speeches and contexts.

[35] Boogie Down Productions, *By All Means Necessary*, LP album (Jive © 1988).

[36] The phrase 'by any means necessary' is repeated several times in the speech by Malcolm X. For example, it occurs in the much-cited section: 'We declare our right on this Earth to be a man, to be a human being, to be respected as a human being, to be given the rights of a human being, in this society on this earth in this day, which we intend to bring into existence by any means necessary'. See Breitman 1992: 84. The speech is often alluded to in hip-hop lyrics. For example, in the song 'Break the Grip of Shame' on the debut album *The Devil Made Me Do It* by Paris (Tommy Boy Records © 1990), the above section is quoted in full. Artists such as Jay-Z, Rakim, Scarface and Kendrick Lamar have all used the phrase 'by any means necessary' in various songs.

The album cover depicts KRS-One mimicking the famous 'window-photo' of Malcolm X.[37] KRS-One is wearing a custom-made Dapper Dan Boogie Down Productions leather tracksuit, sunglasses and a baseball cap, while holding a Micro-Uzi submachine gun. He peeks out of a window in the same way as Malcolm X did in the iconic original photo.[38] The photo is also on parade in the music video for the first song on the album, 'My Philosophy'.[39] Both of these photos are equally on display in a slideshow behind KRS-One when he is performing on stage.

KRS-One was one of the chief architects behind the Stop the Violence Movement, a response to the violence plaguing hip-hop culture. Together with some of the biggest names on the New York hip-hop scene at the time, he recorded the charity song 'Self-Destruction' (1989).[40] The song sampled

[37] According to the back cover of the album, the photo is credited to the photographer Doug Rowell. Rowell took several photos of hip-hop artists at that time – for example, the cover photo to Whodini's album Back in Black (Jive © 1990) and DJ Jazzy Jeff & the Fresh Prince's He's the DJ, I'm the Rapper (Jive © 1988). The original photo is most likely from a series of photos taken for an article published in September 1964 in the monthly magazine *Ebony*. The article 'Mystery of Malcolm X' (written by Hans Jürgen *Massaquoi) contained a similar photo taken from another angle.* The article was reprinted in the 1993 February issue of *Ebony* with different photos, this time illustrated with the iconic photo. There are no photo credits in the article.

[38] The original *Ebony* photo was also used as the blueprint for the singer and song writer Bilal's album *Airtight's Revenge* (Plug Research © 2010). On the cover, Bilal is seen holding a microphone, peering through what seems to be red stage curtains. The picture was also reproduced by Nicki Minaj on the cover for her single 'Lookin' Ass Nigga' (2014 © Cash Money Records), to the dissatisfaction of both the Malcolm X Estate and parts of the hip-hop community. The 2008 Green Party Vice-Presidential candidate and hip-hop activist Rosa Clemente organised a petition calling for Nikki Minaj to withdraw the cover, which she did only a couple of days after the official release. According to Clemente, Minaj's usage of the photo was 'dishonouring the life and contributions of one of the greatest leaders of the twentieth century'. http://rosaclemente.net/nicki-minaj-young-money-records-remove-the-picture-of-malcolm-x-now/ (accessed 14 September 2023).

[39] Boogie Down Productions, *By All Means Necessary*, 'My Philosophy', LP album (Jive © 1998).

[40] Stop the Violence Movement (KRS-One, D-Nice & Ms. Melodie, Delite, Daddy-O, Wise, Frukwan Sun-Star, Allah-Bey, Kool Moe Dee, MC Lyte, Doug E. Fresh, Just-Ice, Heavy D and Chuck D and Flavor Flav), 'Self-Destruct', 12-inch single (Jive © 1989). According to the back cover of the single, all the earnings from the records would be donated to the National Urban League and their programme Black on Black Crime and Youth Education. For an account of the Stop the Violence Movement, see George and National Urban League 1990.

Figure 6.2 Three album covers inspired by the image of Malcolm X at the window with a Micro-Uzi submachine gun: Boogie Down Productions' *By All Means Necessary* (1988), Bilal's *Airtight's Revenge* (2010) and Nicki Minaj's *Lookin' Ass Nigga* (2014).

part of Malcolm X's 'Message to the Grassroots' speech given in Detroit on 10 November 1963 in its intro.[41] The video also features the late MC Heavy D and Frukwan Sun-Star Allah-Bey performing in front of an enormous Malcolm X mural in central Harlem.

In the early 1990s, the use of Islamic semiotic resources in hip-hop climaxed. Artists were inspired by Islamic interpretive traditions ranging from the cognitive universe of NGE and NOI to different Sunni interpretations. Hip-hop acts such as X Clan, Brand Nubian, Lakim Shabazz, King Sun, The Jaz (Jaz-O), Kool Moe Dee, The Poor Righteous Teachers, Big Daddy Kane, Ice Cube, Paris, A Tribe Called Quest, Movement Ex and Gang Starr contributed heavily to this development. Islamic semiotic resources thereby underpinned different aural, visual and textual articulations of the hip-hop of this era. In this context, Malcolm X proved to be a significant source of inspiration; references to his example and legacy abound and may even be seen as central to the message of hip-hop.

This trend accelerated with Spike Lee's guerrilla marketing campaign for his biographical film *Malcolm X* (1992). Lee strategically gave away his self-designed iconic black baseball cap with a silver 'X' on the front to sports stars, hip-hop artists and other prominent figures in the African American community.[42] The popularity of the Malcolm X brand was also fuelled by the extensive bootlegging of Spike Lee's design. Soon the market was flooded with consumer products, including coffee mugs, lighters, fridge magnets, air fresheners and potato chips containing Spike Lee's silver 'X' or other renditions of Malcolm X's life and legacy.[43] Manning Marable has described this development as 'Malcolmania', and Malcolm X-related products reached an estimated annual sales figure of $100 million.[44] Between 1989 and 1992, the book sales of *The Autobiography of Malcolm X* (1965) saw a 300 per cent increase. This can, at least in part, be attributed to the assimilation of Malcolm X in hip-hop culture and the latter's power to influence a broad audience with purchasing power.[45]

[41] The section sample is: 'We all agree tonight, all of the speakers have agreed, that America has a very serious problem. Not only does America have a very serious problem, but our people have a very serious problem. America's problem is [. . .]'. See Breitman 1989: 16.

[42] Lee et al. 1993: 21.

[43] Ibid. p. 25.

[44] Marable and Aidi 2009: 303.

[45] Lord and Thornton 1992.

Figure 6.3 Malcolm X on the cover of *The Source* (March 1990).

In March 1990, *The Source*, one of the most respected hip-hop magazines in the US, ran a cover story on Malcolm X with the headline: 'After 25 Years Hip-Hop Keeps His Message Alive'. The cover featured a picture of Malcolm X taken in Egypt in 1964.[46]

When the airplay and visibility of hip-hop music increased, the legality of sampling came under increased scrutiny. In December 1991, Federal Judge Kevin Thomas Duffy issued a 1,600-word ruling against unauthorised sampling in hip-hop music. Even though several sampling cases had previously been settled out of court, the ruling effectively changed the soundscape of hip-hop. The judge issued a temporary injunction preventing the sales and distribution

[46] As a testimony of the importance of the influence of Islam in hip-hop in the early 1990s, one may mention that *The Source* magazine 1991 March/April issue had rappers Paris, Big Daddy Kane and Lakim Shabazz on the cover together with a crescent and star symbol. The issue featured a lengthy article by acclaimed hip-hop journalist Harry Allen, called 'Righteous Indignation'. In the article, Allen discussed different interpretive traditions of Islam and their influence on hip-hop music, together with some prominent artists of the time. The issue also featured an 'Islamic Rap Review' that rated ten albums with 'Islamic theme'.

of Biz Markie's album *I Need a Haircut* (1991).[47] The ruling required that the original copyright owners should approve all future samples.[48] The court case, in combination with the release of the album *The Chronic* (1992) by Dr Dre, moved the cultural epicentre of hip-hop from the East Coast to the West Coast, from the boroughs of New York to South Los Angeles. The South Bronx, Brooklyn and Harlem were replaced by salutations to neighbourhoods such as Compton, Crenshaw, Long Beach and Inglewood. The soundscape of hip-hop changed and diversified with the new, less sample-heavy West Coast sound. For many observers, this shift marks the end of hip-hop's Golden Era.

South Los Angeles's reputation for gang violence and drug-trafficking had been cemented in the popular imagination of hip-hop fans since the late 1980s, by artist such as Da Lench Mob, N. W. A and Compton's Most Wanted. One of the pivotal figures on the so-called gangsta rap scene was a former member of N. W. A., Ice Cube. Around the same time as Dr Dre released *The Chronic*, at the end of 1992, Ice Cube released his hugely successful third album, *The Predator*.[49] Even though Ice Cube had introduced Malcolm X and a number of Islamic semiotic resources in his blend of social critique and gangster attitude on earlier solo albums, in *The Predator* these uses became much more explicit.[50]

The cover of the album features Ice Cube wearing a *kufi* while smoking what is likely marijuana from a skull-shaped pipe.[51] The image captures both Ice Cube's gangsta bravado as a weed-smoking hoodlum and his conscious support, but not necessarily membership, of NOI. This relationship to NOI is captured in the song 'The Predator' (1992), where Ice Cube declares: 'You call me a Muslim, no I'm not a resident / Still got my vote in – Farrakhan for president'.[52]

[47] Biz Markie, *I Need a Haircut*, CD album (Cold Chillin' and Warner Bros. Records © 1991).

[48] Cateforis 2007: 279.

[49] Ice Cube, *The Predator*, CD album (Priority Records © 1992).

[50] For example, on the song 'Horny Lil' Devil' on the album *AmeriKKKa's Most Wanted*, CD album (Priority Records © 1990).

[51] Although it is not clear from the photo that it actually is a *kufi* that Ice Cube is wearing, at least one of Ice Cube's many interpreters suggests so, and I agree with this suggestion. See Woldu 2008: 46.

[52] Ice Cube, *The Predator*, 'The Predator', CD album (Priority Records © 1992). This dualism is also on display on the back cover of *Death Certificate*, where Ice Cube is seen reading Nation of Islam's newspaper *Final Call*. Behind him, on the right side, his 'crew' Da Lench Mob, all dressed in black, are on display. On his left, standing to attention, wearing bow-ties, members of NOI are presented. Ice Cube in the centre seemingly serves as a bridge between the two camps.

The album features several references to Malcolm X. On the first single released, 'Wicked', Ice Cube compares himself to Malcolm X, and at the same time associates himself with artists like KRS-One and Public Enemy, by referencing the window photo as well as namechecking the song 'Bring the Noise'. Ice Cube states: 'People wanna know how come / I got a gat [slang for a gun] and I'm lookin out the window like Malcolm / Ready to bring that noise'. In the song, 'When will they Shoot?' Ice Cube asks: 'Ice Cube is out-gunned, what is the outcome? / Will they do me like Malcolm?'[53] On the two-and-a-half-minute long interlude, 'Integration (Interlude)', Ice Cube juxtaposes long passages from Malcolm X's address to the Oxford Union on 3 December 1964 with passages from an interview with Farrakhan conducted by Phil Donahue, which aired on 13 March 1990. The topic, as the title suggests, is integration.[54]

Ice Cube's album was released around the same time as the Rodney King trial in 1992. This trial involved four Los Angeles police officers charged with the use of excessive force after a videotape captured them beating Rodney King during his arrest. The officers' acquittal triggered widespread riots in Los Angeles, highlighting deep-seated issues of police brutality and racial injustice. Not surprisingly, the album's aggressive soundscape and lyrics are often said to reflect the African American community's feelings at the time. Furthermore, *The Predator* was a commercial success, reaching #1 on both the R&B and rap charts, selling over three million copies and remaining Ice Cube's most successful album to date.

In the sleeve notes to the album, Ice Cube thanks several prominent Black leaders throughout history: Marcus Garvey, Elijah Muhammed and Malcolm X, together with other 'brothers that were labelled enemies of the state'. It is clear that Ice Cube also considered himself to be an outspoken enemy of the state, using Islamic semiotic resources as multimodal weapons in his music.

[53] Ice Cube, *The Predator*, 'When Will They Shoot?', CD album (Priority Records © 1992).

[54] The section sampled from the Oxford address goes as follows: 'Speaking as a Black man from America, which is a racist society, no matter how much you hear it talk about democracy, it's as racist as South Africa or as racist as Portugal, or as racist as any other racialist society on this earth. The only difference between it and South Africa: South Africa preaches separation and practices separation; America preaches integration and practices segregation. This is the only difference. They don't practice what they preach, whereas South Africa preaches and practices the same thing. I have more respect for a man who lets me know where he stands, even if he's wrong, than the one who comes up like an angel and is nothing but a devil'. The whole address can be found in Ambar 2014.

'I'm Like the Fly Malcolm X, Buy Any Jeans Necessary' (1993–Present)

Much of the media reporting on hip-hop culture in the 1990s was dominated by the rivalry between East Coast and West Coast hip-hop, embodied in West Coast rapper Tupac Shakur and his Los Angeles record label Death Row Records, and East Coast rapper The Notorious B. I. G. and his New York label Bad Boy Records. The feud ultimately ended with the murders of both rappers.

Another notable aspect of hip-hop in the 1990s was the increased commodification of hip-hop culture. Author and scholar Mark Anthony Neal has related:

> In less than a decade, hip-hop culture had been transformed from a subculture primarily influenced by the responses of black urban youth to postindustrialization into a billion-dollar industry in which such responses were exploited by corporate capitalist and the petit bourgeois desires of the black middle class.[55]

While one would be hard-pressed to deny that there is something inherently political embedded in hip-hop culture, many critics and observers have argued that hip-hop lost at least some of its political edge in favour of commercialism in the first years of the 1990s. The emergence of so-called gangsta rap has also been seen as a rejection of the more political (that is, Black nationalistic and Afrocentric) New York-based hip-hop of the late 1980s and early 1990s. But it would be more accurate to speak in terms of a diversification of hip-hop culture, and hip-hop's development from a marginalised subculture into a multibillion-dollar industry was certainly not without friction. The increased commodification of hip-hop culture did not, however, put an end to the use of Malcolm X and Islamic semiotic resources within the culture.

Indeed, several artists from different Islamic interpretative traditions maintained the Islamic legacy within hip-hop culture. In 1993, a number of commercially successful albums were released, which solidified hip-hop music as an arena for the spread of ideas from different interpretive traditions: for example, Wu-Tang Clan's debut album *Enter the Wu-Tang* (*36 Chambers*) and Brand Nubian's sophomore album *In God We Trust* both promoted

[55] Neal 1999: 150.

Islamic semiotics from the teachings of NGE. The first single from Brand Nubian's album is entitled 'Allah U Akbar'. In the song, Brand Nubian samples the call to prayer (*adhan*). The song also includes several references to NGE's Supreme Mathematics. In the video, the group is seen performing in the classroom of the Allah School in Mecca, Harlem, the world headquarters of NGE. Several songs in the album directly mention the teachings and beliefs of NGE, among which one can find 'Ain't No Mystery', 'Meaning of the 5%', 'Allah and Justice' and 'The Godz'.

The Wu-Tang Clan became one of the driving forces behind hip-hop in the 1990s. The group that originally included nine members has to date released seven studio albums, along with at least nineteen compilation albums as a group, and most of the members have launched successful solo careers. To this must be added several affiliated artists, a successful clothing company and various record labels. The group's unofficial leader is RZA, the chief architect of the unique Wu-Tang Clan soundscape, as well as the mastermind of the group's distinctive philosophical blend of NGE teachings, different strands of Eastern philosophy, Kung Fu movie themes and other elements of popular culture. RZA has developed his viewpoints in two books: *The Wu-Tang Manual* (2004) and *The Tao of Wu* (2009). The books have not discussed Malcolm X and his legacy, although sometimes he has been mentioned in passing. In the books, RZA has seemed to view Malcolm X as a role model, writing: 'Years ago, I was like a lot of brothers who grew up militant in the hood; if I had to choose between Martin Luther King and Malcolm X, I'd always go with Malcolm'.[56] RZA has also pointed to the classic conversion narrative discussed in Chapter 5 and to Malcolm X's transformation from a thug to a successful, pious man. He has written:

> History is full of bad men who redeem themselves to become great. Malcolm X – he came up chasing white women and sniffing cocaine, but found Allah and changed. But what about people who have knowledge and go back to doing wrong? For that you usually have to look at our superheroes.[57]

Over the years, several Wu-Tang Clan members have made references to Malcolm X. For example, on 'Wu-Revolution' (featuring Papa Wu and Uncle

[56] RZA and Norris 2009: 189.

[57] Ibid. p. 157.

Pete), the opening track of Wu-Tang Clan's second studio double disc album *Wu-Tang Forever* (1994), the lyrics give a lengthy introduction to the teachings of NGE, as presented by Papa Wu in a call-and-response sermon style. On the track, Uncle Pete is heard chanting 'Malcolm X! Malcolm X! Malcolm X!' as a response to Papa Wu's sermon.

Ghostface Killah, an original member of the Clan, has named a song after Malcolm X. The song is simply entitled 'Malcolm' and features on his acclaimed solo album *Supreme Clientele* (2000). Ghostface Killah wrote the song before a four-month-long incarceration. The track begins and ends with a sample from Malcolm X's 'After the Bombing' speech, delivered on Valentine's Day, 1965. The sample section of the speech contains the following words:

> But they try and project the image to the public that this is being done by thieves, and thieves alone. And they ignore the fact that no, it is not thievery alone. It's a corrupt, vicious, hypocritical system that has castrated the Black man; and the only way the Black man can get back at it is to strike it in the only way he knows how.[58]

In the song, Ghostface Killah enters the mind of a troubled young African American man who is living a crime- and drug-ridden life. Killah starts the song by comparing himself to Malcolm X: 'I'm like Malcolm out the window with the joint / Hooded up blood in my eye'.[59] In the hook, Ghostface Killah encourages the antagonist of the song to walk the same path as Malcolm – in other words, to straighten up and leave his criminal life.

Other Wu-Tang Clan members and affiliates – RZA, Cappadonna, Killah Priest, U-God and Sunz of Man – have paid homage to Malcolm X in various ways on their records. The lesser-known Wu-Tang-affiliated Rhyme Recka named his debut album *The Autobiography of Rapper X* (2008) in order to pay tribute to Malcolm X and his autobiography. The album's intro samples a

[58] Breitman 1989: 200. The speech was held after Malcolm X's home in East Elmurst, Queens, was attacked with Molotov Cocktails. Malcolm X and his family were sleeping in the house when this attack happened. The house was seriously damaged, but Malcolm X and his family managed to escape unharmed.

[59] Ghostface Killah, *Supreme Clientele*, 'Malcolm', CD album (Epic, Razor Sharp Records © 2000).

large portion of Malcolm X's speech to the Oxford Union.[60] The song 'T. A. R. X.' (abbreviation for The Autobiography of Rapper X) contains a collage of snippets of Malcolm X's voice from various speeches and interviews.

Other rappers carried on the tradition of invoking Malcolm X in their lyrics. For example, Styles P, critiquing what he perceives as the superficial and materialistic features of hip-hop culture in his song 'Sensei Style', mentions Malcolm X: 'Learn the game and everything that you're getting from it / Might be the next Malcolm X in a stripper's stomach / Or Martin though [. . .] or Huey though / But niggas only care about Gucci and wearing Louis clothes'.[61] According to Styles P, hip-hop artists are more interested in designer labels such as Gucci and Louis Vuitton than learning about African American political icons such as Malcolm X and Huey P. Newton (the co-founder of the Black Panther Party).

Another rapper who has invoked Malcolm X several times in his lyrics is Killer Mike. His song 'Belly of the Beast' offers a powerful critique of the prison-industrial complex:

> I carved that guard, more years I'm facin'
> Now the inmates call a young nigga Satan
> Something like Malcolm before he joined the Nation
> Back and forth in solitary, I'm pacin'
> Five in the morning, I hear the Muslims praying
> Six in the morning, the guards congregating.[62]

Killer Mike invokes Malcolm X's experiences as described in his autobiography. In prison, before joining NOI, Malcolm was called 'Satan' by the other inmates. Because he cursed God and the Bible so much, he would often end up in solitary confinement.

[60] The section sampled is as follows: 'And in my opinion, the young generation of whites, blacks, browns, whatever else there is, you're living at a time of extremism, a time of revolution, a time when there's got to be a change. People in power have misused it, and now there has to be a change and a better world has to be built, and the only way it's going to be built – is with extreme methods. And I, for one, will join in with anyone – I don't care what color you are – as long as you want to change this miserable condition that exists on this earth'. Ambar 2014: 180.

[61] Styles P, *Master of Ceremonies*, 'Sensei Style' (D-Block, E1 Music © 2011).

[62] Killer Mike, *Sunday Morning Massacres*, 'Belly of the Beast', MP3, 2014, Not On Label (Killer Mike self-released).

Another example from Killer Mike's catalogue is the song 'Pressure' (featuring Ice Cube) from the album *I Pledge Allegiance to the Grind II* (2008), where Killer Mike samples Malcolm X's voice from two different occasions.[63] In the song, Killer Mike and Ice Cube relate the conditions for African Americans post-9/11 to the transatlantic slave trade. The duo rallies against police brutality and corrupt political leadership. According to Killer Mike, it does not matter how successful you are, or how much money you make, as an African American you will always be considered a lesser human being, and the ultimate price for freedom is death: 'Liberation costs more than a damn dollar / It costs what Christ gave / King gave / X gave / A billion dollars don't make you an ex-slave'.[64]

Other rappers have had a more politically quiescent attitude to Malcolm X. Kanye West invokes Malcolm X when it comes to fashion in the song 'Good Morning': 'I'm like the fly Malcolm X, buy any jeans necessary / Detroit Red cleaned up' is a nod to Malcolm X's catchphrase 'by any means necessary' and to his well-known fashion sense.[65] Another example of such a commercialised use is when Drake cleverly invokes Malcolm X in the song 'Forever' – 'Labels want my name beside an X like Malcolm' – and in the song 'Uptown' – 'I drive two black cars / I named 'em Malcolm X and Martin Luther'.[66]

[63] The two sections sampled are: 'Who are you? You don't know? Don't tell me 'Negro' that's nothing. What were you before the white man named you 'Negro'? What was your name? It couldn't have been 'Smith' or 'Jones' or 'Bush' or 'Powell' that wasn't your name. They don't have those kinds of names where you and I come from. No, what was your name? And why don't you know what your name was then? Where was your history? How did a man wipe out your history? How did the man, what did the man do to make you as dumb, as you are right now?' And: 'No negro leaders have fought for civil rights, they have begged for civil rights. They have begged the white man for civil rights, they have begged the white man for freedom, and any time you beg another man to set you free, you'll never be free. Freedom is something that you have to do for yourselves. And until the American Negro lets the white man know that we are really ready and willing to pay the price that is necessary for freedom, our people will always be walking around here second-class citizens or what you call twentieth century slaves. [What price are you talking about sir?] The price of freedom is death'.

[64] Killer Mike, *I Pledge Allegiance to the Grind II*, 'Pressure' (featuring Ice Cube) (Grind Time Official and SMC Recordings © 2008).

[65] Kanye West, *Graduation*, 'Good Morning', CD album (Roc-A-Fella, Def Jam © 2007).

[66] Drake (featuring Kanye West, Lil Wayne and Eminem), 'Forever', MP3 (Zone 4/Interscope/Shady/Aftermath © 2009), and Drake, *So Far Gone (Mixtape)*, 'Uptown', MP3 (October's Very Own © 2008).

In addition to these uses, artists have sought to commemorate the legacy of Malcolm X in the form of visual expressions. New York rapper Nas famously sports a tattoo of the iconic photo of Malcolm X with his finger pointed to his temple on the side of his stomach. Similarly, the Washington DC rapper Wale appeared on the cover of the 2013 summer edition of the tattoo magazine *Urban Ink*, styled in the same way as Malcolm X was in the window photo previously discussed, showing off the same photo tattooed on his left arm.[67] The headline of the article reads: 'Revolution is ink!'

The rap phenomenon Young Jeezy used the same photo of Malcolm X and his words from a speech as inspiration for his mixtape *Trap or Die 2: By Any Means Necessary* (2010). The group The Roots, meanwhile, used a 1944 mug shot of Malcolm X (then Malcolm Little) for their album *The Tipping Point* (2004). On the fiftieth anniversary of Malcolm X's death in 2015, hip-hop magazine *The Source* commemorated him with a special edition cover. Under the headline 'X Legacy: Wake up, Clean Up, Stand Up', rappers from Chuck D and Raekwon to Ludacris and Kendrick Lamar expressed how Malcolm X had influenced their art and music. The legacy of Malcolm X today extends beyond the US cultural landscape. Malcolm X has widely been viewed as the most powerful representative of Islam in the US, and as such his legacy has reached a diverse set of Islamic organisations in Africa and the Middle East. These organisations and movements represent a myriad of interpretive traditions, among which one may find Sufis in Senegal and Wahhabi Muslims in Saudi Arabia.[68]

Yasiin Bey (formerly known as Mos Def) has explained the significance of Malcolm X in an interview with Sohail Daulatzai, in connection to the latter's exhibit 'Return of the Mecca: The Art of Islam and Hip-Hop':

> Speaking out against the injustices that exist in the world and dealing with our struggle in America not as an isolated – domestic – issue, but as an international problem. It's really inspiring but it's also really intimidating for a lot of people, you know. If you are an individual that's not afraid of anything then people tend to be afraid or threatened by you. That attitude is expressed in hip-hop. So it is very dynamic for anyone who has ever been poor, hungry or hunted.[69]

[67] Inside the magazine, Wale is seen posing in a rendition of the window photo.

[68] Marable 2011: 486.

[69] Yasiin Bey (aka Mos Def) on Malcolm X, for 'Return of the Mecca: The Art of Islam and Hip-Hop', https://www.youtube.com/watch?v=jln12UJ8H8U (accessed 14 September 2023).

Yasiin Bey's attitude is manifested in many songs from his catalogue. One of the more interesting examples is the opening song 'Supermagic' on the album *Ecstatic* (2009). The song starts with Yassiin Bey uttering the *Shahada* (the Islamic creed) in Arabic, followed by a lengthy Malcolm X sample from the dramatic closing minutes of his address to the Oxford Union:

> You're living at a time of extremism, a time of revolution, a time when there's got to be a change. People in power have misused it, and now there has to be a change and a better world has to be built, and the only way it's going to be built – is with extreme methods. And I, for one, will join in with anyone – I don't care what color you are – as long as you want to change this miserable condition that exists on this earth.[70]

Malcolm X's Oxford Union address, delivered at the famous debating society at Oxford University on 3 December 1964, has been described as 'the lost jewel of the civil rights movement'.[71] Saladin Ambar, author of the book *Malcolm X at Oxford Union* (2014), has written about the speech in the following way:

> Malcolm at Oxford represented the most comprehensive, best articulated, and clearest sense of his personal and political vision on the future of race relations – not only as a domestic concern, but also a global one. [. . .] Oxford suggests a pivotal moment in human history, as the majority of the world's population begins to unyoke itself from colonial or imperial rule while simultaneously struggling with, or anticipating, the challenges of racially pluralistic societies developing along egalitarian lines. The demands of the future, rather than a mere articulation of present or past problems, brought the very best out of Malcolm X – and it happened in Oxford.[72]

In many ways, 'Supermagic' sets music to Malcolm X's internationalist vison. The song is basically a burst of freestyle energy, where Bey showcases his skills as a lyricist. The phrase 'Super magic black origin freshly out of dopeness' is repeated throughout the song. The words are a homophone-twist of the tongue-twisting phrase 'Supercalifragilisticexpialidocious' from the 1964

[70] Ambar 2014: 180.

[71] Ibid. p. 33.

[72] Ibid.

Disney movie *Mary Poppins*. It is not Yasiin Bey's lyrics that communicate an international outlook: the soundscape conveys that message. Bey does not, like Public Enemy, build the song around a James Brown drum break. Instead, 'Supermagic' is built around guitar riffs from the song 'İnce İnce Bir Kar Yağar' by the Turkish protest singer Selda Bağcan – which in turn is a rendition of composer and poet Aşık Mahzuni Serif's (1940–2002) song by the same name. The funky 'oriental' guitar loop together with portions of the highly politically charged Turkish lyrics that highlight the conditions of poor people in eastern Turkey, combined with Malcolm X's warning, carries the song across nations and establishes a sonic bond between disenfranchised groups around the world. Yasiin Bey takes the words of Selda out of the local Turkish context and inserts them on a global scale. ('Yandık yandık, bize okul, bize yol, bize hayat, etme ağam, n'olur, n'olur, n'olur, n'olur' [We're doomed, education to us, roads to us, life to us / Come now, sir, please, please, please, please]).

Another illustration of the internationalisation of the semiotic resources extracted from Malcolm X's life is the cooperation between the Egyptian hip-hop trio Arabian Knightz and the Brooklyn-based rapper General Steele (from the duo Smif-N-Wessun). In April 2011, in the midst of the uprisings of the Arab Spring, they recorded the song 'I am Malcolm X' (2011).[73] The lyrics of the song link the Arab uprisings to the Civil Rights Movement in the US. The opening of the first verse accentuates the legacy of Malcolm X as the Sunni Muslim El-Hajj Malik El-Shabazz. The lyrics call for a new civil rights movement in Egypt (known as *Umm Al-Dunya*, the Mother of Civilisation), premised on an 'Islamic truth': 'Malik was a king that had a dream like Martin Luther / Built an Islamic truth for constitution revolution / our generation needs a new one / the mother of the civilization needs Civil Rights

[73] The title of the song is a reference to the ending scenes of Spike Lee's movie *Malcolm X* (1992). The film ends with a scene of an African American teacher in an American classroom. Behind her on the blackboard are the words 'MALCOLM X DAY'. She tells the class that it is Malcolm X's birthday: 'Malcolm X is you, all of you, and you are Malcolm X', she says. Some of the students in the classroom rise, and one after another shout: 'I am Malcolm X!' The scene cuts to a classroom in Soweto in South Africa where students also stand up and shout: 'I am Malcolm X!' The movie climaxes with the recently released anti-apartheid activist, the late Nelson Mandela, reciting one of Malcolm X's speeches. The message, both of the song and of the movie scene, is clear: Malcolm X's struggle was not confined to American soil but constituted a global struggle to free all oppressed people in the world.

Movement'.[74] The video clip accompanying the song underlines this message and illustrates it with powerful video footage showing the crossing of Edmund Pettus Bridge, when Alabama state troopers attacked civil rights demonstrators outside the town of Selma in 1965. These images are crosscut with more recent footage of demonstrators being brutally attacked by police on Cairo's Tahrir Square in 2011.[75]

Conclusion: The Many Faces of Malcolm X

With this semiotic inventory in place, I will now address the pattern that has emerged in mapping the use of Malcolm X-related semiotic resources in US hip-hop. I have found that the typical ways of invoking Malcolm X and his legacy are name-dropping, image-dropping and sound-dropping. More extensive uses mainly involve key quotes from Malcolm X or lengthy sound bites of classic speeches. The use of certain iconic photos is comparable to key quotes, as these are clearly meant to trigger established associations.

The references during what I have identified as the first period of hip-hop may be described as semiotic resources used in order to signal an understanding of and engagement with African American political thought, in which Islam plays an important role. As shown in Chapter 4, the earliest hip-hop pioneers incorporated semiotic resources perceived as Islamic. By doing so, they sustained a practice from previous artists, as described in Chapter 3. With the emergence of hip-hop culture, and the above-mentioned pioneers, the use of semiotic elements from the cognitive universe of Islam was extended into the post-civil rights era, but it was not until the end of the 1980s that Islamic semiotic resources became widely visible and mobilised by hip-hop artists through aural, visual and textual articulations. Interwoven with these multimodal Islamic semiotic resources were frequent references to Malcolm X and his legacy. These can also be described as Islamic semiotic resources, since they can be linked to an Islamic past, present and future.

[74] Arabian Knightz: 'I AM MALCOLM X (featuring General Steele)', https://www.youtube.com/watch?v=qGbPccT5ChY (accessed 14 September 2023).

[75] Linking Malcolm X and his legacy to local uprisings and struggles is not unique to Arabian Knightz. A similar strategy was deployed by the Basque separatist hip-hop group Negu Gorriak in the early 1990s. The group's use of Malcolm X and his legacy in aural and visual modes is described in Urla 2001.

Manning Marable, the author of the comprehensive biography *Malcolm X: A Life of Reinvention* (2011), has called Malcolm X 'the most remarkable historical figure produced by black America in the 20th century'.[76] Malcolm X is certainly a visible figure in American popular culture, and the semiotics of Malcolm X have, in various ways, triggered the imagination of US hip-hop artists since the early days of the genre. It is clear that invoking Malcolm X – whether on a T-shirt, or by quoting one of his speeches – for many denotes an engagement in African American political culture.[77] The Malcolmania of the early 1990s and the increased use of references to Malcolm X and his legacy among hip-hop artists played an important role in establishing Malcolm X as an international American Muslim revolutionary icon on par with Nelson Mandela, Ghandi or Che Guevara. Self-evidently, this did not exclude other uses of Malcolm X and his legacy. In some cases, semiotic resources signalling Malcolm X were only deployed because they were perceived as cool. Kayne West and Drake exemplify such usage.

Malcolm X's unique life story provides potential for several different kinds of meaning-making. His life can, as the title of Marable's book suggests, be illustrated by his ability to re-invent himself.[78] These re-inventions are manifested in the many personas adopted by Malcolm X: the most famous being Detroit Red, Malcolm X and El-Hajj Malik El-Shabazz. To these, one can add lesser-known personas such as Jack Carlton, the name Malcolm X used when he performed as dancer and musician at nightclubs in Harlem during

[76] Manning Marable interviewed by Amy Goodman in *Democracy Now!*, 'The Undiscovered Malcolm X: Stunning New Info on the Assassination, His Plans to Unite the Civil Rights and Black Nationalist Movements & the 3 "Missing" Chapters from His Autobiography', http://www.democracynow.org/2005/2/21/the_undiscovered_malcolm_x_stunning_new (accessed 14 September 2023).

[77] Joe Wood has equated invoking Malcolm X to a 'Black Mask': when someone wears or invokes Malcolm 'he wants to tell Blackfolk he really is Black, he bears Malcolm'. Wood has exemplified this with New York Mayor David Dinkins August 1991 visit to Crown Heights, Brooklyn, in an effort to calm African American rioters after a Hasidic rabbi had killed Gavin Cato, a seven-year-old boy of Caribbean descent, in a car accident. Dinkins did not dress in the usual political suit and tie, but rather a track-suit jacket, T-shirt and a Malcolm X baseball cap. See Wood 1992: 9.

[78] For a rich biographical account of Malcolm X's life, see Marable 2011.

the 1940s; and Prisoner 22843, the number Malcolm received during his stint in Charlestown State Prison.

Each of these personas represents significant phases in Malcolm X's life. Each phase has been emphasised or de-emphasised by artists, activists and scholars in order to conjure a Malcolm X tailored after a pre-figured narrative expressive of the desires of these meaning-makers.[79] Sometimes these different interpretations of Malcolm X's life and legacy cause heated debates. This is illustrated by the words of Spike Lee, describing the confrontations that he faced when making his movie about the life of Malcolm X:

> I know the challenge in front of me. Malcolm X was so many things to so many people, and then there are the people who think they know all about him, but they don't know anything that's true. And I also know for a fact that around ten million motherfuckers are going to come out of the walls saying that they were down with Malcolm, and that's bullshit. Malcolm X causes reactions, so there is no way the film won't do the same thing.[80]

Malcolm X means many different things to innumerable people: just one of these is his potential for being perceived as an Islamic icon, and as such, a semiotic resource. The 'Islamic' aspects of Malcolm X do not exclude other popular interpretations of his life and legacy; for example, the interpretation of Malcolm X as someone who did not compromise about important principles, someone who came from hardship and 'nothing' yet built something for himself and spoke truth to power.[81] In his book *Making Malcolm: The Myth and Meaning of Malcolm X* (1995), Michael Eric Dyson has explored some aspects of these interpretations. According to Dyson, there has been a tendency to 'obscure and reduce the complex nature of his achievements and failures' and a bent for 'idolising or demonising' Malcolm's life and deeds.

In my analysis, Malcolm X's personal journey is a moral exemplar, implicit and explicit, for someone who undergoes a transformation from a lost soul to a

[79] See Dyson 1995.

[80] Lee et al. 1993: 10–11.

[81] Hip-hop musicians have also testified that there was something in Malcolm X's aural expression that spoke to them. Many artists seemed to have been inspired by his 'cadence and flow'. See, for example, https://www.youtube.com/watch?v=akksBpeLFd0 (accessed 14 September 2023).

righteous, proud and self-respecting Muslim. To become the latter, one needs to transform, and Islam is signalled to be the path towards that transformation. Transformation, or conversion, narratives are important to all missionary religions; in this case, the transformation narrative of Malcolm X is used by NOI, The Five Percenters and, since Malcolm X became a global household name, by Sunni Muslims worldwide. Furthermore, talking truth power is not only politically brave, but also constructed as an Islamic virtue in many Islamic interpretive traditions, and very much so by both NOI and the Five Percenters. Thus, by dropping the names, images and sounds of Malcolm X and his legacy, artists not only associate themselves with resistance against racial discrimination, but they also associate themselves with Islam. I believe that it is not implausible, even when artists perhaps namecheck Malcolm X to be cool, that Malcolm X still functions as a semiotic resource that carries Islamic connotations. This connection between Malcolm X and Islam has established itself over time through repeated associations made by influential artists and by the film and biography about Malcolm X.

There has been a tendency to separate 'politics' from 'religion' in the literature on African American Islam. Curtis has pointed out when discussing Eric Lincoln's pioneering work on NOI:

> [R]eligion and politics as analytical categories ultimately obscured more than they revealed since he [Eric Lincoln] underemphasized the legitimately religious aspects of the movement's nationalistic activity. In reality, of course, the line between religion and politics was and is often more blurry than he indicated. Indeed, politics and religion were wedded in fascinating and problematical ways within the movement.[82]

The same can be said about Malcolm X. For many individuals, Muslim as well as non-Muslim, Malcolm X's importance goes far beyond that of racial politics in the US. Malcolm X has come to represent an alternative political Islam not rooted in the constructed divide between 'the West' and 'the East', but rather a collective symbol for a shared experience of marginalisation, may it be in the so-called 'West' or the so called 'East'. As the prolific author and scholar Hamid Dabashi has written:

[82] Curtis 2002: 2.

> The significance of Malcolm X is that he rises from the heart of the metropolitan disenfranchised poor in the USA and moves out to reach one of the most massively manufactured civilisational other of 'the West' in the Islamic world. [. . .] There is no other evolutionary figure who like Malcolm X so gracefully and courageously climbs over that dilapidated wall which mercenary Orientalists have constructed between the Western part of their own perturbed imagination and the rest of the world.[83]

The legacy of Malcolm X within hip-hop culture goes beyond national borders, religious beliefs and political goals. Muslims as well as non-Muslims around the globe have utilised his words and pictures.

Malcolm X and his legacy as Islamic semiotic resources have the potential to connect him both to his African American Islamic heritage as a member of NOI and as a universal Islamic semiotic resource. As a universal symbol, artists have highlighted Malcolm X's final years following his *hajj* to Mecca in 1964. In doing so, hip-hop artists have helped to turn Malcolm X into one of the cornerstones of what the author Alex Lubin has called the Afro-Arab Political Imaginary.[84] This can also be seen as a manifestation of what Manning Marable has termed the 'perhaps most important' re-invention of Malcolm X: his function as a 'bridge between the American people and more than one billion Muslims throughout the world'.[85]

The cultural resonance of Malcolm X within hip-hop is key in order to understand the worldview of many young Muslims around the globe. Nowhere is this more applicable than in the contemporary Muslim struggle for civil rights, which has spread through several heterogeneous organisations, initiatives and movements around the world, where Islam has become a path to social, political and religious liberation. Yet, as Graeme Abernethy, the author of *The Iconography of Malcolm X* (2013) has reminded us: 'Malcolm's Islamic faith has always been among the aspects of his life least embraced and understood'.[86] Malcolm X's unique and complex story has inspired – and will most likely continue to find new ways to inspire – hip-hop artists in their artistic expressions.

[83] Dabashi 2008: 23.

[84] Lubin 2014.

[85] Marable 2011: 486.

[86] Abernethy 2013b: 227.

7

AMERICA UNDER ATTACK! DEPICTING 9/11 IN HIP-HOP

The atrocities of 11 September 2001, when nineteen hijackers from the Al-Qaeda terrorist network conducted four coordinated attacks that amounted to the deadliest attack on US soil since the Civil War, have emphatically had a lasting influence on the creators of popular culture.[1] This chapter examines how 9/11 and its legacy have been creatively interpreted by US hip-hop artists in the post-9/11 era.[2] Using aural, visual and textual examples, I will demonstrate how both Muslims and non-Muslims have made different use of Islamic semiotic resources when reacting to 9/11. Furthermore, I will stress semiotic inventiveness in connection to 9/11, where new semiotic resources with the potential to be perceived as Islamic have been introduced. This seeks to show that the events of 9/11 serve as semiotic resources stimulating cultural production relating to Muslims, Islamic interpretive traditions and social justice. I will also demonstrate shifts in the nature of these articulations over time,

[1] Some examples from the field of post-9/11 studies that deal with this ever-growing material include Quay and Damico 2010; Bragard, Dony and Rosenberg 2011; DeGenaro 2012; Melnick 2011; Miller 2014.

[2] To my knowledge, few articles have dealt exclusively with hip-hop responses to 9/11 and its aftermath. One well-informed and important text published online is '9/11 and its Aftermath in Hip-Hop Culture: The Hip-Hop Critique of 9/11 and the Bush Administration' (2013) by Jimmy Jenkins. However, several of the works mentioned in the previous footnote touch on hip-hop music.

revealing how 9/11 and the narratives of the 'War on Terror' have become a necessary framework for understanding the use of Islamic semiotic resources within US hip-hop.

For the purposes of clarity and analytical structure, I have grouped these articulations into three conceptual clusters. The first revolves around patriotic articulations in the immediate aftermath of 9/11. The most famous patriotic musical responses originated from other musical genres, most prominently country music, but hip-hop also produced jingoistic responses to 9/11 in the direct aftermath, and in doing so made use of Islamic semiotics. However, it did not take long for artists to reinterpret 9/11 into a different framework; these articulations are grouped into the second and third clusters. The second cluster revolves around the production of counter-knowledge, here defined as practices that aim to reframe social problems while maintaining entertainment value.[3] Islamic semiotic resources in this cluster are utilised in relation to popular conspiracy theories: for example, the 9/11 truth movement (loosely associated groups of conspiracy theorists), and former sports broadcaster David Icke's conspiratorial universe – which includes shape-shifting reptilians and secret societies such as the Illuminati. The third cluster revolves around creating provocations, a practice that has firm historical roots within hip-hop culture. Needless to say, these clusters are fluid in nature as they intersect and overlap.

In contrast to Chapters 4 and 5, which approached the use of Islamic semiotic resources in hip-hop through a specific song and role model, respectively, this chapter looks at responses to an event. Chapter 4 has demonstrated how an original song with a rather straightforward message can end up in a web of associations produced by a more or less arbitrary use of Islamic semiotic elements and Orientalist representations; Chapter 5 has explicated how African American political awareness and Islamic awareness quite often become indistinguishable. This chapter, however, will engage a more haphazard use of semiotic resources related to different Islamic semiotic regimes.

The unexpected events of the 9/11 terror attacks spawned unusual responses among a wide variety of artists who, to varying degrees, mobilised Islamic resources. However, the responses were eventually framed within a more established semiotic regime within hip-hop, meaning that the semiotic

[3] The definition of the term 'counterknowledge' is borrowed from Gosa 2011.

resources thrown around in the first wave of patriotic reactions were re-coded and appropriated by artists wanting to provoke and challenge the US establishment and state. Thus, 9/11 gave rise to new connotations and ways of using semiotic resources.

Where Were You (When the World Stopped Turning)?

For the art historian W. J. T. Mitchell, 9/11 not only constituted the inaugural event of a new era, with all signs pointing towards the invasions of Afghanistan and Iraq, but it also marked the beginning of another type of war – 'the war of images'. Mitchell has argued that the use of imagery has always been crucial in war and politics, but the difference in the aftermath of 9/11 was the magnitude of images that flooded the media. He has described this development in virological terms:

> Images have always possessed a certain infectious, viral character, a vitality that makes them difficult to contain or quarantine. If images are like viruses or bacteria, this has been a period of breakout, a global plague of images. And like any infectious disease, it has bred a host of anti-bodies in the form of counter images.[4]

These 'viral' images are well-known to contemporary audiences: from pictures of President George W. Bush delivering his 'Bullhorn' speech, over emergency rescue workers in the rubble of Ground Zero, to his opening pitch at Yankee Stadium less than two months after the attacks (he wore a New York City Fire Department fleece and delivered a perfect strike from the mound, while the crowd held up homemade signs draped in red, white and blue, with patriotic slogans such as 'Home of the Brave', 'USA Fears Nobody, Play Ball' and 'United We Stand'). Many people have also probably heard, to expand on Mitchell by adding sounds to images, the chilling phone calls from inside the planes, or the clamour of rescue workers chanting 'USA! USA! USA! USA!' during the president's 'Bullhorn' speech.

A good number of people are also now aware of the 'antibodies', the counter-images that were formed in response to the nationalist fire stoked by the

[4] Mitchell 2010: 2.

9/11 attacks. The iconography of patriotism – often fused with the idealisation of perceived nationalist ideals such as 'grit', 'the American spirit' and 'work ethic' – informed counter-images depicted on bumper stickers, T-shirts and magazine covers.[5] Yet these critical voices failed to make themselves heard, or they were present in public spaces only in their absence. The fact that Clear Channel Communications, the biggest radio station owner in the US, distributed a list of 160 'potentially inappropriate songs' to over 1,200 radio stations across the US did not help to ease the feverishly patriotic atmosphere.

The list included songs such as 'Rock the Casbah' (1982) by The Clash, and The Bangles' 'Walk Like an Egyptian' (1986). Surprisingly few hip-hop songs made the list, but the Beastie Boys are present with both 'Sabotage' and 'Sure Shot' from their album *Ill Communication* (1994).[6] The alternative rock band Rage Against the Machine was the only band to see all of its songs branded as 'potentially inappropriate'.[7] When investigating the history of depicting disasters in US folk songs, the ethnomusicologist James Revell Carr has described the capacity for certain songs about war and disaster to become 'aural monuments': 'They are enduring structures of sound that enshrine the memories of the deceased and the intense emotions of the survivors. Monument building is essential to the healing of psychic wounds following major social dramas'.[8] Carr has further argued that, because 9/11 straddled religion, war and patriotism, the artistic responses focused on the socio-political implications of the attacks rather than detailed descriptions of the tragedy.

Aural monuments, according to Carr, are characterised by their social importance rather than their form or genre. One such aural monument was a song produced in reaction to 9/11, titled 'Where Were You (When the World Stopped Turning)' (2002) by country music singer Alan Jackson. Jackson's finely honed 'Joe-Sixpack-patriotism' resonated beyond his country fanbase

[5] DeGenaro 2012: 260.

[6] Beastie Boys, *Ill Communication*, CD album (Capitol and Grand © 1994).

[7] 'The 164 Songs That Were Banned from American Radio after 9/11', https://www.kerrang.com/here-are-the-164-songs-that-were-banned-from-american-radio-after-9-11 (accessed 6 May 2024).

[8] Carr 2004: n. p.

and had crossover appeal, topping the country, pop and Christian country music charts. The chorus of the song reads as follows:

> I'm just a singer of simple songs
> I'm not a real political man
> I watch CNN but I'm not sure I can tell
> You the difference in Iraq and Iran
> But I know Jesus and I talk to God
> And I remember this from when I was young
> Faith, hope and love are some good things He gave us
> And the greatest is love
> Where were you when the world stopped turning on that September day?[9]

Different in tone from Jackson's melancholic ballad is another country music artist's reaction to 9/11: the song 'Courtesy of The Red, White and Blue (The Angry American)' (2002) performed by Toby Keith. In the video, Keith, surrounded by American flags and playing on a guitar painted with the Star-Spangled Banner, demands that the perpetrator who delivered the 'mighty sucker punch' should be punished in 'the American way':

> Justice will be served
> And the battle will rage
> This big dog will fight
> When you rattle his cage
> And you'll be sorry that you messed with
> The U.S. of A.
> 'Cause we'll put a boot in your ass
> It's the American way.[10]

References to Christianity, most prominently to 'Jesus' and 'God', are common in country songs, and they also appear in the responses to 9/11, one example being Alan Jackson's above-mentioned song. Less common are direct references to Islam, but there are exceptions. Following 9/11, Toby Keith also

9 Alan Jackson, *Drive*, 'Where Were You (When the World Stopped Turning)', CD album (Arista Nashville © 2002).

10 Toby Keith, *Unleashed*, 'Courtesy of the Red, White and Blue (The Angry American)', CD album (Dreamworks Nashville © 2002).

wrote 'The Taliban Song' (2003), a live version of which was included on the album *Shock'n Y'all* (2003). The title of the album is a reference to the Bush administration's 'Shock and Awe' tactics utilised during Operation Iraqi Freedom, which aimed to subdue the enemy's will to fight through displays of overwhelming military might. In the song, Keith places Islamic semiotic elements like 'Allah' and 'Taliban' in a derogatory context:

> Now we prayed to Allah with all of our might
> Until those big U.S. jets came flyin' in one night
> They dropped little bombs all over the holy land
> Man you should've seen 'em run, like rabbits they ran, the Taliban
> Ooo, ooo the Taliban, baby
> But you know someday soon we're both gonna saddle up and it'll be
> Ride camel, ride.[11]

Country music might be the genre that is mostly associated with patriotic responses to the 9/11 attacks, but other genres have also spawned aural responses. Republican presidential candidate Ted Cruz, in the lead-up to the presidential election of 2016, stated that he stopped listening to rock music in favour of country music: 'I actually intellectually find this very curious, but on 9/11, I didn't like how rock music responded', he stated. 'And country music, collectively, the way they responded, it resonated with me'.[12]

Artists such as Bruce Springsteen, singer-songwriter Tori Amos and the Irish rock band The Cranberries released songs in the wake of 9/11, songs that addressed the attacks, but rarely utilised Islamic semiotic resources. However, hip-hop artists, using Islamic semiotic resources, were able to articulate patriotic responses to 9/11 that stand like aural monuments over the events.

The First Responders: 'Mr Bush, Sit Down, I'm in Charge of the War!'

The prelude to hip-hop music after 9/11 is almost prophetic in nature. During the summer of 2001, the hip-hop duo Coup, recognised for their left-leaning lyrics, produced the cover art for their album *Party Music* (2001), which was

[11] Toby Keith, *Shock'n Y'all*, 'The Taliban Song', CD album (DreamWorks Nashville © 2003).

[12] http://www.politico.com/story/2015/03/ted-cruz-rock-music-116353.html#ixzz3fBqQipnF (accessed 15 September 2023).

Figure 7.1 The Coup's original album cover (LP) for *Party Music*, 2001.

scheduled for an early September release. It depicts the duo, Boots Riley and DJ Pam the Funktress, standing before the exploding Twin Towers of the World Trade Center. DJ Pam is holding two conductor sticks, while Riley holds what appears to be a detonator but actually is a guitar tuner. The distribution company Warner Brothers quickly pulled the album once news of its untimely cover art was leaked to US mainstream media following 9/11.[13]

The album was released with a different cover in November 2001, this time depicting a flaming gasoline Martini on a bar top.[14] In an article published on

[13] In his richly detailed book *The City's End: Two Centuries of Fantasies, Fears, and Premonitions of New York's Destruction* (2010), Max Page has investigated the fantasies of destruction created by American writers, musicians, computer game developers and image-makers. Apart from the *Party Music* album, Page has also mentioned *E. L. E.* (*Extinction Level Event*): *The Final World Front* (Flipmode, Elektra © 1998), the third studio album by American rapper Busta Rhymes. The album cover art, inspired by disaster movies, depicts a fireball explosion over Manhattan. See Page 2008.

[14] Davey D, 'Boots Speaks out about 9-11', http://www.daveyd.com/bootsonthewarpolitics.html (accessed 14 September 2023).

the CNN website, Boots Riley stated that the intention of the album cover art had been to use the World Trade Center as a symbol for capitalism, and that his thoughts were with the victims of the tragic event and their families.[15]

In hip-hop lore, 9/11 is remembered for another unfortunate coincidence. On the morning of that ill-fated Tuesday, the album *The Blueprint* hit record stores across the US.[16] This was the sixth studio album by rapper Jay-Z. Despite the 9/11-tragedy, the album sold more than 420,000 copies in its first week, which was a lot in a climate where digitally (both legally and illegally) distributed music had already gained ground. In a piece published by CNN as a part of its ten-year remembrance of 9/11, the prominent hip-hop scholar Tricia Rose has reflected on why Jay-Z's record sales did not plummet, while those of other artists who released albums in connection to 9/11 did:

> Young people not directly affected are always more removed from the onset of national tragedy [. . .]. While the much older fans of Mariah Carey or Bob Dylan would likely be too busy and worried about terrorist attacks to rush out and purchase a CD the week of 9/11, Jay-Z's teen and early 20s fans, already hyped up about this release long beforehand, remained focused on their idol.[17]

But the hip-hop generation was not as 'removed' from the national tragedy as Rose has argued in her article, and hip-hop artists have produced patriotic responses to the events of 9/11. During the summer leading up to 9/11, the North Carolina rapper Petey Pablo released 'Raise Up' as the lead single on his debut album *Diary of a Sinner: 1st Entry* (2001).[18] In the aftermath of 9/11, Pablo remixed the song and re-released it as 'Raise Up (USA Remix)' (2001): the promo CD single was draped in a printed American flag, and Pablo had altered the lyrics to fit the patriotic climate of the time. Instead of screaming 'Who am I? Petey Pab' motherfucker!!!' Pablo kicks off the first verse by stating: 'Say it loud, United States of America!!!' Instead of spinning their shirts,

[15] 'Album Cover of WTC Blast Pulled', http://edition.cnn.com/2001/SHOWBIZ/Music/09/13/wtc.cover/ (accessed 14 September 2023).

[16] Jay-Z, *The Blueprint*, CD album (Roc-A-Fella, Def Jam © 2001).

[17] 'Jay-Z's Music on 9/11', http://edition.cnn.com/2011/SHOWBIZ/Music/09/08/jayz.music.september.11/ (accessed 14 September 2023).

[18] Petey Pablo, *Diary of A Sinner: 1st Entry*, ' Raise Up', CD album (Jive © 2001).

as in the earlier version, in the second version Pablo encourages the listeners to wave their US flags: 'Take the flag, put it in the air, spin it like a helicopter'.[19]

Pablo also replaced the North Carolina neighbourhood shout-outs in the original version with shout-outs to the US Armed Forces, such as the Marines and the Air Force, as well as to the New York Police Department (NYPD). Pablo further salutes well-known US Armed Forces installations such as Fort Bragg and Parris Island, and in a show of support for the American troops he states: 'Even got me dressed in Army fatigues, how ya love that?' In the second verse, Pablo displays a blunt nationalism, which is usually not found in hip-hop lyrics:

> Wave the flag strong
> And could somebody tell Mr. bin Laden
> He got a lot of people lookin' for him
> My house, my home, my hood
> My brother, my sister, my cuz
> Land of the free, home of the brave, it's the land I love.[20]

In the outro of the song, the radio show host Steph Lova is heard thanking Petey Pablo for his efforts to deliver a message of unity to 'everybody from every corner of the earth, who lost a loved one' on 9/11. 'Raise Up (USA Remix)' stands as a powerful hip-hop statement released in direct response to 9/11. It clearly was both influenced by and contributed to the patriotic spirit of the time, speaking to a different audience than the country fans of artists such as Toby Keith. It is a potential aural monument for the hip-hop generation, remembering the tragic events of 9/11 and its aftermath, the War on Terror.

On 7 October 2001, Operation Enduring Freedom began with Tomahawk missile and air strikes against perceived terrorist targets inside Afghanistan. At

[19] The producer Timbaland produced both the original version and the remix of 'Raise Up'. The bouncy soundscape created by Timbaland has a clear 'oriental' or 'Middle Eastern' vibe to it. This can be attributed to the sample loop utilised throughout the song. The sample used is based on a section of 'Enta Omri' ['You Are My Life'] by the Egyptian composer Hossam Ramzy, in turn a rendition of world-renowned Egyptian singer Umm Kulthum's iconic 'Enta Omri'. The oriental violin loop might not seem an obvious choice for a red, white and blue flag-waving song in the aftermath of 9/11.

[20] Petey Pablo, ' Raise Up (USA Remix)', CD promo single (Jive © 2001).

the end of the same month, the rapper Canibus released his third studio album, *C! True Hollywood Stories* (2001). The album contained the track 'Draft Me!', a war-mongering outburst supporting the US-led invasion of Afghanistan. The song can best be described as a bigoted fantasy where Canibus expresses his desire to enlist in the US Armed Forces:

> Draft me! I wanna fight for my country
> Jump in a Humvee and murder those monkeys!
> and Razor blades cut ya face and leave a scar so you remember me
> Lurkin, to leave y'all with bloody red turbans
> Screamin 'Jihad! while y'all pray to a false god.[21]

His fascination with the ongoing invasion is also expressed in the song 'Box Cutta' Blade Runna' (2001) from the same album, wherein he states: 'I'll create the time and scene / Somewhere in Afghanistan, U.S.A. survival teams / Keep an eye on their surroundings in the jihad regime / A total riot scene, back and forth'.[22]

Another response, released in December 2001, is more cautious in its patriotic support of the dominant narratives of 9/11. It came with the release of the Wu-Tang Clan's fourth studio album, *Iron Flag.*[23] On the cover, the members of the group are seen raising a black and yellow Wu-Tang flag in a rendition of Joe Rosenthal's iconic photograph of soldiers raising the American flag on the Japanese island of Iwo Jima during World War II. Photojournalist Thomas E. Franklin took a comparable photo in the immediate aftermath of the 9/11 attacks, which is known as the 'Ground Zero Spirit', or 'Raising the Flag at Ground Zero'. The photo depicts three dust-covered FDNY firefighters raising a US flag in the rubble of the World Trade Center. The photo instantly became a symbol of American patriotism, and both of the iconic photos have been depicted on US postal stamps.

[21] Canibus, *C! True Hollywood Stories*, 'Draft Me!' (Featuring C-4), CD album (Archives Music © 2001).

[22] Canibus, *C! True Hollywood Stories*, 'Box Cutta' Blade Runna', CD album (Archives Music © 2001). True to his feelings presented on the album, Canibus actually joined the US Army in 2002, a decision that garnered a great deal of attention within the hip-hop community. He was discharged two years later, when Army officials found him smoking cannabis while on duty.

[23] Wu-Tang Clan, *Iron Flag*, CD album (Loud Records © 2001).

Figure 7.2 Wu-Tang Clan's album cover (LP) for *Iron Flag* (2001), inspired by Jo Rosenthal's classic *Raising the Flag on Iwo Jima* of 1945.

On the second song from the album, 'Rules', the Wu-Tang Clan seems poised to go to war. In the opening verse, Ghostface Killah appears to be ready to defend both his hometown of New York City and his country. He states:

> Who the fuck knocked our buildings down?
> Who the man behind the World Trade massacres, step up now
> Where the four planes at huh is you insane bitch?
> Fly that shit over my hood and get blown to bits!
> No disrespect, that's where I rest my head
> I understand you gotta rest yours true, nigga my people's dead
> America, together we stand, divided we fall
> Mr. Bush, sit down, I'm in charge of the war![24]

Asking, rhetorically, 'who the fuck knocked our buildings down?' and recognising the carnage of the attacks, Ghostface Killah demands that the perpetrator 'step up'. Ghostface Killah makes it obvious that no one attacks his 'hood' and his 'people' without feeling his rage. He stands for unity and tells the president to step aside and make way for him. This sudden blast of overwhelming patriotism is otherwise highly uncommon in the lyrics of the Wu-Tang Clan.

But not all articulations in the direct aftermath of 9/11 were coloured by patriotic sentiment. Rapper Sage Francis offered the reflective song 'Makeshift Patriot'.[25] In the song, Francis criticises what he perceives to be the sheepish and rash patriotism vented by many Americans. The track also clearly expresses worries for things to come. The line 'Freedom will be defended at the cost of civil liberties' is eerily predictive when describing the aftermath of 9/11. The song also offers comments on the 'Bullhorn' speech:

> He's got a megaphone, and he's promising to make heads roll
> So we cheer him on, but asbestos is affecting our breath control
> The less we know, the more they fabricate
> The easier it is to sell souls.[26]

[24] Wu-Tang Clan, *Iron Flag*, 'Rules', CD album (Loud Records © 2001).
[25] Sage Francis, 'Makeshift Patriot', promo 7-inch single (Strange Famous Records © 2001).
[26] Ibid.

Sage Francis's critical approach was later echoed by other hip-hop artists. The rapper Heems has offered one of the more lucid hip-hop statements in connection to 9/11. On his solo debut album *Eat Pray Thug* (2015), several songs deal with his experience as a Punjabi American living in New York in the aftermath of 9/11, a time when so many within the community experienced discrimination and hatred as they were confused with Muslims. The song 'Flag Shopping' (2015) contains the following:

> I know why they mad
> But why call us A-rabs
> We sad like they sad
> But now we buy they flags
> Spying on our Muslim brother
> While staring at our mother
> Lover they some bad motherfuckers
> We're going flag shopping
> We're going flag shopping
> The kids are throwing stones
> We complain but they ain't stopping
> On your way to the top
> And now they want you to stop
> Your mama pray to god
> But your dad'll lose his job.[27]

The song 'Patriot Act' (2015), which speaks about Heems's feeling of forced assimilation, has this to say:

> Bright American flags that read 'I am not Osama'
> And we ironed our polo shirts and we combed our hair
> And we proudly paid our taxes
> And we immediately donated to a local white politician
> And we yelled 'I'm just like you' as quietly and calmly as we could.[28]

In the immediate wake of 9/11, some hip-hop artists, as discussed, embraced the flag-waving approach of the majority of the US population, as inspiration for both aural monuments and violent patriotic outbursts. Others, like Sage Francis

[27] Heems, *Eat Pray Thug*, 'Flag Shopping', CD album (Megaforce © 2015).

[28] Heems, *Eat Pray Thug*, 'Patriot Act', CD album (Megaforce © 2015).

and Heems, contested these responses and the effects that they had on US foreign policy and mainstream America's attitudes towards minorities in the wake of the attacks. They especially targeted the close association made by the public between terrorism and those perceived to be of Arab or Muslim descent, a phenomenon that coincided with the enactment of stricter social controls intended to prevent new terror attacks and punish alleged terrorists. Others still, as will now be shown, went further and rejected the conventional interpretation of the events.

In the patriotic articulations, Islamic semiotic resources such as 'Taliban', 'bin Laden', '9/11' and 'Jihad' are used alongside derogatory declarations such as 'monkeys', 'False God' and (bloody) 'red turbans' in order to denounce the perceived enemy. In other words, some hip-hop artists produced patriotic songs much in line with similar songs in other genres, such as country. Some of these songs can be viewed as aural monuments that foment patriotic sentiments against the perceived enemy of Islam, or at least certain expression of Islam, even though nuances are seldom stressed. The less patriotic songs avoid direct Islamic semiotic resources, but they still address issues relevant to Muslims who felt more discrimination. Why this is the case is difficult to say; it could be coincidence, or it could be a fear of utilising the semiotic resources that signalled the enemy at the time. However, that emotional attitude and its accompanying use of Islamic resources was to change soon.

'Black Helicopters in the Skies'

In 2002, hip-hop acts started to challenge the official narratives of 9/11. The Florida-based hip-hop duo Dead Prez, consisting of stic.man and M-1, released the song 'Know Your Enemy' (2002), where they portray the Bush administration as the real enemy: 'Know your enemy, know yourself / That's the politic / George Bush is way worse than bin Laden is / Know your enemy, know yourself / That's the politic / FBI, CIA, the real terrorists'. Like Sage Francis, they also took aim at US foreign policy: 'You wanna stop terrorists? / Start with the U.S. imperialists / Ain't no track record like America's, see / bin Laden was trained by the CIA'. Like Heems, Dead Prez also criticised the increased social control: 'You got to watch what you say in these days and times / It's a touchy situation, lotta fear and emotion'. 'Now everybody walkin' round patriotic / How we gon' fight to keep freedom when we ain't got it?' But Dead Prez went one step further, suggesting that the attacks were part of a wider scheme to put African Americans back into slavery: 'They try to make us think we crazy / But

I know what they doin, they tryna put us back in slavery'.[29] As the conspiratorial snowball started to roll, an increasing number of artists jumped on the bandwagon. Prolific artists such as Chuck D, frontman of legendary hip-hop group Public Enemy, and multi-platinum solo artist Busta Rhymes called on their fans to investigate the background to 9/11 and its aftermath.[30]

In April 2002, the New York-based alternative hip-hop outfit Non Phixion released their album *The Future Is Now* (2002). Non Phixion invites listeners to a gloomy and paranoid post-9/11 world, and the album popularised the use of conspiracy themes in hip-hop music. Over drone and murky beats, Non Phixion depicts a world where black helicopters hover in the sky, an all-seeing surveillance-industrial complex records every step of citizens, and the US government engineers the AIDS virus. The album puts the events of 9/11 in a larger New World Order conspiratorial framework, arguing that the Bush administration, together with a small but ominous cabal, sought to establish a One World Government through various drawn-out clandestine operations involving the use of government bodies (including the Pentagon and the CIA), international organisations such as the UN, major corporations and banks.[31] In the song 'Suicide Bomb' (2002), Ill Bill's opening verse states:

[29] Dead Prez, *Turn Off the Radio: The Mixtape Vol. 1*, 'Know Your Enemy', CD album (Full Clip Records © 2002).

[30] 'Draft Me!' www.theguardian.com/culture/2002/jan/22/artsfeatures1 (accessed 14 September 2023).

[31] The New World Order is a widely spread conspiracy theory within the radical right in the US. According to the conspiracy theorists, the idea of a New World Order is thought to have its roots in the rhetoric of world leaders such as Woodrow Wilson and Winston Churchill, originally describing the shift in the power balance after World War I and World War II. The idea is then thought to have been developed in the rhetoric of President George H. W. Bush in his second State of the Union address describing the Gulf Crisis and the first war in Iraq. This, in combination with what was perceived as increased governmental interference and regulations by both the Bush and Clinton administrations, triggered the imagination of the radical right in the US, according to which increased regulation was interpreted as the first sign of a forthcoming doom, crafted by a secret 'World Government' bent on world dominion and enslavement of the population. The ultimate goal of this scheme is to replace sovereign nations with a technocratic world state. These conspiracy theories encompass everything from CIA mind control experiments, concentration camps across the US linked by the railroad system, gun control, UFOs and Freemasonry. The spread of the New World Order theory was fuelled by the publication of several books concerning a perceived federal government authoritarianism and a UN invasion. These books include Pat Robertson's *The New World Order* (1991)

> Suicide bomb, from Al-Qaeda to the Quran
> Represent your clique and our Jihad, bangin' from God to Enron
> Bin Laden is still CIA
> John Walker captured in Kandahar, Afghanistan with shit stains on his face
> I seen the planes hit the world trade then I seen the world change
> Ideological earthquake, people exploding
> Explodin' on the same streets where the prophets increase
> Walking on water, now we be throwin' rocks at police.[32]

The song alludes to conspiracy theories linking the Bush administration to the energy company Enron (made famous by the Enron scandal, which erupted in October 2001), and of course 9/11. A common theory among New World Order conspiracy theorists posits that the Bush administration had knowledge about the attacks and allowed them to happen, as a pretext for an invasion of Afghanistan, in order to be able to build a pipeline through the country to the large landlocked oil and gas reserves in Central Asia, to save Enron from bankruptcy. The lyrics also suggest that bin Laden was a CIA agent, and that John Walker Lindh (the 'American Taliban') allegedly became interested in Islam after watching Spike Lee's biopic *Malcolm X* (1992), after which he read *The Autobiography of Malcolm X* (1965) and became interested in hip-hop culture.[33]

and Gary Kah's *En Route to Global Occupation* (1991). Elements of the New World conspiracy beliefs can be found within right-wing militia movements, tax protesters, sovereign or state citizens and Christian apocalyptics. However, as pointed out by, for example, Kaplan and Lööw in their edited volume *The Cultic Milieu: Oppositional Subcultures in an Age of Globalization* (2002), oppositional subcultures often make strange bedfellows. This is best illustrated by Mattias Gardell's contribution 'Black and White Unite in Fight?' where Gardell explores the unlikely friendship between leaders of NOI and the White Aryan Resistance, as they come together over the question of racial separation. In the case of hip-hop culture, one can see a similar tendency. For example, award-winning rapper Prodigy (from the duo Mobb Deep) appeared on 'The Alex Jones Show', sharing his insights about conspiracy theories. To take another example, Non Phixion has expressed its fascination with New World Order conspiracies, thus indirectly associating themselves with right-wing fringe movements.

[32] Non Phixion, *The Future is Now*, 'Suicide Bomb' (featuring Juju, Marley Metal, Psycho Les, Moonshine and Al Tariq), CD album (Uncle Howie Records © 2002).

[33] Hisham Aidi, 'America's Hip-Hop Foreign Policy', http://www.theatlantic.com/international/archive/2014/03/americas-hip-hop-foreign-policy/284522/ (accessed 14 September 2023).

The conspiratorial 'Suicide Bomb' skilfully weaves in the words 'suicide bomb', 'Al-Qaeda', 'Qur'an', 'Jihad' and 'bin Laden' and connects these Islamic semiotic resources to the post-apocalyptic conspiracy framework. The words also work as semiotic entries that encompass stories, or hints of stories, about the wider historical narrative of the post-9/11 US, in which Muslims are vilified by the authorities. Coupled with other songs from the album, such as 'Black Helicopters' and 'The CIA is Trying to Kill Me', Non Phixion's album clearly set the tone for many other interpretations of the 9/11 era that followed.

Several other artists reinterpreted 9/11 within a similar paranoid mindset. For example, Immortal Technique, a rapper and avid social commentator, released the controversial song 'Bin Laden' (2005), in which he claims that 9/11 was an inside job:

> They tell you to listen
> But they don't really tell you they mission
> They funded Al-Qaeda and now they blame the Muslim religion
> Even though Bin Laden was a CIA tactician
> They gave him billions of dollars and they funded his purpose
> Fahrenheit 9/11
> That's just scratching the surface.[34]

The song follows the narrative of filmmaker Michael Moore's documentary *Fahrenheit 9/11* (2004), which questions the Bush administration's intentions behind the invasion of Iraq and highlights the connections between the Bush and bin Laden families. The song also claims that the CIA had provided arms and funding to the Arab mujahidin in Afghanistan, including Osama bin Laden, during the 1980s. The hook of the song bluntly states: 'Bush knocked down the towers'. This statement is sampled from another song that explicitly questions the official narrative concerning 9/11, 'Why?' (2004) by the hip-hop artist Jadakiss.[35]

[34] Immortal Technique, 'Bin Laden Remix (Bin Laden Pt. 2)', EP 12-inch (Babygrande and Viper Records © 2005).

[35] The song 'Why?' by Jadakiss appears on the album *Kiss of Death*, CD album (Ruff Ryders, Interscope © 2004). It contains the line 'Why did Bush knock down the towers?' This line received a lot of attention in mainstream US media. Jadakiss claimed that he was contacted and confronted by the Bush administration about the statement. He also appeared on the conservative pundit Bill O'Reilly's Fox News programme *The O'Reilly Factor* and defended his line. Interview with Jadakiss by Mats Nileskär, Swedish Radio, Musikguiden i P3, 15 July 2015.

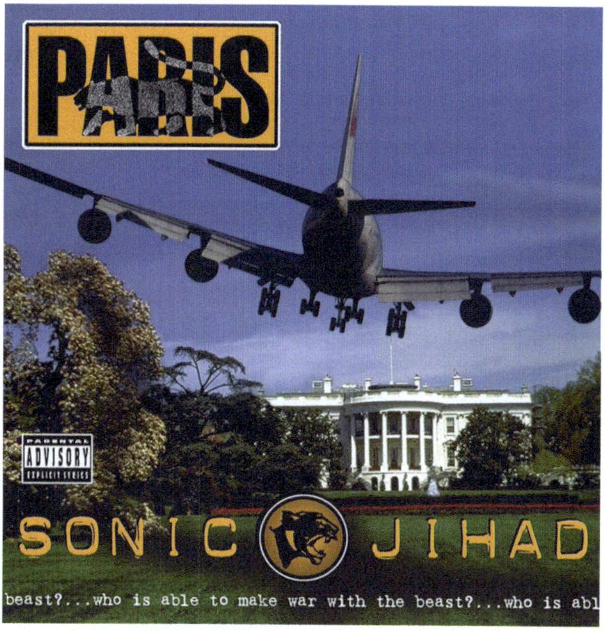

Figure 7.3 Paris' album cover (LP) for *Sonic Jihad*, 2003.

Immortal Technique has been branded a 'poster boy' for the truth movement by the influential cultural critic Jeffrey Melnick.[36]

Another example is *Sonic Jihad* (2003), the fifth studio album by the rapper Paris.[37] The cover depicts a plane soaring beneath a clear blue sky over the White House South Lawn, en route to crashing into the building. The title of

[36] Melnick 2011: 101.

[37] Paris, *Sonic Jihad*, LP album (Guerrilla Funk Recordings © 2003). Paris already had a long history of controversial records behind him and was no stranger to controversy before the release of *Sonic Jihad*. His first album *The Devil Made Me Do It* (1990) contained two singles that were banned from MTV. Likewise, his sophomore album *Sleeping with the Enemy* (1992) stirred controversy, containing the song 'Bush Killa', where Paris fantasises about how he assassinates George Bush, Sr. The lyrics of the song and the artwork for the album (showing Paris peeking out behind a tree on the White House lawn, ready to assassinate a waving and smiling George Bush, Sr) was leaked by an employee at Tommy Boy Records before the release. As a result, the album was pulled. Paris himself later issued the album on his newly formed label Scarface Records. In 1998, Paris left the recording industry. Having earned a degree in economics from the University of California at Davis, he started a career as a licensed stockbroker. He was actually trained at the World Trade Center in New York.

the album, *Sonic Jihad*, is printed in yellow capitals at the foot of the cover, the words surrounding the head of a roaring black panther. Underneath the title, the words 'beast? . . . who is able to make war with the beast? . . . who is ab . . .' appear like a scrolling news ticker. In the left corner, Paris's logo contains the silhouette of a black panther.

The album cover is meant to depict the presumable scenario of United Airlines Flight 93 (the only plane that did not reach its intended target on 9/11) crashing into its supposed target, the White House. The title *Sonic Jihad* is a combination of the Qur'anic term *jihad*, most commonly understood as a 'Holy War' waged by Muslims, and 'Sonic', possibly to both allude to the sonic speed of the plane crashing into the presidential mansion and the sound waves produced by Paris on the album. The two words thus signify 'A Holy War of Sound Waves' waged by Paris against perceived injustices.[38]

The words 'who is able to make war with the beast?' are seemingly a biblical reference to the Book of Revelation 13:4: 'So they worshiped the dragon who gave authority to the beast; and they worshiped the beast, saying, 'Who is like the beast? Who is able to make war with him?' John's apocalyptic story (often seen as John the Apostle) of a battle against the beast, with its wide variety of interpretations, has inspired many artists over the years.[39] One common interpretation is that the beast is human, a powerful leader who received his power from the Devil. In the case of Paris, it is obvious that the beast refers to President George W. Bush. Paris uses the same biblical reference in the song 'Bush Killa' (1992), here referring to the older George H. W. Bush: 'Now who

[38] The translation of *jihad* as 'Holy War' is controversial, among both Muslims and non-Muslims. The term is often understood in dualistic terms, as having two meanings: one reads *jihad* as an inner spiritual struggle (the 'greater *jihad*'), and the other reads it as a physical struggle against the enemies of Islam (the 'lesser *jihad*'). The 'lesser *jihad*' may take violent or non-violent forms. For a further discussion of the use of the word *jihad*, see, for example, 'Djihad', *The Encyclopaedia of Islam. 2: C-G.*

[39] For example, John Steinbeck's book *The Grapes of Wrath* (1939). The 'grapes of wrath' is a Biblical allusion to the Book of Revelation 14:19–20: 'So the angel swung his sickle to the earth and gathered the clusters from the vine of the earth, and threw them into the great wine press of the wrath of God'. The equally famous song 'Number of the Beast', *Number of the Beast*, CD album (EMI © 1982) by Iron Maiden starts with spoken quotes from Revelation 12:12 and Revelation 13:18, and the theme of the song is that 666 is the number of the beast, as stated in Revelation 13:18: 'Let he that has understanding count the number of the beast, for the number is that of a man; and his number is six hundred and sixty-six'.

is able to make war with the beast? / It starts with 'P' / Trumpets sound when I push the program / And set my sight on a serpent man'. The trumpets, also a biblical reference, are referring to the sound of the seven trumpets believed to announce the coming of the Apocalypse. The serpent man alludes to Satan taking the form of a snake in order to tempt Eve to eat the forbidden fruit in the garden of Eden, which led to the fall of mankind.[40]

The additional album artwork features concentric circles surrounding a red seal that contains the 'Eye of Providence' (the all-seeing eye of God), situated above an unfinished thirteen-stepped pyramid, as depicted on the reverse side of the Great Seal of the United States, which is prominently displayed on the dollar bill. At the top of the seal is the Latin phrase '*annuit cœptis*', which translates as: 'He [God] favours our undertaking'. At the bottom of the seal is an arced banner with the words '*novus ordo seclorum*', meaning 'New Order of the Ages', which, on the dollar bill, is a reference to a new American era. On the base of the pyramid are the Roman numerals MDCCLXXVI (1776), the year when the Continental Congress approved the US Declaration of Independence from Great Britain.

The collage of sepia-toned photographs surrounding the seal suggests how Paris sees the 'New Order of the Ages': a world of chaos. There are pictures of gang members posing with tattoos, American riot police in confrontation with African American protesters, crack cocaine 'rocks', exploding buildings, homeless people and bomb planes loading their deadly cargo, melding with images of starving children with swollen bellies, what appear to be Palestinians throwing stones and people dying on the streets of an unidentifiable Middle Eastern town. In turn, these pictures are juxtaposed with photos of Ariel Sharon, George W. Bush, Osama bin Laden, Saddam Hussein and Yasser Arafat. Paris has also provided the score for, and narrated, the movie *Aftermath: Unanswered Questions from 9/11* (2002),[41] a documentary-style movie purporting to answer what it believes are unanswered questions surrounding the 9/11 attacks and their effects on US society.

[40] The story is described in the Qur'an, *Sura Al-A'raf* (7:19–23). The events that lead to the fall of man are described, and *Sura Ibrahim* (14:26) refers to the 'Forbidden Tree'.

[41] The documentary is available online: https://www.youtube.com/watch?v=K86oRRGXDGE (accessed 11 September 2023). The movie is directed by Stephen Marshall (Guerrilla News Network © 2003). Among others, Alex Jones is featured in the movie.

The conspiratorial themes of songs like 'Bin Laden' and artwork such as that seen on *Sonic Jihad* coincide with the rise and mobilisation of the so-called truth movement. In the direct aftermath of 9/11, the truth movement became an umbrella term for a diverse and loosely-knit network of organisations and individuals that have questioned the official accounts of the 9/11 events. In 2004, the truth movement made a concerted effort to reach out with its message, pushing for official hearings and organised conferences where different theories surrounding the 'truth' behind 9/11 were debated. The movement marketed numerous, more or less well-produced movies and digitally produced presentations as possible alternative scenarios to the actual events of 9/11. These were spread and gained viral status online.[42]

The concept album *The 911 Report: The Ultimate Conspiracy* (2006) might be the utmost manifestation of counter-knowledge production relating to 9/11 in hip-hop and other cultural forms. If the truth movement had a soundtrack, this album would be it. It was recorded by the Philadelphia group Lost Children of Babylon, known for its eclectic blend of semiotics from the cognitive universe of Islam, Egyptian mythology, New World Order conspiracy theories and Illuminati conspiracy theories.[43] The album cover depicts a man with the Star-Spangled Banner wrapped turban-like around his head, holding up an American flag in a burning inferno, with the exploding Twin Towers in the background. The cover includes the name of the group (the name is also printed in Arabic), as well as the name of the album printed in capital letters. The cover, moreover, includes the *shahada*, the Islamic creed declaring one's belief in the oneness of God and the acceptance of Muhammad as God's messenger, which is printed over the burning Twin Towers. In addition to the track list, the back cover of the album depicts the silhouette of the

[42] Fenster 2008: 246–47. Several hip-hop artists appeared on the soundtrack to one of the most famous 9/11 movies, *Loose Change* (first released in 2005). The soundtrack *The Beats of Loose Change*, CD album (Third i Records © 2006) contains music by hip-hop artists DJ Skooly, Swae, Smoke and Nick Tha 1da. The full movie, which appears in several renditions, can be watched online: https://www.youtube.com/watch?v=ynROamW80O0 (accessed 14 September 2023).

[43] The group consists of nine members: Rasul Allahu, The Breath of Judah, Richard Raw, Cosmic Crusader, Ancient Kemite, Amun Sen Hotep Re, Atum Sen Geb the Eloheem, Stretch the Mad Scientist and Wazulu the Ill Dravidian.

Figure 7.4 The Lost Children of Babylon's album cover (LP, front and back) for *The 911 Report: The Ultimate Conspiracy*, 2006.

second plane, United Airlines Flight 175, on its way to hit the South Tower on 9/11. The names of the songs are printed in Arabic as well as in English. The sleeve notes contain the following dedication:

> THIS ALBUM IS DEDICATED TO ALL THE VICTIMS OF THE TRAGEDY WHICH OCCURRED ON SEPTEMBER 11, 2001 [. . .] TO THE FAMILIES AND FRIENDS WHO LOST A LOVED ONE [. . .] TO ALL THE FALLEN HEROES WHO DIED TRYING TO SAVE THE LIVES OF THE INNOCENT [. . .] TO ALL THOSES [sic] WHO STRIVE TO REVEAL THE REAL MOTIVES BEHIND THIS TRAGIC INCIDENT [. . .] MAY TRUTH AND JUSTICE PREVAIL.

The intro of the album opens with a sample from a weather report from the morning of 11 September 2001, set to chilling and eerie background music. The weather announcer reports: 'It's going to be a beautiful day today, sunshine throughout, low humidity [. . .]. Really a splendid September day!' This is followed by the fictitious voice of a female flight attendant welcoming the passengers onboard American Airlines Flight 11 flying from Boston to Los Angeles. In the background of the announcement, the *adhan* (Islamic call to prayer) is heard. After the announcement, the actual words of hijacker Mohamed Atta, as recorded by the air traffic controllers in Boston, are sampled: 'We have some planes. Just stay quiet and you'll be okay. We are returning to the airport. Nobody move. Everything will be okay. If you try to make any moves, you'll endanger yourself and the airplane. Just stay quiet'. The intro ends with the sound of American Airlines Flight 11 crashing into the North Tower of the World Trade Center.

The song that follows the intro is called 'Warning: Boxcutterz on an Airplane': the word 'box cutter' is in reference to the 9/11 hijackers' alleged weapon of choice. The song contains verses seeking to capture the point of view of hijacker Mohamed Atta, mixing fact and fiction to reconstruct the course of events on American Airlines Flight 11. The song also contains verses from the point of view of an unnamed US government official pleading with the hijackers to not go through with the attack.

The production of the song is accredited to DJ Loose Change, who took his stage name from a famous 9/11 conspiracy theory movie series. The soundscape of the song centres on two samples that add intertextuality and depth. DJ Loose Change cuts two phrases well-known to most hip-hop listeners: the line 'I am a hijacked Delta', from Nas's song 'NY State of Mind' (1994), referring to a series of hijacking attempts that Delta Airlines suffered during the 1970s and 1980s;[44] and Notorious B. I. G.'s line 'blow up like the World Trade', from the song 'Juice' (1994).[45] The line is a reference to the 1993 bomb that went off in the basement of the World Trade Center, planted by a group of terrorists trained by Al-Qaeda. The plot was masterminded by Khalid Shaikh Mohammed, considered to be the principal architect of the 9/11 attacks.

In total, *The 911 Report: The Ultimate Conspiracy* contains nineteen tracks. They all interpret various aspects of the 9/11 events within the conspiratorial framework of the truth movement. The 9/11 terrorists are described as puppets in a larger conspiracy, and the main target for the fury of the Lost Children of Babylon is US foreign policy, personified by Dick Cheney and George W. Bush. The album remains one of the most comprehensive and controversial attempts to explore the official narrative of the 9/11 events. Although the album failed to achieve larger mainstream success, it still stands as a hip-hop underground classic. Within this counter-knowledge cluster, Islamic semiotic resources are woven into a larger narrative of a 'One World Government', and the belief that 9/11 was an 'inside job'. 'Al-Qaeda' and 'bin Laden' are portrayed as puppets in a larger scheme orchestrated by a cabal of dark interests that seeks world domination. In this context, Islamic semiotic resources such as 'Jihad' are appropriated to symbolise a struggle against perceived social injustices. Some of the songs discussed above can be characterised as 'magnetic songs', becoming leitmotifs for the so-called truth movement. Ron Eyerman and Andrew Jamison have suggested that magnetic songs (a term coined by the author Serge Denisoff) are

44 Nas, *Illmatic*, LP album (2004 © Columbia). Nas was not the first rapper to refer to airplane hijackings. The first hip-hop song containing a reference to airplane hijackings is 'The Message' (1982) by Grandmaster Flash and the Furious Five.

45 The song was released in August 1994, as the first single from his debut album *Ready to Die*. Hip-hop fans have vividly discussed why Biggie allegedly knew about the attack already in 1994. Some have even connected him to Illuminati conspiracy. In the aftermath of 9/11, many radio stations in the US censored the song under the assumption that it added fuel to conspiracy theories. http://www.billboard.com/articles/columns/hip-hop/7767469/notorious-big-juicy-biggie-9-11-radio-censorship (accessed 14 September 2023).

songs that have the ability to attract non-participants to join social movements or reinforce the commitment level of the supporters.[46] Many of the songs in this cluster clearly seek to fill the function of magnetic songs by acting as marketing tools for conspiracy theories around the 9/11 events.

Boxcutter Pazzy, Al Qaeda Jada and Taliban Bundy

Even today we hear the events of 9/11 echo in the aural, visual and textual production of US hip-hop artists. These echoes occur in punchlines, metaphors and provocative allusions designed to accentuate artists' credentials as hard-core gangsters or simply mean and dangerous individuals. One example of such usage is Cage's line, 'too bad no planes flew into MTV / I'll never get a platinum plaque for MP3' from his song 'Escape to 88' (2002).[47]

Other artists have used aliases that connect to the legacy of the attacks. The front man of the Philadelphia group Jedi Mind Tricks, Vinnie Paz, is sometimes known as Odrama vin Laden or Boxcutter Pazzy: the alias Odrama vin Laden is an obvious word play on Osama bin Laden, while Boxcutter Pazzy is once again a reference to box cutters being the 9/11 hijackers' alleged weapon of choice. The alias is carefully chosen since it signals both Muslim gangster bravado and the fact that Vinnie Paz is conversant in conspiracy theories. In the video for the song 'End of Days' (2010), Paz is seen wearing a *kufi* and a t-shirt with the text: '9/11 was an inside job'. In the song, he states:

> Whoever built the pyramids had knowledge of electrical power
> And you know that that's the information
> That they suppress and devour
> Who you think the motherfuckers that crashed in the tower?
> Who you think that made it turn into ash in an hour?[48]

The song starts with a lengthy sample of the British former BBC-commentator-turned-conspiracy-evangelist David Icke, known for combining New Age philosophical considerations with his 'Reptoid hypothesis', according to which high-ranking world leaders and politicians belong to an inter-dimensional race

[46] Eyerman and Jamison 1991: 43.

[47] Cage, *Movies for the Blind*, 'Escape to 88' (Eastern Conferenc © 2002).

[48] Vinnie Paz (featuring Block McCloud), *Season of the Assassin*, 'End of Days', CD album (Enemy Soil © 2010).

of reptilian humanoids. Icke has argued that this race of shape-shifting reptilians, known as the Babylonian Brotherhood, or the Illuminati, influence world events in order to keep humans in constant fear so that they can feed off this negative energy. In Icke's universe, 9/11 becomes one such event, created by the shape-shifting reptilians in order to induce fear on a mass scale.[49]

By weaving Islamic semiotic elements into the audio-visual setting of the video, Vinnie Paz seems to suggest that Islam and Muslims are not to blame for the 9/11 attacks. In the song's lyrics, he states: 'They want you to believe the lie that the enemy Saudi / The enemy ain't Saudi, the enemy around me'. Thus, he suggests that Muslims have been scapegoated by the real enemy. He also states in the song that 'the Shaitan army, they display it proudly', using one of the Arabic names for the Devil. In the context of the song, 'the Shaitan army' should be understood to mean the Illuminati or the Babylonian Brotherhood, echoing Icke's conspiracy theories.

In the same way in which many hip-hop artists over the years have displayed an inclination towards the aesthetics of the Italian American Mafia and other organised crime syndicates, some hip-hop artists have used the 'Jihad aesthetics' of Al-Qaida in their videos and on their records. Jadakiss, for example, has released a series of mixtapes named 'Al Qaeda Jada'. On the cover of 'Al Qaeda Jada Pt. 7', he is seen with his head wrapped in a black and white *keffiyeh*, sporting a *jihad*-style bandana with the *shahadah* printed on it.[50] Does this mean that Jadakiss is an avid Al Qaeda supporter? Most likely not. A more plausible interpretation is that this is just the latest way for Jadakiss to transgress authority and social norms in US society, being famous for his provocative allusions to religious imagery. Jadakiss also released the mixtape *The Passion of the Kiss* (2009), alluding to the famous biblical movie *The Passion of the Christ* (2004). On the record cover, Jadakiss is seen with a crown of thorns and a bloodied face, mimicking the movie's poster.

Another example is the Harlem crew The Diplomats, infamous for its 'Taliban-dropping' – constant provocative references to the Taliban movement and 9/11. Their double-album *Diplomatic Immunity* (2003) is filled with

[49] Robertson 2013. Icke has developed these theories in books such as *The Biggest Secret* (1999), *Alice in Wonderland and the World Trade Center Disaster: Why the Official Story of 9/11 is a Monumental Lie* (2002) and *Children of the Matrix* (2017).

[50] In 2008, Jadakiss also released a series of four webisodes titled 'Al Qaeda Jada'.

more or less provocative references to the attacks. The Diplomats embraced Islamic semiotic resources such as 'Taliban', Al-Qaeda' and 'bin Laden' as lyrical catchphrases (in hip-hop widely known as ad-libs) used out of context as space fillers, salutations, or to give words an inverted meaning. For example, 'He Taliban!' could mean that someone is a straight-up person or someone to trust. Another example could be 'I feel good man, Taliban!' In this context, the word Taliban is used as an affirmative space filler.

The album also contains one of the most controversial bars about the 9/11 attacks delivered in hip-hop, in which the Diplomats' rapper Juelz Santana states his admiration for the courage of Mohammed Atta: 'I worship the prophet / The great Mohammed Omar Atta / For his courage behind the wheel of the plane / Reminds me when I was dealin' the 'caine'.[51] In an interview with the *NME*, Santana defended his words:

> No matter what anybody says, that was courage right there. If anybody wants to say I worship them, well I know how I feel – I don't worship them. I don't appreciate anything they ever did. I'm not with them, not 1%, not 2% not 10% but I've looked in the dictionary and I've defined the word courage.[52]

The implication is that, even if Juelz Santana does not agree with the actions of the 9/11 hijacker, he still admires his courage. In the same interview, Santana suggested that America itself is to blame for the 9/11 attacks:

> It's because United States have been going over there trespassing, stealing their stuff [. . .]. now they make it seem like they came over here and bombed us for nothing. How did the United States let this happen. How can you talk about my words when the big question is how can you let this happen.[53]

Despite standing his ground at the time, Juelz Santana later changed the lyrics to 'I worship the late prophet / The great Muhammad Ali / The words he spoke / They stung like a bee', in reference to the boxer Muhammad Ali's famous quote 'float like a butterfly, sting like a bee'.

[51] The Diplomats, *Diplomatic Immunity*, 'I Love You', CD album (Roc-A-Fella Records © 2003).

[52] 'Cam'ron's Crew Defends 9/11 Lyric', https://www.nme.com/news/music/camron-4-1380851 (accessed 15 September 2023).

[53] Ibid.

Several other artists are known for making use of 9/11 in tandem with Islamic semiotic resources. The hip-hop act Three 6 Mafia from Memphis, Tennessee, recorded the song 'Bin Laden' (2003), celebrating their favourite marijuana blend called 'Bin Laden Weed'.[54] 'Bin Laden' in this context signals that the marijuana is extraordinarily potent.

A further example is the Southern hip-hop artist Taliban Bundy, whose name combines 'Taliban' with the name of the notorious American serial killer Ted Bundy. The rapper T. I. states that he is 'Wild as the Taliban / Nine in my right, forty-five in my other hand / I'm in trouble man, always in trouble man' in his song 'Rubber Band Man' (2003), indicating that he has a lot of cash in rubber bands and is equipped with a 9mm pistol in one hand and a 45mm gun in the other.[55] In the song 'Jumpman' (2015) by Drake and Future, Drake starts by rapping: 'If Young Metro don't trust you I'm gon' shoot you / Yeah, yeah / Halloween / Taliban, Taliban / I'm gon' shoot you / Yeah'.[56] When the song was featured in a commercial for Apple Music, with mainstream singer-songwriter Taylor Swift seen working out to the track, 'Taliban' was removed, which underlines the contentious nature of this particular word. However, these references should not be linked directly to the Taliban movement in Afghanistan, which harboured Osama bin Laden and other leaders of Al-Qaeda. In the above-mentioned song, the word Taliban is only indirectly linked to the Sunni militant outfit and more directly to the name of the notorious Eastside Atlanta street gang Taliban.

In this final cluster, one can see Islamic semiotic resources such as 'Taliban' and 'bin Laden' being utilised in a way that implies a challenge to and transgression of boundaries and limits – a practice not unfamiliar in hip-hop culture. Hip-hop has a history of consciously provoking strong reactions, ranging from the gangsta rap of Schoolly D and Ice-T in the mid-1980s to the recent unapologetic sexually explicit music of Nicki Minaj and Cardi B. Fondness for the 'Jihad aesthetics' of Al-Qaeda and the use of Islamic semiotic resources such as 'Taliban' might just be the latest formula for artists to keep pushing and exploring the limits of US popular culture.

[54] Three 6 Mafia, *Da Unbreakables*, 'Bin Laden', CD album (Loud Records © 2003).

[55] T. I., *Trap Muzik*, 'Rubber Band Man' (Grand Hustle Records © 2003).

[56] Drake and Future, *What a Time to Be Alive*, 'Jumpman' (Young Money, Cash Money, Republic Freebandz A1 and Epic © 2015).

Conclusion: Conflicting Meanings and Narratives Using Islamic Semiotic Resources in the Post-9/11 Era

In summary, this chapter has discussed a raft of examples where Islamic semiotic resources have been put to use by US hip-hop artists in relation to 9/11 and its aftermath. I have demonstrated that Islamic semiotic resources have been situated and applied in different contexts by Muslims as well as non-Muslims for a variety of purposes, highlighting the way in which the events of 9/11 have stimulated cultural production relating to Muslims and different Islamic interpretive traditions and forms of social justice. Islamic semiotic resources are torn in different directions and joined together in ways that give rise to competing and conflicting narratives. I have given many examples of this, organising the resource usage into three clusters: patriotic articulations, articulations that aim to create counter-knowledge, and articulations used to provoke and transgress boundaries and social norms in US society.

In the aftershock of 9/11, hip-hop artists mirrored other musical genres, country music standing out among these, and produced patriotic responses to the terrorist attacks. Some of these hip-hop songs can be viewed as aural monuments to the attacks, standing as sound structures commemorating the memory of lost ones and channelling the intense feelings of the survivors. As with country music, hip-hop also produced more aggressive nationalistic responses utilising Islamic semiotic resources in a derogatory context aimed at ridiculing Islam and Muslims. But it did not take long for American hip-hop artists to start reinterpreting the 9/11 attacks within a conspiratorial framework. Such a reframing was an attempt to address new social problems – citizen surveillance and Islamophobia being significant ones – in US society following 9/11. In doing so, Islamic semiotic resources were used alongside, and intertwined with, well-known conspiracy theories in order to challenge the official accounts of the attacks. Some of these songs became magnetic songs, used as marketing tools for conspiracy theories in order to attract new followers and reinforce the commitment of the already convinced. In this cluster, the use of Islamic themes can be seen as semiotic entries that encompass narratives, or suggestions of storylines, about the wider narrative of the post-9/11 era in the US, where many Muslims feel vilified by the authorities' anti-terror surveillance aimed at mosques, schools, Muslim organisations and individuals. Muslims also felt the flames of hostility, fanned by those who see Islam as essentially fomenting hatred and violence.

The last cluster encompasses what I have termed, for the lack of a better word, provocations. 9/11 created new taboos for US hip-hop artists to transgress and challenge. Within this cluster, Islamic semiotic resources are re-invented and bring new meanings in new contexts. The meanings of words such as 'Taliban', 'bin Laden' and 'Al Qaeda', as we have seen, have been inverted to mean something positive, in contrast to their often more mainstream negative connotations. Sometimes objects have also been re-described as Islamic semiotic resources: one interesting example discussed above is box cutters, tools associated with the 9/11 hijackers. When evoking the image of box cutters in a context of upfront provocation, spiced with semiotic resources commonly associated with Islam, box cutters are drawn into the associational sphere of Islam and invented as semiotic resources that can be perceived as Islamic, or at least as associated with other semiotic resources that often are perceived as Islamic.

This semiotic inventiveness and the responsiveness of the artists accountable for making semiotic resources change meaning or broaden their associational scope are important factors to consider in any study of social semiotics. To gain a richer and more accurate understanding of a word such as 'Taliban', contextualisation is necessary. Contextualisation here cannot be reduced to merely stating that the word Taliban features in hip-hop lyrics but must be taken to mean an engagement with how those lyrics came to be, their intertextuality (often expressed in abbreviated narratives) and their political positionality.

8

CONCLUSION
THE SEMIOTICS OF ISLAM, CREATIVITY AND BLURRED LINES

In this study, I have sought to unpack the intricate relationship between Islamic semiotic resources and US hip-hop culture. I began by stressing that the use of such resources in African American music-making predates hip-hop culture. Based mainly on a literature review, I have argued that Muslims as well as non-Muslims have used Islamic themes in their artistic productions throughout the history of African American music-making. To fully understand the use of Islamic semiotic resources in contemporary hip-hop music, it is essential to recognise the historical legacy that shapes it. Key elements of this legacy have been repeatedly evoked over time in lyrics, sounds and imagery. To be fair, this history is not the exclusive property of hip-hop. Many of the organisations and actors described in this book have triggered the imagination of other artists drawing from African American history or trying to shape its future. These organisations and actors have become key reference points and therefore Islamic semiotic resources in their own right. I discovered that the relationship between semiotic resources from different Islamic interpretive traditions and African American music-making was reciprocal and mutually bolstering.

With their roots in African American Islamic or Islam-inspired spirituality – particularly in the Black Arts Movement and Nation of Islam – the pan-religious organisation Universal Zulu Nation (which accepts Islam as a valid religious tradition to be drawn from) and the Nation of Gods and Earths (not Islamic but consciously drawing from Islam) have been presented in the study as being imperative in creating a paradigm within hip-hop culture. Within this paradigm, Islamic semiotic resources have become an integral part. The Universal Zulu Nation and the Nation of Gods and Earths have linked historical African American movements, including Nation of Islam and Marcus Garvey's Universal Negro Improvement Association (UNIA), with contemporary musical culture.

I have argued that Christopher Partridge's concept of occulture is especially useful for interpreting this development and, therefore, that the use of Islamic semiotic resources in this occultural milieu cannot exclusively be explained as a form of protest against perceived inequalities. Indeed, this milieu is also a reaction to materialism, self-centredness and lack of spirituality – all symptoms of the re-enchantment of popular culture, characterised by a spiritual re-awakening that emphasises personal progress and well-being rather than organised worship.

In order to further the understanding of the associations and functions of Islamic themes in hip-hop culture in their multimodality, this book includes three in-depth studies of hip-hop and Islamic themes. Firstly, Chapter 5 has analysed the serendipities of the production of Islamic semiotic resources in the song 'Paid in Full (Mini Madness: The Coldcut Remix)' (1987), performed by Eric B. & Rakim and remixed by the British electronic music duo Coldcut. This chapter has also discussed its accompanying music video, directed by Bruno Tilley. I have highlighted the individual efforts made by the different figures involved in the production of the music video, showing how together, through different yet intertwined agendas, they shaped representations of Islam. By recognising the Islamic semiotic elements produced in the song and music video, I have argued that a new possible interpretation of the song opens up – namely, the song taps into and replicates a conversion narrative common in the African American Islamic experience, stressing the transformative power inherent in the individual spiritual encounter. This narrative is embodied, most famously, in the life of Malcolm X and his journey from a lost street hustler to a prominent African American figure who rose to leadership and moral certainty through embarking on a righteous path.

In Chapter 6, I have discussed the multimodal semiotic resources of Malcolm X and his legacy in hip-hop. The central argument of this chapter was that hip-hop artists creatively – by name-dropping, image-dropping and sound-dropping – have contributed to the processes of re-inventing Malcolm X and his legacy, not only by casting him as a symbol of local African American resistance against racial inequalities, but also by casting him as a global Sunni Muslim revolutionary with a worldwide impact that reaches far beyond hip-hop culture. Malcolm X's life story provides a potential for several different kinds of meaning-making. I have suggested that it makes no sense to separate the categories of politics and religion in artists' usage of the life and legacy of Malcolm X. Indeed, politics and religion are intertwined and co-dependent. Further, I have argued that recognising the cultural resonance of Malcolm X within hip-hop is crucial in order to understand contemporary Muslim struggles for civil rights, found in several unrelated organisations, initiatives and movements around the world where *Islam* has become a path to social, political and religious liberation.

In Chapter 7, I have recognised the crucial role that 9/11 has played in US hip-hop when it comes to framing and creatively re-inventing Islamic semiotic resources. Islamic semiotic resources, so I have found, were pulled in diverse directions and added together in competing and conflicting narratives. I have demonstrated how Islamic semiotic resources were deployed in derogatory contexts, through what I have called 'patriotic articulations'. I have also described Islamic semiotic resources used in connection to popular conspiracy theories in order to reframe social problems facing Muslims, or people that are perceived as Muslims, in the post-9/11 era. Finally, I have discussed the fact that concepts can be invented, or radically re-described, as Islamic semiotic resources, as well as the fact that the meanings of Islamic semiotic resources can become inverted to mean something positive in contrast to their often more mainstream negative connotations.

Blurred Lines: The Problem of Islamic Hip-Hop

Throughout this study, I have engaged in a conversation about what the literature labels as 'Muslim hip-hop' or 'Islamic hip-hop'. Firstly, I have contributed with a new voice to this conversation, which takes a different perspective on the topic itself. I recognise that not all hip-hop made by Muslims can be labelled 'Muslim' or 'Islamic': just because a person who consider himself or herself Muslim decides to record a song does not necessarily mean that this person's artistic output is de facto 'Islamic'. Scholars in the field would most likely agree with this claim. Apart from some artists, such as Native Deen, who present themselves as devout Muslims doing Islamic hip-hop, much hip-hop that includes Islamic semiotic resources is far more difficult to classify as 'Islamic hip-hop'. A label like Islamic hip-hop, as I have argued, can in such cases be a hindrance to understanding musical culture and expressions.

Secondly, I have shown that both non-Muslims and Muslims alike contribute to establishing Islamic themes within hip-hop culture. As demonstrated throughout, Islamic semiotic resources are used in different contexts by Muslims as well as non-Muslims, for a variety of reasons. Most scholars of Islamic studies have moved away from earlier attempts in the field to define a timeless essence of Islam. Today, scholars fruitfully pay attention to how people who self-identify as Muslim construct Islam and live 'everyday Islam' through concrete, contingent and accidental practices, affective registers and forms of thought. In this book, my intention has been to expand the borders of Islamic studies and recognise the fact that non-Muslims (outsiders) also participate in the processes that shape what is perceived as 'Islam' and/or 'Islamic', and that their production of 'Islam' is an area eminently worthy of study. These factors include, for example, pundits, politicians and academics who write and talk about Islam in public arenas. However, there are also other actors who participate in these complex processes. Central to the understanding of the empirical material studied within this book is the movement Nation of Gods and Earths (NGE), which clearly identifies with and uses Islamic symbols and concepts but does not consider itself to be Muslim.

The framework of social semiotics in this study has served as an explanatory device (open to questions and challenges, to be sure) that has helped me break down stereotypes and point to the diversity of 'Islamic' expressions and interpretive traditions. It has also helped me unlock the actual meaning-making produced with Islamic semiotic resources. At times, the usage of Islamic semiotic resources has been treated in a rather simplistic manner by researchers, who often overlook the actual ideas and intentions of the sender. But by addressing references to the Qur'an, the Taliban and box cutters as semiotic resources that can come to be perceived as Islamic, the intertextuality and cut-up techniques of hip-hop culture can be addressed with appropriate precision.

Finally, I have addressed the serendipities of Islamic semiotics and suggested that sometimes the use of Islamic semiotic resources is scattered or inverted in meaning. If my material had been interpreted based on Talal Asad's notion of an Islamic discursive tradition, one would sooner or later have run into serious problems which have not been addressed by Asad, such as the role of non-Muslims in the construction of Islamic traditions.

Ultimately, this study encourages future scholarship to consider the diverse, fluid nature of popular culture and multimodal expressions. It advocates for a social semiotic approach as one way to unpack stereotypes and appreciate the diversity of Islamic expressions. I wanted to underscore the importance of cultural literacy in societies that are not only interconnected but also multimodal, engaging with various forms of media and communication. The ability to interpret and understand diverse cultural signs and symbols across different platforms becomes crucial in navigating the complexities of global interactions in our increasingly interconnected multimodal societies. By promoting cultural literacy, we enhance our capacity for empathy, collaboration and mutual respect in a world where the fusion of cultural expressions is the norm rather than the exception.

Throughout this book, it has been my intention to provide tools and examples of how to understand and work with the dialectics between Muslims and non-Muslims in shaping what is perceived as Islam and/or Islamic, something that is highly relevant even for those not interested in hip-hop music. This emerging and important field of study invites researchers to engage with the manifold realities of being Muslim. It illuminates how interactions between Muslims and non-Muslims construct multilayered representations that shape global cultural discourses on what Islam is and can be.

BIBLIOGRAPHY

Abdat, Fathie (2014), 'Before the Fez: The Life and Times of Noble Drew Ali 1886–1924', *Journal of Race, Ethnicity and Religion*, vol. 5 (8), pp. 1–19.

Abernethy, Graeme (2013), *The Iconography of Malcolm X*, Culture America, Lawrence: University Press of Kansas.

Ackfeldt, Anders (2012), '"Imma March" Toward Ka'ba: Islam in Swedish Hip-hop', *Contemporary Islam*, vol. 6 (3), pp. 283–96.

Ackfeldt, Anders (2013), '"I Am Malcolm X": Islamic Themes in Hip-hop Video Clips Online', *CyberOrient*, vol. 7 (2), pp. 67–86.

Ackfeldt, Anders (2016), 'Music, Modern', in Richard C. Martin (ed.), *Encyclopedia of Islam and the Muslim World*, 2nd edn, Farmingham Hills: Macmillan Reference USA, pp. 774–76.

Ahmed, Amer F. (2021), 'Islam and Hip Hop in Black America: Oral Tradition as Critical Liberatory Praxis', in C. L. Wijeyesinghe (ed.), *The Complexities of Race: Identity, Power, and Justice in an Evolving America*, New York: New York University Press.

Aidi, Hisham (2002), 'Jihadis in the Hood: Race, Urban Islam and the War on Terror', *Middle East Report* (224), p. 36.

Aidi, Hisham (2003), 'Let Us Be Moors: Islam, Race and "Connected Histories"', *Middle East Report* (229), pp. 42–53.

Aidi, Hisham (2004), 'Verily, There Is Only One Hip-hop Umma: Islam, Cultural Protest and Urban Marginality', *Socialism and Democracy* 18 (2), pp. 107–26.

Aidi, Hisham (2011), 'The Grand (Hip-Hop) Chessboard: Race, Rap and Raison d'Etat', *Middle East Report* (260), pp. 25–39.

Aidi, Hisham (2014), 'Hip-Hop Diplomacy: US Cultural Diplomacy Enters a New Era', *Foreign Affairs*, 16 April.

Alim, H. Samy (2005), 'A New Research Agenda: Exploring the Transglobal Hip Hop Umma', in Miriam Cooke and Bruce B. Lawrence (eds), *Muslim Networks from Hajj to Hip Hop*, Chapel Hill: University of North Carolina Press, pp. 264–75.

Alim, H. Samy (2006), *Roc the Mic Right: The Language of Hip Hop Culture*, New York: Routledge.

Allen, Harry (1994), 'Time Bomb: Clocking the History of Hip Hop 15 Years after "Rapper's Delight"', *Vibe*, vol. 2 (10), p. 71.

Alridge, Derrick P. (2005), 'From Civil Rights to Hip Hop: Toward a Nexus of Ideas', *The Journal of African American History*, vol. 90 (3), pp. 226–52.

Ambar, Saladin M. (2014), *Malcolm X at Oxford Union: Racial Politics in a Global Era*, New York: Oxford University Press.

de Araújo, Shadia Husseini and Matthias Gebauer (2016), 'Islamic Shores Along the Black Atlantic: Analysing Black and Muslim Countercultures in Post-Colonial Societies', *Journal of Muslims in Europe*, vol. 5 (1), pp. 11–37.

Asad, Talal (2009), 'The Idea of an Anthropology of Islam', *Qui Parle*, vol. 17 (2), pp. 1–30.

Austin, Allan D., ed. (1984), *African Muslims in Antebellum America: A Sourcebook*, Critical Studies on Black Life and Culture, vol. 5, New York: Garland Publishing.

Bakker, Justine M. (2015), 'On the Knowledge of Self and Others: Secrecy, Concealment and Revelation in Elijah Muhammad's Nation of Islam (1934–1975)', in Stephen C. Finley, Margarita Simon Guillory and Hugh R. Page (eds), *Esotericism in African American Religious Experience: 'There is a Mystery'*, Aries book series, vol. 19, Leiden: Brill, pp. 138–51.

Baraka, Imamu Amiri, and Larry Neal, eds (2007), *Black Fire: An Anthology of Afro-American Writing*, Baltimore: Black Classic Press.

Basu, Dipannita, and Sidney J. Lemelle, eds (2006), *The Vinyl Ain't Final: Hip Hop and the Globalization of Black Popular Culture*, London: Pluto.

Berman, Marshall (1996), '"Justice/Just Us": Rap and Social Justice in America', in Andy Merrifield and Erik Swyngedouw (eds), *The Urbanization of Injustice*, London: Lawrence & Wishart Ltd., pp. 1–31.

Bevelander, Pieter, and Jonas Otterbeck (2010), 'Young People's Attitudes towards Muslims in Sweden', *Ethnic and Racial Studies*, vol. 33 (3), pp. 404–25.

Beynon, Erdmann Doane (1938), 'The Voodoo Cult among Negro Migrants in Detroit', *American Journal of Sociology*, vol. 43 (6), pp. 894–907.

Bivins, Jason (2015), *Spirits Rejoice! Jazz and American Religion*, New York: Oxford University Press.

Blyden, Edward Wilmot (1994), *Christianity, Islam and the Negro Race*, Baltimore: Black Classic Press.

Boyd, Todd (2002), *The New H. N. I. C. (Head Niggas in Charge): The Death of Civil Rights and the Reign of Hip Hop*, New York: New York University Press.

Bradley, Adam, and Andrew DuBois, eds (2010), *The Anthology of Rap*, New Haven: Yale University Press.

Bragard, Véronique, Christophe Dony and Warren Rosenberg (2011), *Portraying 9/11: Essays on Representations in Comics, Literature, Film and Theatre*, Jefferson: McFarland & Co.

Breitman, George (1989), *Malcolm X Speaks: Selected Speeches and Statements*, 8th cloth edn, New York: Pathfinder.

Breitman, George, ed. (1992), *By Any Means Necessary: Malcolm X*, 2nd edn, New York: Pathfinder.

Cateforis, Theo, ed. (2007), *The Rock History Reader*, New York: Routledge.

Cato, Johan (2012), *När islam blev svenskt Föreställningar om islam och muslimer i svensk offentlig politik, 1975–2010*, Lund Studies in History of Religion, Lund: Centre for Theology and Religious Studies.

Cepeda, Raquel (2007), *Bling: A Planet Rock*, DVD documentary, VH1 Rock Docs.

Chang, Jeff (2005), *Can't Stop, Won't Stop: A History of the Hip-Hop Generation*, New York: St Martin's Press.

Chang, Jeff (2007), 'It's a Hip-Hop World', *Foreign Policy* (163), pp. 58–65.

Charnas, Dan (2010), *The Big Payback: The History of the Business of Hip-Hop*, New York: New American Library.

Chase, Christopher W. (2010), 'Prophetics in the Key of Allah: Towards an Understanding of Islam in Jazz', *Jazz Perspectives*, vol. 4 (2), pp. 157–81.

Coleman, Brian (2007), *Check the Technique: Liner Notes for Hip-Hop Junkies*, New York: Villard Books.

Cooper, Martha (2015), *Subway Art* [s. l.], London: Thames & Hudson.

Cooper, Martha, Zeb.roc.ski and Nika Kramer (2013), *Hip Hop Files: Photographs, 1979–1984*, Berlin: From Here to Fame; London: Turnaround [distributor].

Costello, Mark, and David Foster Wallace (1990), *Signifying Rappers: Rap and Race in the Urban Present*, 1st edn, New York: Ecco Press.

Culler, Jonathan (1992), 'In Defence of Overinterpretation', in Umberto Eco and Stefan Collini (eds), *Interpretation and Overinterpretation*, Cambridge and New York: Cambridge University Press, pp. 109–24.

Curtis, Edward E. (2002), *Islam in Black America: Identity, Liberation, and Difference in African-American Islamic thought*, Albany: State University of New York Press.

Curtis, E. (2007), 'Islamism and Its African American Muslim Critics: Black Muslims in the Era of the Arab Cold War', *American Quarterly*, vol. 59 (3), pp. 683–709.

Curtis, Edward E. (2009), 'Debating the Origins of the Moorish Science Temple: Toward a New Cultural History', in Edward E. Curtis and Danielle Brune Sigler (eds), *The New Black Gods: Arthur Huff Fauset and the Study of African American Religions*, Bloomington: Indiana University Press.

Dabashi, Hamid (2008), *Islamic Liberation Theology: Resisting the Empire*, London and New York: Routledge.

Daulatzai, Sohail (2012), *Black Star, Crescent Moon: The Muslim International and Black Freedom Beyond America*, Minneapolis: University of Minnesota Press.

DeGenaro, William (2012), 'Performing Working-Class Patriotism: Musical Responses to 9/11', in M. Keith Booker (ed.), *Blue-Collar Pop Culture: From NASCAR to Jersey Shore*, Santa Barbara: Praeger, pp. 134–50.

d'Eramo, Marco (2004), *Slakthuset och skyskrapan: Chicago – en berättelse om vår framtid*, translated by Gunnar Sandin, Lund: Arkiv.

Diouf, Sylviane A. (2004), 'African Muslims in Bondage: Realities, Memories and Legacies', in Joanne M. Braxton and Maria Diedrich (eds), *Monuments of the Black Atlantic: Slavery and Memory*, New Brunswick: LIT; distributed in North America by Transaction Publishers.

Diouf, Sylviane A. (1998), *Servants of Allah: African Muslims Enslaved in the Americas*, New York: New York University Press.

Dirks, Jerald (2006) *Muslims in American History: A Forgotten Legacy*, 1st edn, Beltsville: Amana Publications.

Dyson, Michael Eric (1995), *Making Malcolm: The Myth and Meaning of Malcolm X*, Oxford: Oxford University Press.

Edwards, Holly (2000), 'A Million and One Nights: Orientalism in America, 1870–1930', in *Noble Dreams, Wicked Pleasures: Orientalism in America 1870–1930*, Princeton: Princeton University Press, pp. 11–58.

Eyerman, Ron, and Andrew Jamison (1991), *Social Movements: A Cognitive Approach*, University Park: Pennsylvania State University Press.

Fenster, Mark (2008), *Conspiracy Theories: Secrecy and Power in American Culture*, revised and updated edn, Minneapolis: University of Minnesota Press.

Finley, Stephen C., ed. (2015), *Esotericism in African American Religious Experience: 'There is a Mystery'*, Aries Book Series: Texts and Studies in Western Esotericism, vol. 19, Leiden and Boston: Brill.

Floyd-Thomas, Juan M. (2003), 'A Jihad of Words: The Evolution of African American Islam and Contemporary Hip-Hop', in Anthony B. Pinn (ed.), *Noise and Spirit:*

The Religious and Spiritual Sensibilities of Rap Music, New York: New York University Press, pp. 49–70.

Ford, Arnold J. (1922a), 'The Negro and Music', *Negro World*, 1 July.

Ford, Arnold J. (1922b), *The Universal Ethiopian Hymnal*, [New York]: Beth B'nai Pub. Co.

Forman, Murray (2002), *The 'Hood Comes First: Race, Space, and Place in Rap and Hip-Hop*, Middletown: Wesleyan University Press.

Gardell, Mattias (1995), *Countdown to Armageddon: Minister Farrakhan and the Nation of Islam in the Latter Days*, Stockholm: Stockholm University.

Gardell, Mattias (1996), *In the Name of Elijah Muhammad: Louis Farrakhan and the Nation of Islam*, Durham: Duke University Press.

Gates, Henry Louis, and Cornel West (2000), *The African-American Century: How Black Americans Have Shaped Our Country*, New York: Free Press.

Gates, Henry Louis, and Evelyn Brooks Higginbotham, eds (2004), *African American Lives*, New York: Oxford University Press.

Gates, Henry Louis (2012), in Abby Wolf (ed.), *The Henry Louis Gates, Jr Reader*, New York: Basic Civitas Books.

Geertz, Clifford (1999), *Islam Observed: Religious Development in Morocco and Indonesia*, 15th printing, Chicago: University of Chicago Press.

George, Nelson, and National Urban League, eds (1990), *Stop the Violence: Overcoming Self Destruction*, New York: Pantheon Books.

Gibson, Dawn-Marie (2012), *A History of the Nation of Islam: Race, Islam, and the Quest for Freedom*, Santa Barbara: Praeger.

Gillespie, Dizzy (2009), *To Be, or Not to Bop*, 1st edn, Minneapolis: University of Minnesota Press.

Gomez, Michael A. (1994), 'Muslims in Early America', *The Journal of Southern History*, vol. 60 (4), pp. 671–710.

Gomez, Michael Angelo (2005), *Black Crescent: The Experience and Legacy of African Muslims in the Americas*, New York: Cambridge University Press.

Gosa, Travis L. (2011), 'Counterknowledge, Racial Paranoia, and the Cultic Milieu: Decoding Hip Hop Conspiracy Theory', *Poetics*, vol. 39 (3), pp. 187–204.

Hager, Steven (2002), *Adventures in the Counterculture from Hip Hop to High Times*, Berkeley: High Times Books.

Hager, Steven (2004), 'Afrika Bambaataa's Hip-Hop', in Raquel Cepeda (ed.), *And It Don't Stop: The Best American Hip-Hop Journalism of the Last 25 Years*, New York: Faber & Faber, pp. 12–26.

Halliday, Michael Alexander Kirkwood (1978), *Language as Social Semiotic: The Social Interpretation of Language and Meaning*, London: Edward Arnold.

Halper, Jeff, Edwin Seroussi and Pamela Squires-Kidron (1989), 'Musica Mizrakhit: Ethnicity and Class Culture in Israel', *Popular Music*, vol. 8 (2), pp. 131–41.

Hebdige, Dick (2004), 'Rap and Hip-Hop: The New York Connection', in Mark Anthony Neal and Murray Forman (ed.), *That's the Joint! The Hip-Hop Studies Reader*, New York: Routledge, pp. 223–32.

Hennessey, Thomas J. (1994), *From Jazz to Swing: African-American Jazz Musicians and their Music, 1890–1935*, Jazz History, Culture, and Criticism series, Detroit: Wayne State University Press.

Higgs, Robert (1976), 'The Boll Weevil, the Cotton Economy and Black Migration, 1910–1930', *Agricultural History*, vol. 50 (2), pp. 335–50.

Hjärpe, Jan (1997), 'What Will be Chosen from the Islamic Basket?' *European Review*, vol. 5 (3), pp. 267–74.

Hughes, Aaron W. (2014), *Theorizing Islam: Disciplinary Deconstruction and Reconstruction*, 1st publication in paperback, Durham: Acumen.

Icke, David (1999), *The Biggest Secret – The Book That Will Change the World*, Wildwood: Bridge of Love Publications.

Icke, David (2002), *Alice in Wonderland and the World Trade Center Disaster: Why the Official Story of 9/11 is a Monumental Lie*, Wildwood: Bridge of Love Publications.

Icke, David (2017), *Children of the Matrix: How an Interdimensional Race Has Controlled the World for Thousands of Years – and Still Does*, Isle of Wight: David Icke Books.

Jenkins, Robert L., and Mfanya Donald Tryman, eds (2002), *The Malcolm X Encyclopedia*, Westport: Greenwood Press.

Jonnes, Jill (2002), *South Bronx Rising: The Rise, Fall, and Resurrection of an American City*, 2nd edn, New York: Fordham University Press.

Kah, Gary (1992), *En Route to Global Occupation*, Lafayette: Huntington House Publishers.

Kepel, Gilles (1997), *Allah in the West: Islamic Movements in America and Europe*, Mestizo Spaces series, Palo Alto: Stanford University Press.

Keyes, Cheryl Lynette (2004), *Rap Music and Street Consciousness*, 1st paperback edn, Urbana: University of Illinois Press.

Khabeer, Su'ad Abdul (2016), *Muslim Cool: Race, Religion, and Hip Hop in the United States*, New York: New York University Press.

Khabeer, Suad Abdul (2007), 'Rep that Islam: The Rhyme and Reason of American Islamic Hip Hop', *The Muslim World*, vol. 97 (1), pp. 125–41.

Kline, Daniel (2013), 'The New Kids: Indigo Children and New Age Discourse', in Egil Asprem and Kennet Granholm (eds), *Contemporary Esotericism*, Gnostica series, Bristol, CT: Equinox Publishing, pp. 351–71.

Knight, Michael Muhammad (2006), *Blue-Eyed Devil: A Road Odyssey Through Islamic America*, Brooklyn: Soft Skull Press.

Knight, Michael Muhammad (2007), *The Five Percenters: Islam, Hip Hop and the Gods of New York*, Oxford: Oneworld Publications.

Knight, Michael Muhammad (2012), *William S. Burroughs vs. the Qur'an*, Berkeley: Soft Skull Press; distributed by Publishers Group West.

Kress, Gunther R. (2010), *Multimodality: A Social Semiotic Approach to Contemporary Communication*, London and New York: Routledge.

Kubik, Gerhard (1999), *Africa and the Blues*, Jackson: University Press of Mississippi.

Lateef, Yusef (2006), *The Gentle Giant: The Autobiography of Yusef Lateef*, 1st Morton Books edn, Irvington: Morton Books.

Lee, Spike, Ralph Wiley, James Balwin, Arnold Perl, Alex Haley and Malcolm X (1993), *By Any Means Necessary: The Trials and Tribulations of the Making of Malcolm X*, London: Vintage.

Lomax, Alan (2002), *The Land Where the Blues Began*, New York: New Press.

Lord, Lewis, and Jeannye Thornton (1992), 'The Legacy of Malcolm X', *US News & World Report*.

Lubin, Alex (2014), *Geographies of Liberation: The Making of an Afro-Arab Political Imaginary*, The John Hope Franklin series in African American History and Culture, Chapel Hill: The University of North Carolina Press.

Mandaville, Peter (forthcoming), 'Islamism and Subalternity Global Jihadis and Modern Social Power', *IR's Worlding and Alternative World Claims I*.

Marable, Manning (2011), *Malcolm X: A Life of Reinvention*, New York: Viking.

Marable, Manning, and Hisham Aidi, eds (2009), *Black Routes to Islam*, New York: Palgrave Macmillan.

Martin, Tony (1983), *Literary Garveyism: Garvey Black Arts and the Harlem Renaissance*, The New Marcus Garvey Library, no. 1., Dover, MA: The Majority Press.

McAlister, Melani (1999), 'One Black Allah: The Middle East in the Cultural Politics of African American Liberation, 1955–1970', *American Quarterly*, vol. 51 (3), pp. 622–56.

McAlister, Melani (2005), *Epic Encounters: Culture, Media, and US Interests in the Middle East since 1945*, updated edn with a post-9/11 chapter, Berkeley: University of California Press.

McMurray, Anaya (2008), 'Hotep and Hip-Hop: Can Black Muslim Women Be Down with Hip-Hop?' *Meridians*, vol. 8 (1), pp. 74–92.

Meir-Glitzenstein, Esther (2014), *The 'Magic Carpet' Exodus of Yemenite Jewry: An Israeli Formative Myth*, Brighton and Chicago: Sussex Academic Press.

Melnick, Jeffrey Paul (2009), *9/11 Culture: America under Construction*, West Sussex, UK, and Malden, MA: Wiley-Blackwell.

Melnick, Jeffrey (2011), *9/11 Culture*, Hoboken: John Wiley & Sons.

Miah, Shamim, and Virinder Kalra (2008), 'Muslim Hip-Hop: Politicisation of Kool Islam', *South Asian Cultural Studies Journal*, vol. 2 (1) (2008), pp. 12–25.

Miller, Kristine, ed. (2014), *Transatlantic Literature and Culture after 9/11: The Wrong Side of Paradise*, Hampshire, UK: Palgrave Macmillan.

Miller, Monica R. (2013), *Religion and Hip Hop*, New York: Routledge.

Miller, Monica R., Anthony B. Pinn and Bun B. eds (2015), *Religion in Hip Hop: Mapping the New Terrain in the US*, London and New York: Bloomsbury Academic.

Miller, Terry (2009), 'A Myth in the Making: Willie Ruff, Black Gospel and an Imagined Gaelic Scottish Origin', *Ethnomusicology Forum*, vol. 18 (2), pp. 243–59.

Miller, Monica R., and Anthony B. Pinn, eds (2015), *The Hip Hop and Religion Reader*, 1st edn, New York: Routledge.

Mitchell, W. J. T. (2010), *Cloning Terror: The War of Images, 9/11 to the Present*, Chicago and London: University of Chicago Press.

Miyakawa, Felicia M. (2005), *Five Percenter Rap: God Hop's Music, Message, and Black Muslim Mission*, Profiles in Popular Music, Bloomington: Indiana University Press.

Mohaiemen, Naeem (2008), 'Sound Unbound', in Paul D. Miller, aka DJ Spooky that Subliminal Kid (ed.), *Sound Unbound: Sampling Digital Music and Culture*, Cambridge, MA: The MIT Press, pp. 313–37.

Motley, Carol M., and Geraldine Rosa Henderson (2008), 'The Global Hip-Hop Diaspora: Understanding the Culture', *Cross-Cultural Business Research*, vol. 61 (3), pp. 243–53.

Nance, Susan (2002), 'Mystery of the Moorish Science Temple: Southern Blacks and American Alternative Spirituality in 1920s Chicago', *Religion and American Culture: A Journal of Interpretation*, vol. 12 (2), pp. 123–66.

Nasir, Kamaludeen Mohamed (2020), *Representing Islam: Hip-Hop of the September 11 Generation*, Bloomington: Indiana University Press.

Navas, Eduardo (2012), *Remix Theory: The Aesthetics of Sampling*, New York: Springer.

Neal, Mark Anthony (1999), *What the Music Said: Black Popular Music and Black Public Culture*, New York: Routledge.

Nieuwkerk, Karin van, Mark LeVine and Martin Stokes, eds (2016), *Islam and Popular Culture*, 1st edn, Austin: University of Texas Press.

Nuruddin, Yusuf (1994), 'The Five Percenters: A Teenage Nation of Gods and Earths', in Yvonne Yazbeck Haddad and Jane I. Smith (eds), *Muslim Communities in North America*, SUNY Series in Middle Eastern Studies, Albany: State University of New York Press.

Ogg, Alex, and David Upshal (2001), *The Hip Hop Years: A History of Rap*, New York: Fromm Intl.

Oliver, Paul (1970), *Savannah Syncopators: African Retentions in the Blues*, London: Studio Vista.

Onaci, Edward (2010), 'I Can be Your Sun, You Can be My Earth: Masculinity, Hip Hop and the Nation of Gods and Earths', in Derrick P. Alridge, James B. Stewart and V. P. Franklin (eds), *Message in the Music: Hip Hop, History, and Pedagogy*, Washington DC: The ASALH Press.

Otterbeck, Jonas (2000), *Islam på svenska: Tidskriften Salaam och islams globalisering*, Stockholm: Almqvist & Wiksell International.

Otterbeck, Jonas, and Göran Larsson (2017), 'Islam and Popular Music', in Christopher H. Partridge and Marcus Moberg (eds), *The Bloomsbury Handbook of Religion and Popular Music*, London: Bloomsbury Publishing, pp. 111–21.

Page, Max (2008), *The City's End: Two Centuries of Fantasies, Fears, and Premonitions of New York's Destruction*, New Haven: Yale University Press.

Palmer, Susan J. (2010), *The Nuwaubian Nation: Black Spirituality and State Control*, Surrey, UK, and Burlington, VT: Ashgate Publishing.

Paniccioli, Ernie, and Kevin Powell (2014), *Who Shot Ya? Three Decades of Hip Hop Photography* [s. l.]: Harper Paperbacks.

Partridge, Christopher H. (2004), *The Re-Enchantment of the West: Alternative Spiritualities, Sacralization, Popular Culture, and Occulture*, London and New York: T. & T. Clark International.

Partridge, Christopher (2013), 'Occulture is Ordinary', in Egil Asprem and Kennet Granholm (eds), *Contemporary Esotericism*, Gnostica series, Bristol, CT: Equinox Publishing, pp. 113–33.

Peretti, Burton W. (2009), *Lift Every Voice: The History of African American Music*, The African American History series, Lanham: Rowman & Littlefield Publishers.

Perkinson, James W. (2014), *Shamanism, Racism, and Hip Hop Culture: Essays on White Supremacy and Black Subversion*, New York: Palgrave Macmillan.

Petersen, J., and A. Ackfeldt (2022), 'The Case for Studying Non-Muslim Islams', *Method and Theory in the Study of Religion*, vol. 35 (2–3), pp. 241–59.

Peterson, James (2006), 'Dead Prezence: Money and Mortal Themes in Hip Hop Culture', *Callaloo*, vol. 29 (3), pp. 895–909.

Poutiainen, Ari, and Inka Rantakallio (2016), 'Discursive Construction of African-American Identities and Spirituality: A Comparison of Muslim Hip Hop and 1960s Jazz Avant-Garde', *Popular Music and Society*, vol. 39 (2), pp. 186–201.

Porter, Eric (2002), *What Is This Thing Called Jazz? African American Musicians as Artists, Critics, and Activists*, Music of the African Diaspora series, vol. 6, Berkeley: University of California Press.

Quay, Sara E., and Amy M. Damico, eds (2010), *September 11 in Popular Culture: A Guide*, Santa Barbara: Greenwood.

Rantakallio, Inka (2013), 'Muslimhiphop.com: Constructing Muslim Hip Hop Identities on the Internet', *CyberOrient*, vol. 7 (2), pp. 8–41.

Redmond, Shana L. (2013), *Anthem: Social Movements and the Sound of Solidarity in the African Diaspora*, New York: New York University Press.

Rehn, Alf, and David Sköld (2005), '"I Love the Dough": Rap Lyrics as a Minor Economic Literature', *Culture and Organization*, vol. 11 (1), pp. 17–31.

Rivera, Raquel Z. (2003), *New York Ricans from the Hip Hop Zone*, New Directions in Latino American Cultures series, 1st edn, New York: Palgrave Macmillan.

Robertson, David G. (2013), 'David Icke's Reptilian Thesis and the Development of New Age Theodicy', *International Journal for the Study of New Religions*, vol. 4 (1), pp. 27–47.

Robertson, Pat (1998), *The New World Order: A Reality You Cannot Afford to Ignore, A Book You Cannot Afford to Miss*, Bucks: Word Entertainment Ltd.

Rose, Gillian (2001), *Visual Methodologies: An Introduction to the Interpretation of Visual Materials*, London and Thousand Oaks: Sage.

Rose, Tricia (1994), *Black Noise: Rap Music and Black Culture in Contemporary America*, Hanover, NH: University Press of New England.

Rose, Tricia (1989), 'Orality and Technology: Rap Music and Afro-American Cultural Resistance', *Popular Music and Society*, vol. 13 (4), pp. 35–44.

RZA and Chris Norris (2009), *The Tao of Wu*, New York: Riverhead Books.

RZA and Chris Norris (2005), *The Wu-Tang Manual*, 1st Riverhead trade paperback ed., New York: Riverhead Books.

Safi, Omid, and Juliane Hammer, eds (2013), *The Cambridge Companion to American Islam*, Cambridge, UK, and New York: Cambridge University Press.

Salvatore, Armando (1995), *Islam and Political Modernity: Western and Islamic Discourses*, International Politics of the Middle East series, vol. 4, Reading, UK: Ithaca Press.

Sanchez, Sonia (1974), 'NEW POEMS by Sonia Sanchez', *Black World*, January, pp. 22–35.

Saphire, Queen ([n. d.]), *The Green Book: Universal Zulu Nation Infinity Archive 1973–2000*, vol. 1, https://uznnoble9.wordpress.com/wp-content/uploads/2015/01/green_book.pdf.

Schmidt, Garbi (1998), *American Medina: A Study of the Sunni Muslim Immigrant Communities in Chicago*, Stockholm: Almqvist & Wiksell.

Schneider, Eric C. (2011), *Smack: Heroin and the American City*, Philadelphia: University of Pennsylvania Press.

Sernett, Milton C. (1997), *Bound for the Promised Land: African American Religion and the Great Migration*, The C. Eric Lincoln Series on the Black Experience, Durham: Duke University Press.

Shibli, Fatima El (2007), 'Islam and the Blues', *Souls*, vol. 9 (2), pp. 162–70.

Smethurst, James Edward (2005), *The Black Arts Movement: Literary Nationalism in the 1960s and 1970s*, Chapel Hill: University of North Carolina Press.

Stenberg, Leif (1996), *The Islamization of Science: Four Muslim Positions Developing an Islamic Modernity*, Lund Studies in History of Religions, vol. 6, Stockholm: Almqvist & Wiksell International.

Steinskog, Erik (2018), *Afrofuturism and Black Sound Studies: Culture, Technology, and Things to Come*, 1st edn, Cham: Palgrave Macmillan.

Stjernholm, Simon (2011), *Lovers of Muhammad: A Study of Naqshbandi-Haqqani Sufis in the Twenty-First Century*, PhD thesis, Lund University.

Swedenburg, Ted (1997), 'Islam in the Mix: Lessons of the Five Percent', PhD thesis, University of Arkansas.

Toop, David (2000), *Rap Attack 3: African Rap to Global Hip Hop*, 3rd edn, London: Serpent's Tail.

Turner, Richard Brent (2013), 'African Muslim Slaves and Islam in Antebellum America', in Omid Safi and Juliane Hammer (eds), *The Cambridge Companion to American Islam*, Cambridge and New York: Cambridge University Press, pp. 28–44.

Turner, Richard Brent (2003), *Islam in the African-American Experience*, 2nd edn, Bloomington: Indiana University Press.

Urla, Jacqueline (2001), '"We are all Malcolm X!" Negu Gorriak, Hip Hop and the Basque Political Imaginary', in Tony Mitchell (ed.), *Global Noise: Rap and Hip-Hop Outside the USA*, Middletown: Wesleyan University Press, pp. 171–93.

Van Leeuwen, Theo (2005), *Introducing Social Semiotics*, London and New York: Routledge.

Van Sertima, Ivan (2003), *They Came Before Columbus: The African Presence in Ancient America*, New York: Random House Trade Paperbacks.

Vannini, P. (2007), 'Social Semiotics and Fieldwork: Method and Analytics', *Qualitative Inquiry*, vol. 13 (1), pp. 113–40.

Waardenburg, Jacques (1985), 'Islam as a Vehicle of Protest', in Ernest Gellner (ed.), *Islamic Dilemmas: Reformers, Nationalists, Industrialization: The Southern Shore of the Mediterranean*, Religion and Society, vol. 25, Berlin and New York: Mouton Publishers.

Wijeyesinghe, Charmaine L. (2021), *The Complexities of Race: Identity, Power, and Justice in an Evolving America*, New York: New York University Press.

Williams, Justin A., ed. (2015), *The Cambridge Companion to Hip-Hop*, Cambridge, UK: Cambridge University Press.

Wilson, Peter Lamborn (1993), *Sacred Drift: Essays on the Margins of Islam*, San Francisco: City Lights Books.

Wilson, Peter Lamborn (1988), *Scandal: Essays in Islamic Heresy*, Brooklyn: Autonomedia.

Wintz, Cary D., and Paul Finkelman, eds (2004), *Encyclopedia of the Harlem Renaissance*, New York: Routledge.

Woldu, Gail Hilson (2008), *The Words and Music of Ice Cube*, The Praeger Singer-Songwriter Collection. Westport: Praeger Publishers.

Womack, Ytasha (2013), *Afrofuturism: The World of Black Sci-fi and Fantasy Culture*, 1st edn, Chicago: Chicago Review Press.

Wood, Joe, ed. (1992), *Malcolm X: In Our Own Image*, 1st edn, New York: St Martin's Press.

INDEX

EU Authorised Representative:
Easy Access System Europe Mustamäe tee 50, 10621 Tallinn, Estonia
gpsr.requests@easproject.com

Printed and bound by CPI Group (UK) Ltd, Croydon, CR0 4YY
07/10/2026
02229141-0001